IN OUR OWN HANDS

IN OUR OWN HANDS

Essays in Deaf History, 1780–1970

Brian H. Greenwald and Joseph J. Murray
EDITORS

GALLAUDET UNIVERSITY PRESS
Washington, DC

Gallaudet University Press
Washington, DC 20002
http://gupress.gallaudet.edu

Printed in the United States of America

Editors' Note: The cover art, "Fluttering Butterfly Girl," is a linocut print by David Call, a deaf artist based in California. The work portrays a young girl signing BUTTERFLY in American Sign Language. The image of a butterfly is a contemporary symbol used by some deaf communities to symbolize deaf people and sign language. The exuberance of the young girl at the center of this artwork speaks to the theme of agency that runs through the historical essays in the book. A common thread in the essays is that deaf people repeatedly sought to "manage their own affairs" and fought back when they were denied the opportunity to do so. The title *In Our Own Hands* reflects both the assertion of agency and the use of sign language, the latter being an issue of particular prominence in several of the essays in this volume.

Library of Congress Cataloging-in-Publication Data
Names: Greenwald, Brian H., editor. | Murray, Joseph J., editor.
Title: In our own hands : essays in deaf history, 1780-1970 / Brian H. Greenwald, Joseph J. Murray, editors.
Other titles: In our own hands (Gallaudet University Press)
Description: Washington, DC : Gallaudet University Press, 2016.
Identifiers: LCCN 2016005244 | ISBN 9781563686603 (paperback)
Subjects: LCSH: Deaf--United States--History. | BISAC: HISTORY / Social History.
Classification: LCC HV2530 .I52 2016 | DDC 305.9/0820973--dc23
LC record available at http://lccn.loc.gov/2016005244

This book is dedicated to Michael J. Olson, archivist at Gallaudet University for his constant support of teachers, researchers, and students working in deaf history. The value of the Gallaudet University Archives is without parallel elsewhere in the world.

CONTENTS

ACKNOWLEDGMENTS

THIS COLLECTION CAME TOGETHER through a fortuitous combination of personal research, presentations, work with former students, and dialogue with others on current research trends in the field of deaf history. The editors noticed that agency, or attempts to claim deaf autonomy, was a commonality among these articles. This framework is consistent throughout the book and we believe these contributions also add to a greater understanding of the pressures that different groups of deaf people faced in their work to claim agency at different places and times.

We are grateful to the contributors for their enthusiasm and persistence. At different points, we have met with these contributors and engaged in delightful conversations about their research. Their work shown here adds new layers to our understanding of the complexities of agency in deaf women, African Americans, religion, organizations, schools, and transnationalism. Deaf people claimed autonomy in some arenas more successfully than in others.

Michael J. Olson, interim director of the Gallaudet University Archives, and staff including Seung Hahn, provided indispensable advice, unearthed photographs, offered suggestions, and support. We are very fortunate to be on the same campus as the world's largest archival collection related to deaf history. Many of the articles in this collection used primary source material available at the Gallaudet University Archives, showing, once again, its value to deaf history and ongoing interpretations of deaf lives.

We also express our sincere gratitude to Ivey Pittle Wallace, director of Gallaudet University Press. She has been one of the staunchest supporters in the publication and dissemination of deaf history scholarship over the past two and half decades, and her unwavering support is also true here. Deirdre Mullervy and Valencia Simmons have been very collegial and we thank Gallaudet University Press for their patience, guidance, and support. We are also grateful to our contributors, three of whom are our former graduate students and remain involved in research on deaf lives today.

Brian Greenwald is greatly indebted to the coeditor of this volume. We have organized conferences, presented together, and I hold deep respect for my coeditor's work in human rights and deaf history. Joseph Murray thanks his coeditor for proposing the idea of this volume in the first place. It was a pleasure and honor to work with Dr. Greenwald, who tirelessly advances this field in his research and work with undergraduate and graduate students, within the profession at large, and with the general public.

Brian Greenwald would like to thank his wife Rebecca Greenwald for the many hours spent at the office. Rebecca Greenwald was unfailingly supportive in every possible way, full of encouragement, and love. Joseph Murray thanks his wife, Claudia Murray, and his children, Joshua and Ella, for their support during his hours away, whether overseas or downstairs in his office, during this project. Nothing is better than sharing one's accomplishments with those one loves.

—Brian H. Greenwald and Joseph J. Murray, Editors

INTRODUCTION

Brian H. Greenwald and Joseph J. Murray

THIS COLLECTION OF WORKS in the field of Deaf history is drawn from new research on deaf lives between 1780 and 1970. The contributors examine unexplored areas in Deaf history that intersect with important subthemes in historical studies. These themes include Southern history, religious history, and Western history, as well as new perspectives on the histories of eugenics, African Americans, women, and religion. The commonality of these chapters is that they trace the development of deaf people's attempts to carve out spaces for themselves within the larger society. Most of the contributors focus on developments in the United States, but one offers a perspective from a turbulent period in Australia's history.

Scholarship in Deaf history has traditionally concentrated on the national scale.[1] This book takes a closer look at the local and regional landscapes as deaf people asserted their rights in local and national settings. The chapters in this collection explore deaf peoples' claim to autonomy in their personal, religious, social, and organizational lives, and reveal how these debates overlapped with social trends and spilled out into particular physical and social spaces such as clubs, churches, and even within families. The contributors show how deaf people had agency and used this agency to engage in vigorous debates about issues that constantly tested the values of deaf people as Americans (or Australians).

Yet other earlier works have documented instances where agitation to attain equality was contested by other individuals or organizations. Breda Carty's study of breakaway social organizations in New South Wales and Queensland in Australia during the 1920s and 1930s shows how the presumption of authority by hearing men was unabashedly used to control the Deaf societies in these states. The societies provided religious, welfare services, and were centers of sporting and social activities for deaf people. In a meticulously researched article, Carty details the struggle for autonomy that led to the creation of deaf-controlled organizations in these two states. The Australian government eventually forced the organizations to merge back into the societies, and the process of merger showed the power hearing people maintained over deaf organizations in this time.

Anja Werner's chapter focuses on hearing people's perceptions of deaf people. Werner traces discourses on deaf people and deafness in 1200 newspaper and journal articles that appeared in English-language periodicals between 1780 and 1914. She divides this span into four discrete periods defined by waves of educational change during the time. Werner notes the shift in public discourse over the course of the nineteenth century from talking about deaf people to objectifying deaf people through medical discourses in the latter part of the period covered by her chapter.

The remaining chapters in this volume reveal a more complete portrait of deaf activism in the United States that expands the traditional East Coast focus to studies in the South and the West. Kati Morton Mitchell examines the life and advocacy of Alice Taylor Terry, a deaf female leader and writer in California in the first half of the twentieth century. Terry was politically astute and maintained leadership positions in deaf organizations dominated by deaf males during a time when women agitated for suffrage. Her writing covered many topics of interest to deaf people, including oralism, eugenics, and driving rights, and she constantly exhorted deaf people to support their state organizations in addition to the National Association of the Deaf. She placed deaf agency at the center of her arguments for deaf people's right to a place in larger society.

Two chapters in this volume focus largely on the US South. Carolyn McCaskill, Ceil Lucas, Robert Bayley, and Joseph Hill look at the broad sweep of the history of African American deaf people from 1820 to 1990. They examine agency through the lens of education. Records of African Americans attending schools for the deaf are sporadic up until after the Civil War. Following that war, seventeen schools opened segregated "Colored Departments," sometimes on the same campus as the white school, and other times on a different campus.[2] These separate schools lasted long after the 1954 *Brown vs. the Board of Education of Topeka* decision, the last one closing in Louisiana in 1978. Many of the teachers at these schools were white, and African Americans who wished to teach at these schools could not find teacher-training programs until after World War II.

Jean Bergey's biography of the Reverend Robert and Mrs. Estelle Caldwell Fletcher uses oral history, film, photographs, and family documents to portray the life and work of an Episcopalian preacher from the 1930s to the 1970s. Bergey's chapter introduces new material on deaf leadership in churches, access to religious services, and on the community's role in caring for elderly deaf people. Issues of race, class, and gender are interwoven in the story of how the Fletchers served multiple congregations across the South. Bergey's research on Rev. Fletcher, who lived in Alabama, offers insight into everyday life for white deaf people in the South and, via his work, gives us glimpses into the lives of deaf African Americans.

Organized religious activities played an important role in creating spaces for deaf people to meet and interact. Jannelle Legg's chapter relates the controversy over the loss of one such space, the sale of St. Ann's Church in New York City in the 1890s. Key members of the deaf community, most prominently Edwin Allen Hodgson, used the public press and public forums to advance their arguments for an independent deaf church. Legg underlines the multiple ways in which deaf and hearing lives intersected within both the physical space of the church and the church community. St. Ann's Church played a large role in the deaf community. Aside from its obvious religious functions, it also provided social services such as sign language interpreting and financial assistance, and it served as a space for socializing and conducting cultural activities. However, paralleling to some degree the Australian societies covered in Carty's chapter, St. Ann's Church was run by a hearing pastor and deaf people had little influence over decisions concerning the administration of the church, including its eventual sale. Hodgson's actions (with a hearing ally) show how deaf people seized agency by going outside the boundaries of an ostensibly "deaf-centered" institution and bringing their issues to a larger public.

Several of the chapters in this volume look at how the rise of eugenic theories in the late nineteenth century affected deaf people's lives. Attempts to restrict deaf people's autonomy, most notably through eugenic practices, has most often been studied in Deaf history by looking at the late nineteenth century and, particularly, at Alexander Graham Bell. However, research on the National Association of the Deaf and the Clarke School for the Deaf, a prominent oral school in western

Massachusetts, has revealed that both institutions attempted to curtail deaf people's autonomy by preemptively suggesting certain deaf people should not marry one another.

Brian Greenwald's chapter provides a close textual analysis of Alexander Graham Bell's most widely known publication on deaf people, *Memoir Upon the Formation of a Deaf Variety of the Human Race.* Bell originally presented the paper as an address to the National Academy of Sciences in 1883. Although the *Memoir* typically has been criticized for its eugenic stance, particularly on marriage, Greenwald reveals that Bell also challenged language use and social relationships among deaf people. Ultimately eugenics proved to be less threatening to deaf autonomy than Bell's other concerns, and the widespread educational and social acceptance of Bell's work among hearing educators of the deaf was the real tragedy. Greenwald ends his chapter noting deaf autonomy was contested in many arenas that were influenced by the ideology of Alexander Graham Bell.

Melissa Malzkuhn examines the National Association of the Deaf (NAD) through the lens of eugenics. The NAD promoted full citizenship for its members, a goal articulated at the first NAD convention by Theodore Froehlich—"As deaf-mutes among the other inhabitants of this country, we have interests peculiar to ourselves, and which can be taken care of by ourselves."[3] Malzkuhn combed through NAD conference proceedings and deaf residential school publications and found a tightly focused public "voice" that offers a collective perspective protecting deaf people from the potential impact of eugenicists. While insisting that agency remain firmly in control of deaf bodies, the NAD sought to maintain marriage autonomy for most deaf people by encouraging those with hereditary deafness to abstain from marriage. By this point, the white deaf Americans who made up the leadership of the NAD had apparently acknowledged the impact of eugenic ideas in American life.

Following Malzkuhn's chapter, Marion Schmidt discusses research that the Clarke School for the Deaf undertook starting in 1929. The school established research divisions in audiology, psychology, and heredity that utilized cutting-edge genetic and medical knowledge to learn more about the hereditary background of Clarke's students. Researchers worked to reduce the incidence of deafness in future generations and to identify how best to integrate deaf and hearing students. Schmidt concludes that these researchers held complete agency over the testing, studying, and advising of deaf children who enrolled at Clarke School for the Deaf.

In another chapter on the work of NAD, Octavian Robinson discusses campaigns led by that organization and the National Fraternal Society of the Deaf (NFSD) that projected deaf people as independent citizens and denigrated those who participated in forms of peddling, casting them as paupers and second-class citizens. Using extensive primary sources, Robinson pieces together a story of deaf people seeking to gain economic independence. The NAD and NFSD aggressively mounted anti-peddling campaigns to demonstrate deaf peoples' ability to contribute to the larger society. These organizations utilized ableist discourses while also reinforcing a narrow form of citizenship.

Joseph Murray's chapter looks at how supporters of the National Deaf-Mute College, now Gallaudet University, promoted the university from its founding in 1864 to the 1890s. Murray reviews Presentation Day exercises and other public events chronicled in the college's annual reports to uncover how supporters of the college promoted it as an institution that fostered the national ideal of equal citizenship for all people, including deaf people. The mission of the college was to ensure that students would succeed in "the race of life," and the college's alumni and faculty made sure to publicize the success of its graduates, despite the discrimination women and African Americans faced at the university.

Deaf education was a common battleground where agency was constantly tested. With the heyday of the Progressive Era as a backdrop, Motoko Kimura examines deaf agency in the Chicago public day schools. Combing through a variety of records, including municipal data, Kimura tells the story of a seemingly strong deaf community through the Illinois School for the Deaf at Jacksonville and the Pas-a-Pas club in Chicago. In 1875, with the establishment of the first day school in Chicago, the number of deaf children in Chicago attending the city's public schools grew, subverting traditional placements at the Illinois School for the Deaf. One of the leaders in the initial attempt to establish education for deaf children in Chicago was Philip Alfred Emery. His actions apparently alienated him from the existing deaf community power structure that successfully campaigned for his removal from his post. However, the Chicago Board of Education then resisted efforts by the Pas-a-Pas club to influence the curriculum and other education matters related to deaf education, leaving an opening for oralists to shape deaf education in the city. Their actions minimized opportunities for deaf parents and hearing people from a lower socioeconomic strata to influence public school education for deaf children.

As the chapters in this volume show, deaf people's autonomy in managing their own affairs was often contested by hearing people. Yet, as the contributors demonstrate, deaf people constantly pressed for autonomy in political, social, and religious avenues, and the results were decidedly mixed. In 1880, NAD President Theodore Froehlich called for deaf people to keep "interests peculiar to ourselves" to themselves, a sentiment later echoed in a 1932 call by the *British Deaf Times* for "a fuller appreciation of the rights of the deaf to manage their own affairs."[4] Such calls to agency are especially relevant in contemporary times as deaf people are engaged in questions about the value of residential schools, the rapid progression of medical research on hearing loss, genetic engineering, and even the right to use sign language at home and in organizations and schools.[5] The value of this collection, then, is to remind us that challenges remain. These episodes have much to teach us about the fragility of autonomy and the perils resulting from the loss of agency. We believe that deaf history has much to offer scholars who continue to study deaf people in relation to the societies in which they live.

Notes

1. Some examples of studies of deaf history on a national scale in the United States include Jack R. Gannon, *Deaf Heritage: A Narrative History of Deaf America* (Silver Spring, MD: National Association of the Deaf, 1981); John V. Van Cleve and Barry A. Crouch, *A Place of Their Own: Creating the Deaf Community in America* (Washington, DC: Gallaudet University Press, 1989); Douglas C. Baynton, *Forbidden Signs: American Culture and the Campaign against Sign Language* (Chicago: University of Chicago Press, 1998); John V. Van Cleve, ed., *Deaf History Unveiled: Interpretations from the New Scholarship* (Washington, DC: Gallaudet University Press, 1999); Robert Buchanan, *Illusions of Equality: Deaf Americans in School and Factory, 1850–1950* (Washington, DC: Gallaudet University Press, 1999); Susan Burch, *Signs of Resistance: American Deaf Cultural History, 1900 to World War II* (New York: New York University Press, 2004); Hannah Joyner, *From Pity to Pride: Growing Up Deaf in the Old South* (Washington, DC: Gallaudet University Press; Brenda Jo Brueggemann and Susan Burch, eds., *Women and Deafness: Double Visions* (Washington, DC: Gallaudet University Press, 2006); John V. Van Cleve, ed., *Deaf History Reader* (Washington, DC: Gallaudet University Press, 2007); Susan Burch and Hannah Joyner, *Unspeakable: The Story of Junius Wilson* (Chapel Hill, NC: The University of North Carolina Press, 2007); Brian H. Greenwald and John V. Van Cleve, ed., *A Fair Chance in the Race of Life:*

The Role of Gallaudet University in Deaf History (Washington, DC: Gallaudet University Press, 2008); Carolyn McCaskill, Ceil Lucas, Robert Bayley, and Joseph Hill, *The Hidden Treasure of Black ASL: Its History and Structure* (Washington, DC: Gallaudet University Press, 2011); and R.A.R. Edwards, *Words Made Flesh: Nineteenth-Century Deaf Education and the Growth of Deaf Culture* (New York: New York University Press, 2014).

2. Carolyn McCaskill, Ceil Lucas, Robert Bayley, and Joseph Hill, *The Hidden Treasure of Black ASL: Its History and Structure* (Washington, DC: Gallaudet University Press, 2011), 14–15.

3. Theo. A. Froehlich, "Importance of Association Among Mutes for Mutual Improvement" in *Proceedings of the National Convention of Deaf-Mutes* (New York: New York Institution for the Deaf and Dumb, 1880), 39.

4. "Overseas Page. Australia," *British Deaf Times* 24, no. 337–38 (Jan-Feb 1932): 3. As quoted in Breda Carty, this volume.

5. For example of a discussion on the right to use sign language, see *Sign Language Studies* 15, no. 4 (Summer 2015).

1

Why Give Him a Sign Which Hearing People Do Not Understand . . . ? Public Discourses about Deafness, 1780–1914

Anja Werner

In 1876, an author in the *American Annals of the Deaf and Dumb* asked, "Why give him a sign which hearing people do not understand . . . ?"[1] The statement illustrates the extent to which deaf lives were shaped by hearing expectations at that time. In the late nineteenth century, hearing culture was assumed to be the most highly evolved form of human society, and a majority of hearing people expected their deaf compatriots to adjust to the hearing mainstream. Any type of otherness was perceived as an unfortunate mishap and even a threat rather than an alternative way of being. By contrast, hearing people of the early nineteenth century had been more open-minded. Some deaf people like Laurent Clerc alongside hearing teachers of the deaf who promoted signed forms of communication, such as Thomas Hopkins Gallaudet, had been respected and visible members of American society. Why, then, the change in public opinion? Why did the hearing majority become unwilling and even unable to realize that deaf people who signed could fully exercise their citizenship?

Based on my examination of roughly 1,200 Anglo-American newspaper and journal articles straddling the years from 1780 to 1914, I would argue that the change coincided with changing access to information about deafness. By the mid-nineteenth century, mentions of deaf people in mainstream periodicals significantly decreased. At the same time, more and more deaf periodicals were being founded. These deaf papers

This project was made possible thanks to a research fellowship from the Max Planck Institute for the History of Science (Berlin, Germany).

represented deaf self-consciousness. It was a reply to hearing strategies of exclusion as an oralist lobby was gaining strength and the hearing public's opinion shifted from favoring the manual method to preferring the oral method in educating deaf children. The oral method was also perceived to be more modern and grounded in the latest scientific discoveries.[2]

Since Harlan Lane's 1984 *When the Mind Hears*, deaf and hearing historians alike have added considerably to our understanding of deaf agency in the nineteenth century.[3] My goal was not so much to trace deaf history, as to examine a specific type of source for its significance in understanding the dynamics between hearing and deaf people.[4] In this chapter, I first describe my overall research of nineteenth-century newspapers, which focused on different journals and recurrent themes. I subsequently share a few examples of how discussions about deafness changed over the decades. In doing so, I focus on references to deaf people in mainstream—that is, hearing—periodicals rather than the deaf press. While the idea of "citizenship" was not discussed then as a tool to understanding hearing-deaf relations, it can help us today in examining hearing people's perceptions of deaf people and their tactics of exclusion despite ongoing deaf activism to fight such attitudes.

Articles and Recurrent Themes

I found nearly 1,200 articles from American, British, and Irish periodicals in a systematic search of available online-databases like Journal Storage and those of the American Antiquarian Society. In this chapter, I focus mainly on American sources. However, it was not always possible to identify with certainty a source as British or American in its origin. Moreover, the online-databases are biased with regard to the resources from which they draw their materials. Articles from the "silent press" that came up in my search do not amount to a systematic and comprehensive list. The fact that such articles did come up does, however, allow for conclusions with regard to general trends. For instance, a growing tendency to discuss deaf culture exclusively in publications by and for deaf people may be discerned, while hearing readers increasingly found oralist perspectives reflected in hearing journals.

I included articles from weekly and monthly journals as well as from daily newspapers. The articles cover a broad range of topics, whereby references to deafness could be both literal and metaphorical. Common sayings such as the expression "to be deaf to an idea" were also traced.

Some articles were brief notes on new publications; others amounted to detailed analyses of twenty pages and more. Most articles averaged either the length of a typical newspaper column or two to three journal pages. British and American journals shared information by reprinting articles from the other side of the Atlantic or simply by writing about institutions in both countries. References to periodicals in other European languages were also found. In the United States, articles were often reprinted repeatedly in different journals. Frequently a certain periodical published a number of articles on deafness in the course of a few years or even decades.

In the course of time, articles about deafness and deaf people appeared in journals that addressed very diverse readerships. In other words, different (hearing) professionals succeeded one another in discussing deaf issues. For instance, a significant number of the early articles were found in church newspapers, while many later articles were published in scientific journals. This finding supports the fact that a shift occurred with regard to explaining the need for deaf education, which changed from the idea of providing deaf people with an access to religion to assimilating them into hearing society on the basis of medico-scientific findings. Moreover, for specific decades recurring themes may be traced. Then again, some subjects appear to have been news throughout the century. Among the latter are, of course, discussions of manual and oral methods, excerpts or entire reports from schools for deaf children as well as descriptions of alternative teaching methods. Sometimes the articles addressed clearly defined audiences, such as those of youth, Sunday school, and ladies' journal readers. Poems and stories about deaf people appeared in these journals to teach hearing children and women how to lead good, moral lives. The ladies' journals in particular through the decades touched upon issues of caring about and teaching deaf people.[5]

Among the various alternatives in instructing deaf people that were discussed, visual alphabets—such as the manual alphabet or finger spelling (dactylology)—seemed especially useful in order to facilitate communication on the basis of vocal languages. Besides the one- and two-handed alphabets, educators devised syllabic alphabets in the 1830s.[6] But in the 1860s, alternatives to what was then referred to as "gestures" were sought. Some experimented with the Morse alphabet in combination with drums.[7] Then again, Thomas Gallaudet, a son of Thomas Hopkins Gallaudet, designed alphabets of smell, taste, and even moods to be used in the dark, which were as creative as they were impracticable.[8] But spelling out entire conversations was tedious. Moreover, hearing people had invented manual alphabets long before they became a means to communicate with deaf people.[9] Pictures were employed as well. Especially in Germany, so *The Deaf Mutes' Friend* informed its American readers, "there have been prepared, expressly for the mute, hundreds of pictures illustrating the common objects and employments of life."[10]

Some articles appeared—upon first glance—in curious publication venues, such as agricultural journals. However, farming was one way for a deaf person to make a living, which also meant that deaf farmers might have subscribed to farmers' papers.[11] At least one of these papers, *The Western Farmer & Gardener*, may actually have been aimed for a deaf audience, for it not only printed the "Alphabet of the Deaf and Dumb," but also discussed "Advantages of Being Deaf" during the 1850s.[12] Then again, *Our Dumb Animals*, which in 1874 asked "Are Our Dumb Animals Deaf?," was not part of the "silent press." An article in his journal praised a "deaf and dumb teamster" who was able to manage his oxen much better than his hearing colleagues even though he could not yell at them—he had trained his oxen well.[13]

Articles in law reviews illustrate to what extent hearing persons shifted from perceiving deaf persons in court as mere curiosities and material for entertaining stories to viewing them as a threat to the accustomed order of hearing society.[14, 15] This threat, apparently, had to be dispelled by ridiculing deaf people and by something that, with hindsight, might be termed pseudo-science. The shift seems to have occurred during the 1850s, incidentally a time when articulate deaf people thrived. Articles in law reviews and related journals were comparatively rare—I found eight in journals such as *The Monthly Law Reporter* and *The American Law Register*: one in 1830, three in the 1850s, and one each in 1867, 1881, 1897, and 1904. The low number of such articles might be explained to some extent by the above-mentioned possible bias of my search. But it might also be a statement on the low importance of deaf matters in hearing mainstream society. In the 1850s, curiosity about deafness as well as rising fears of capable deaf people might have motivated the writing of articles on a "deaf juryman" and "competency of witnesses," which also discussed the appropriateness of deafness for an active role in a trial.[16]

An increasing trend toward a more scientific approach to deafness may be observed by the time of the 1880s. In 1881, Davis Smith analyzed the "Contributory Negligence by Persons with Defective Senses," a choice of wording that conveyed the idea of deafness as a medical defect.[17] Similarly, *The American Law Register* in 1904 published an article on "The Survival of the Weakest as Exemplified in the Criminal," which also discussed deaf people. The article illustrates that with eugenics — in hindsight — a questionable branch of scientific research had entered the discourse.[18] The 1867 *Legal and Insurances Reporter* simply examined "A Deaf Subject."[19]

The *Charities Review* was not a law review, but, along with covering a broad range of institutions and occupations of deaf people, it also published an article about a "deaf-mute lawyer" in 1897.[20] The subject seems to be at odds with the general trend of limiting deaf agency. However, the fact that someone wondered about a "deaf-mute lawyer" may serve as an example of how deaf people continued to show hearing people that they could participate as active players in society.

Chronology of Deaf History Derived from Contemporary Journal Articles

On the basis of my analysis of the 1,200 articles, I discerned four time periods that mark specific developments in the history of deaf Americans between 1780 and 1914.[21] I will discuss these four time periods in more detail below. They appear roughly to coincide with five phases of educational stagnation and reform during the nineteenth century: the birth of national American education during the 1760s to 1810s; early attempts to reorganize American education by implementing and further developing European concepts during the 1810s to 1830s; founding new institutions and an increasing interest in natural sciences during the 1830s to 1860s; intense American student migration to Europe alongside educational reform activities in the United States between 1865 and 1898; consolidating American education and a decreasing interest in studying in Europe from 1898 to 1914 (consolidation). Wars and revolutions on both sides of the Atlantic clearly shaped the evolution of American education. Different forms of communication with Europe — such as scientific exchanges but also Americans' educational journeys to the Old World — also influenced how Americans thought about deafness.[22] In other words, developments that affect deaf people are closely intertwined with larger trends in society. The larger trends, in turn, influence the extent to which deaf people were and are able to interact with hearing society, such as in voicing their own concerns about educational issues and thus in having an impact on a fundamental aspect of their identities as deaf Americans.

1780 to 1817—Observing Deafness in Europe and America

Starting with Abbé Charles-Michel l'Epée's activities in Paris, France, between 1760 and 1817 deaf education was institutionalized in the Western world. The earliest relevant English-language articles I could find date from 1780. I traced twenty-eight articles in ten different journals, most of them were either printed in Europe or discussed deafness in Europe. A first truly American subject was introduced in an 1804 article about "Deaf and Dumb Indians." It actually discussed the sign systems of some Native Americans and apparently assumed that, because they were using signs to communicate, they had to be deaf.[23]

Generally speaking, the subject matter of articles shifted from relating miracles about deaf persons in the late eighteenth century to introducing educational institutions for deaf children in the early nineteenth century. In the late 1700s, publications such as the *New Wonderful Magazine and Marvelous Chronicle* depicted deaf people as curiosities, who either displayed criminal intentions or proved to be nothing less than sheer miracles.[24] First reports about deaf education were also found before the turn of the century. [25] In the early nineteenth century, the emphasis on education became more pronounced, and fewer authors published articles about deaf wonders and miracles. Periodicals now dealt with educational institutions for deaf children in Europe, and, by 1817, in the United States.[26]

1817 to 1861—Institutionalizing the American Deaf Community

Nearly eight hundred articles were printed and reprinted during this period, accounting for two-thirds of my entire database. A number of articles were simply reprinted from other publications, often retaining their titles. It means that news about deaf people reached diverse audiences.[27] The wealth of information during this period is more substantial than that of subsequent years, disregarding the fact that I did not systematically include in my list articles from periodicals for deaf people.[28] During this period, articles about deafness reached deaf and hearing people alike; at least more so than in later years.

This period may be sub-divided into two parts: first, the period of establishing early schools for the deaf in the northeast, midwest, and, eventually, in the south, whose annual reports started appearing in journals in the 1820s; and, second, the period of thriving deaf American communities during the 1840s and 1850s, which was reflected in numerous publications by deaf authors. Already in the 1820s, articles and the occasional poem about deafness gave evidence of a strong interest in deaf lives.[29] Societal and religious journals reprinted sign alphabets and annual reports of schools for deaf children and thereby informed the larger public about deaf culture.[30] At the same time, however, medical journals began printing articles about deafness, such as the *Boston Medical Intelligencer*.[31] The idea of teaching deaf persons to articulate aroused curiosity.[32] Christian and medical journals alike wondered about "cures" for deaf people.[33] Many articles simply referred to "The Deaf and Dumb" or an extended version of this phrase such as "Exhibition of the Deaf and Dumb," examples of the latter appeared in three different papers in 1833. One of these articles was published in the *American Railroad Journal & Advocate of Internal Improvements*, a title that suggests an openness toward changing society in constructive ways.[34]

The 1840s mark an ambivalent change in terminology. Although the term "deaf-mute" had occasionally appeared since at least 1826, a lengthy note accompanying an 1845 article in *The Penny Library for School Children* pointed out that the "deaf and dumb are now generally called *Deaf-mutes*."[35] In attempting to differentiate *mute* from *dumb*, the author summarized the success of articulation exercises in Europe and concluded that

> The question is often asked why, since the race of monkeys and baboons have the organs of voice and hearing also, they never learn to talk? . . . The truth is, monkies [*sic*], and the lower animals, do not talk, because they have nothing to say. The tongue is moved by the mind, but where there is no intellect, there is no thought; and where there is no thought, there is no need of any language, except that natural language which enables animals to make known their pains and pleasures, their wants and fears.[36]

Put differently, the term *dumb* implied an absence of thought, whereas the term *mute* simply referred to an absence of sound. By then some deaf children had shown that through oral education they could express themselves in vocal language, which proved that they were capable of thought.

The latter observation is noteworthy, for it accorded deaf people intellectual potential, however it was tied to an assumed superiority of vocal languages over signs. "Joe, the Jersey Mute," who during the 1850s and 1860s authored articles for a variety of very different journals

Masthead of the *Silent World* newspaper, founded in 1870. Courtesy of Gallaudet University Archives.

ranging from *The Social Revolutionist* to *The Home Guardian*, is an example of a deaf voice that reached the hearing public. His articles discussed sensitive matters such as "Injustice to Deaf and Dumb Teachers" and "The Wrongs of the Deaf and Dumb; or, Ignorance and Education."[37] For hearing people, however, it was comforting to learn that deafness did not prevent a deaf person from learning vocal speech; it simply took some effort on the part of hearing teachers (and, incidentally, a major effort on the part of the deaf student).

1861 to 1880: Vibrant Deaf Culture vs. Oralism

A minimum of 250 items were published between 1862 and 1880. They illustrate a growing distance between hearing and deaf worlds after the Civil War. The war had reduced interest in deaf issues despite the fact that in the course of the war the future Gallaudet University had been founded, which was then called the Columbia Institution for the Instruction of the Deaf and Blind.[38] Once peace had been restored, deaf people with connections to schools for deaf children eagerly established a succession of papers, some of them short-lived, to serve the deaf community over the years, including *The Deaf-Mutes' Friend*, which was a follow-up project of the 1867 *National Deaf Mute Gazette*.[39] Meanwhile, medical articles phrased perspectives on deafness in abstract scientific language, such as the article "XIX. Pathological Researches into the Diseases of the Ear, Supplement to Seventh Series: Sebaceous Tumours in the External Auditory Meatus" that was published in the *Medico-Chirurgical Transactions* in 1864.[40] By the 1860s, deaf people had become "patients," as is apparent from an 1866 article on "Leaves from the Journal of an Old Doctor. Number Nineteen. The Deaf and Blind Patient" in the *Street & Smith's Literary Album*.[41] The emerging medico-

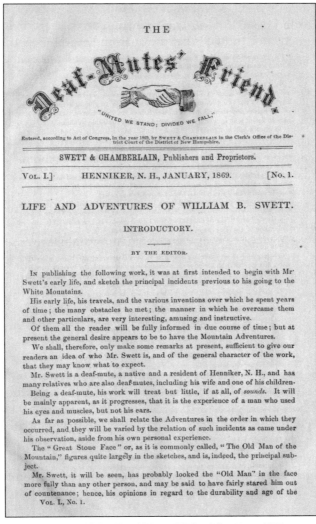

THE

Deaf-Mutes' Friend

"UNITED WE STAND; DIVIDED WE FALL."

Entered, according to Act of Congress, in the year 1869, by SWETT & CHAMBERLAIN in the Clerk's Office of the District Court of the District of New Hampshire.

SWETT & CHAMBERLAIN, Publishers and Proprietors.

VOL. I.]   HENNIKER, N. H., JANUARY, 1869.   [No. 1.

LIFE AND ADVENTURES OF WILLIAM B. SWETT.

INTRODUCTORY.

BY THE EDITOR.

In publishing the following work, it was at first intended to begin with Mr. Swett's early life, and sketch the principal incidents previous to his going to the White Mountains.

His early life, his travels, and the various inventions over which he spent years of time; the many obstacles he met; the manner in which he overcame them and other particulars, are very interesting, amusing and instructive.

Of them all the reader will be fully informed in due course of time; but at present the general desire appears to be to have the Mountain Adventures.

We shall, therefore, only make some remarks at present, sufficient to give our readers an idea of who Mr. Swett is, and of the general character of the work, that they may know what to expect.

Mr. Swett is a deaf-mute, a native and a resident of Henniker, N. H., and has many relatives who are also deaf-mutes, including his wife and one of his children.

Being a deaf-mute, his work will treat but little, if at all, of *sounds*. It will be mainly apparent, as it progresses, that it is the experience of a man who used his eyes and muscles, but not his ears.

As far as possible, we shall relate the Adventures in the order in which they occurred, and they will be varied by the relation of such incidents as came under his observation, aside from his own personal experience.

The "Great Stone Face" or, as it is commonly called, "The Old Man of the Mountain," figures quite largely in the sketches, and is, indeed, the principal subject.

Mr. Swett, it will be seen, has probably looked the "Old Man" in the face more fully than any other person, and may be said to have fairly stared him out of countenance; hence, his opinions in regard to the durability and age of the

VOL. L., No. 1.

The first issue of the *Deaf-Mutes' Friend*, January 1869. Courtesy of Gallaudet University Archives.

scientific turn notwithstanding, a renewed religious interest may also be traced in accounts of churches for deaf people including those that were published in *The Spirit of Missions*.[42] The idea of the "deaf, not dumb" was discussed in British publications, such as *The British Medical Journal*, in 1877.[43]

An article in *The Deaf-Mutes' Friend* reflected heightened deaf self-confidence and desire for self-determination on the part of deaf people when it proclaimed in 1869, "Let the deaf-mutes and their friends support our magazine and it shall support, interest and defend them."[44] The same article also bemoaned, "how little the deaf-mutes are understood by the greater part of the people, and their need of more extended information on the subject."[45] Deaf people were eager to increase deaf literacy, which is why the "silent press" induced parents to start teaching their deaf children words, writing, and the manual alphabet as well as "gesticulation" before they were old enough for school.[46] All of this reflected a deaf thirst for knowledge and desire to excel at school and in society. Senator James Willis Patterson of New Hampshire even encouraged deaf college students "to develop into full fledged Presidents of these United States."[47]

With a perceived "encroachment" of more and more educated deaf people on the hearing mainstream, the oral method became a means for hearing people to retain if not regain control. Hearing instructors took over from deaf teachers—a deaf person, after all, could hardly be an authority on articulation. But when facing hearing rather than deaf teachers, deaf children would only have hearing people as role models. They would be socialized in a hearing world and not be "lost" to a "deaf sub-culture." In 1836, Edward Davenport had still acknowledged that "it may be presumed that one who has felt the full weight of the evils of being deaf and dumb, and has successfully surmounted the obstacles in the path of knowledge, will be best able to point out the course to others similarly situated."[48] By 1867, however, hearing instructors were employed, and the hearing masses favored day schools for deaf students. It prevented deaf students from getting together to sign with each other after the lessons.[49] Moreover, hearing experts pointed out the supposed disadvantages of sign languages.[50] Hearing people viewed all these measures as a way to integrate deaf people into the hearing world.

Hearing experts had realized that, "There is no defect in the vocal organs of deaf-mutes";[51] a hearing impairment should consequently not prevent a person from using their voice. Deaf people did not speak, because *"being unable to hear others speak, they do not learn to use their voices."*[52] After all, "We learn to speak by imitating the speech of others."[53] The 1861 proceedings of the New York Academy of Medicine even claimed that, "All deaf mute children . . . have said 'mamma' and 'papa.'"[54] In order to learn articulation and lipreading, teachers of deaf children had to study the anatomy of the vocal organs and positions of the tongue so that they could demonstrate to their students how to produce specific sounds. Oralism could thus be fashioned as a scientific breakthrough despite the fact that it was centuries old. It did not seem to matter that the "teaching of articulation . . . requires great pains and attention."[55]

Deaf people were by now on their own in pointing out serious weaknesses of the oral approach. They did so in the "silent press." It was consequently lost to hearing readers that the oral method was not entirely successful, and that medical doctors were unable actually "to cure" deafness. If the collaboration of hearing doctors with hearing teachers did not work, the news spread in deaf circles but not among hearing audiences. For instance, as hearing teachers of deaf people began using the oral method more widely, physicians became attached to schools to examine and categorize deaf students. Medicine could have helped determine teaching methods on a case-by-case basis. Instead, deaf students on the whole were labeled as imperfect hearing persons. In early 1869, Orrick Metcalfe, was appointed to the New York institution in order to teach articulation and to examine "the ears of the pupils . . . to ascertain if there are not some cases in which medical skill can restore or ameliorate the faculty of hearing."[56] If successful, "this will become a permanent feature in our Institution."[57] However, *The Deaf-Mutes' Friend* cautioned its readers that they "must not indulge in any very high raised hopes of restoration to hearing."[58] It feared that "Dr. Metcalfe hopes to immortalize his name by some great discovery in Medical Science or Aural Surgery."[59] By November, Metcalfe had returned to his medical practice.[60]

1880 to 1914—Oralist Dogma

Only about 140 articles were traced for the period following the 1880 conference of Milan, Italy, during which mainly hearing teachers voted to ban signed languages from schools for deaf children. The comparatively low number of articles might be a reflection of the mainstream consensus regarding the higher significance of vocal language. A few gems are among the articles such as an item on the "Education of the Deaf in India."[61] Other articles examined "Deaf and Dumb Heroines in Fiction."[62] Europeans had also begun to observe the situation in the United States.[63] Last, but not least, quite a few of the 140 articles were from the *British Medical Journal*, which pursued an aggressive oralist agenda.[64] Voices from the deaf world seemed to be confined to deaf circles now.

Conclusion

In the hierarchically constructed world of late nineteenth-century thinking, an inability to hear created a dilemma with regard to the intellect—it turned a deaf person into an allegedly less highly evolved human being who, according to the logic of the times, could hardly be clever enough to have anything of value to communicate to either a hearing person or another deaf person. Articulate deaf people were thus silenced by an overwhelming hearing majority's consensus regarding their lower intellectual capabilities and certainly regarding their ability to communicate abstract thoughts via signed language.

This development to a degree might be interpreted as a reaction of hearing people to the flourishing deaf communities, which by the mid-nineteenth century had evolved around American schools for deaf children. The increasing support of the oral method may be explained with the advancement of medical perspectives about deaf people in the course of the century. Medical science served to objectify deaf people to a hearing public. Early periodicals had praised signing or "mute" deaf people as autonomous individuals, implicitly assuming that deaf people had the same agency as their hearing counterparts. By contrast, the shift to talking about—rather than with—deaf people in what appeared to be scientific language resulted in denying them the status of autonomous individuals.

By the late nineteenth century, for most hearing Americans the central question with regard to deaf education was not what might be best for deaf children (and adults), but how to assimilate them into the hearing mainstream in order to "improve" their lot. The euphemistic idea of "improvement" allowed hearing people to ignore their fears of an unknown and frightening world apparently without sound and (spoken) language. Hearing people were so busy imagining deaf lives that they, for the most part, were literally unable—and certainly unwilling—to give attention to what deaf people had to say about their education and other issues. This development was reflected in a growing body of publications by and for deaf people, who created a world on their own apart from the—with regard to deaf culture and agency—hearing ignorance surrounding them.

Notes

[Note that in the following, when no author is given, none was provided in the publication that is being cited.]

1. D. Greenberger. "Articulation," *American Annals of the Deaf and Dumb* 21, no. 3 (July 1876), 186.

2. Douglas C. Baynton, *Forbidden Signs: American Culture and the Campaign against Sign Language* (Chicago: The University of Chicago Press, 2011 [1996]).

3. Harlan Lane, *When the Mind Hears: A History of the Deaf* (New York: Vintage Books, 2013 [1984]).

4. A recent monograph that heavily draws on journal articles is Rebecca Anne Rourke Edwards, *Words Made Flesh: Nineteenth-Century Deaf Education and the Growth of Deaf Culture* (New York: New York University Press, 2012).

5. Examples given in chronological order—"Anecdotes of the Deaf and Dumb,"*Youth's Friend* (August 1, 1834), 123–26; "The Affectionate Sisters,"*Sunday School Magazine* (January 1, 1836), 69–71; "The Deaf and Dumb Boy's Thoughts on Prayer," *Sunday-School Journal* 10, no. 5 (September 4, 1839), 500; "The Blind Man and His Deaf Wife; or, Beautiful Compensation," *The Ladies' Repository* (December 1854), 543; "The Deaf Shoemaker. By Phillip Barrett. With other stories for the young. New York: M. W. Dodd," *The Ladies' Home Magazine* (December 1859), 315; "The Education of Deaf Mutes: Shall it be by Signs or Articulation? By Gardiner Green Hubbard, of Cambridge, Mass." Boston: A. Williams & Co. . . . ," *The Ladies Repository* 38, no. 3 (September 1867), 231–32; "The Deaf Uncle [a brief play],"*Our Boys and Girls* 4, no. 88 (September 5, 1868), 572; "Care in Speaking to the Deaf,"*Godey's Lady's Book* (September 1874), 287.

6. Frederick Barnard, "Existing State of the Art of Instructing the Deaf and Dumb," *Literary & Theological Review* 2 (September 1835), 378.

7. "Capacity of the Deaf and Dumb,"*The Telegrapher* 4, no.15 (December 7, 1867), 124; John R. Burnet, "Annual Examination at the New York Institution," *The Deaf-Mutes' Friend* 1, no. 8 (August 1869), 233.

8. *The Deaf-Mutes' Friend* 1, no.11 (November 1869), 340.

9. Rachel Sutton-Spence, "British Manual Alphabets in the Education of Deaf People since the 17th Century," in Leila Monaghan, Constanze Schmaling, Karen Nakamura, and Graham H. Turner, eds., *Many Ways to Be Deaf: International Variation in Deaf Communities* (Washington, DC: Gallaudet University Press, 2003), 25–48.

10. "The Articulation System,"*The Deaf-Mutes' Friend* 1, no. 5 (May 1869), 137.

11. E.g., *American Agriculturist; Central Union Agriculturist and Missouri Valley Farmer; Farmer and Mechanic; Farmer's Monthly Visitor; New England Farmer; New England Farmer, and Gardner's Journal; New England Farmer, and Horticultural Register; New-York Farmer & Horticultural Repository; North Western Farmer; Western Farmer & Gardener; Yankee Farmer, and News Letter; Yankee Farmer, and New England Cultivator.*

12. "Alphabet of the Deaf and Dumb," *Western Farmer & Gardener* 11, no. 51 (December 22, 1854), 203; "Deaf and Dumb Alphabet," *Western Farmer & Gardener* 12, no. 16 (April 20, 1854), 62; "Advantages of Being Deaf," *Western Farmer & Gardener* 15, no. 11 (March 12, 1858), 44.

13. "Are Our Dumb Animals Deaf?," *Our Dumb Animals* 6, no. 8 (January 1874), 69.

14. In the following discussion, I did not include articles on legislation from *The British Medical Journal* of the 1890s.

15. "Trial of Deaf and Dumb Person," *American Jurist & Law Magazine* (January 1, 1830), 158–63.

16. "Bequest of a resident of North Carolina to 'The Deaf and Dumb Institution.' Held, that 'the President and Directors of the North Carolina Institute for the Education of the Deaf and Dumb,' were entitled to take. — President, &c., of the North Carolina Institute vs. Norwood. . . . ," *Livingston' Monthly Law Magazine* 1, no. 9 (September 1853), 571–74; "A Deaf Juryman," *The Monthly Law Reporter* 8, no. 4 New Series (August 1855), 239; "The Competency of Witnesses," *The American Law Register* 8, no.1 (November 1859), 1–27.

17. A. Davis Smith, "Contributory Negligence by Persons with Defective Senses," *The American Law Register* 29, no. 8, New Series Volume 20 (August 1881), 507–16.

18. Gino Carlo Speranza, "The Survival of the Weakest as Exemplified in the Criminal," *The American Law Register* 52, no. 3, Volume 43 New Series (March 1904), 159–66.

19. "A Deaf Subject," *Legal and Insurance Reporter* 9, no. 5 (January 31, 1867), 36.

20. "Day Schools for the Deaf; Gallaudet Celebration; Kindergarten for the Deaf; Deaf Tramps; Illinois Alumni Association; School at Palmacottah; Destruction of New Brunswick Institution by Fire; New York Kindergarten Cottage; Mississippi School and Yellow Fever; Linotype; Jackson Vertical Writing; Deaf Mute Lawyer," *Charities Review* 7, no. 2 (October 1897), 713–15.

21. An excellent account of the first half of the twentieth century is Susan Burch, *Signs of Resistance: American Deaf Cultural History, 1900 to World War II* (New York: New York University Press, 2004).

22. See chapters one and three in Anja Werner, *The Transatlantic World of Higher Education: Americans at German universities, 1776–1914* (New York: Berghahn Books, 2013).

23. "Deaf and Dumb Indians," *Weekly Entertainer or, Agreeable and Instructive Repository* 47 (March 9, 1807), 197.

24. "A Remarkable Case of a Man born Deaf," *New Wonderful Magazine and Marvelous Chronicle* 3, no. 25 (April 1, 1794), 287; "Account of Thomas Mitchel, a Notorious Impostor," *New Wonderful Magazine and Marvelous Chronicle* 4, no. 37 (July 1, 1794), 28–31; "Some Remarkable Observations on Deaf and Dumb PERSONS,"*New Wonderful Magazine and Marvelous Chronicle* 5, no. 49 (October 1, 1794), 103–6; "Historical Wonders, Containing Many Wonderful Facts," *New Wonderful Magazine and Marvelous Chronicle* 3, no. 25 (April 1, 1794), 178–80.

25. E.g., "Observations d'un sourd & muet, &c. — Observations on an elementary Course of Education for the Deaf and Dumb, by One who is Deaf

and Dumb," *London Review of English and Foreign Literature* 11 (January 1780), 59–61.

26. "Deaf and Dumb," *The North American Review and Miscellaneous Journal* 5 (1817), 52; W. B. Chelsea, "Account of the General Institution established in Birmingham, for the Instruction of Deaf and Dumb Children; including Rules of the Society, and a List of the Patrons, Officers, and Subscribers. . . . ," *Gentleman's Magazine* (May 1814), 471–72.

27. E.g., "A Little Deaf and Dumb Boy," *Unitarian Monitor* (March 13, 1833), 187; "A Little Deaf and Dumb Boy," *Youth's Friend* (May 1, 1833), 78; "A Deaf and Dumb Boy," *Sunday School Magazine* (January 1, 1836), 59–61; "A Deaf and Dumb Boy," *Youth's Companion* (September 23, 1836), 76.

28. E.g., *American Annals of the Deaf and Dumb* 1, no. 1 (October 1847).

29. "On the Removal of the Deaf and Dumb to Their New Asylum, Erected by the Liberality of the General Government [poem]," *American Baptist Magazine, & Missionary Intelligencer* (July 1, 1821), 160; "Education of the Deaf and Dumb [From 'Jonathan Kentucky's Journal,' in the 'New Monthly Magazine']," *Weekly Entertainer and West of England Miscellany* 3, no. 21 (May 21, 1821), 385–87.

30. Examples include "Manual Alphabet for the Deaf and Dumb," *Mirror of Literature, Amusement, and Instruction* 3, no. 74 (March 13, 1824), 161–62; "Fifth Report of the Directors of the American Asylum at Hartford, for the Education and Instruction of the Deaf and Dumb. May 12th 1821," *Literary Gazette, or, Journal of Criticism, Science, & the Arts* 1, no. 36 (September 8, 1821), 561–63; "Letter from H. Buell, Deaf and Dumb," *Evangelical Monitor* (December 29, 1821), 149–50.

31. E.g., "Deaf and Dumb Men," *Boston Medical Intelligencer* (November 25, 1823), 161–62; "84. The first number of a new Monthly work appeared on the 31st of March, entitled, 'The Aurist, or Medical Guide for the Deaf.' . . . ," *Gentleman's Magazine* (May 1, 1825), 446–47; "XI. Examination of the Organs of Hearing from the body of a boy, aged 13 years, who had been the subject of Congenital Deafness. By J. Thurnam, Esq., Member of the Royal College of Surgeons in London. Communicated by Dr. Sims," *Medico-Chirurgical Transactions* 19 (1835), 162–66.

32. "A Remarkable Account of Two Children who were deaf and dumb from the birth, being brought to speak articulately. From the register of the academy at Caen, in Normandy," *The Churchman* 7, no. 44 (January 13, 1838), 1.

33. "Cure of the Deaf and Dumb," *Christian Advocate* (March 10, 1827), 107; "Cure of the Deaf and Dumb," *Boston Medical Intelligencer* 4 (May 22, 1827), 21.

34. "Exhibition of the Deaf and Dumb [From the Journal of Commerce of Saturday]," *American Railroad Journal & Advocate of Internal Improvements* (May 18, 1833), 316; "Exhibition of the Deaf and Dumb [Jour. of Com.]," *Christian Magazine* (June 1, 1833), 189–90; "Exhibition of the Deaf and Dumb," *Boston Masonic Mirror* (January 19, 1833).

35. "The Little Deaf Mute," *The Penny Library for School Children* (January

1845), 73–74, here n73; also "On the Instruction of Deaf Mutes," *Christian Observer* (December 1, 1826), 739–46. Emphasis in the original.

36. "The Little Deaf Mute," n74. *The Penny Library for School Children* (January 1845).

37. E.g., "Injustice to Deaf and Dumb Teachers," *The Social Revolutionist* 4, no. 2 (August 1857), 36–38; "Recollections of a Deaf and Dumb Teacher. . . . Amusing Sketches of the Deaf and Dumb Pupils," *The Ladies' Repository* (August 1857), 487–89; "Missionaries and Deaf Mutes," *Baptist Family Magazine* 2, no. 9, New Series (September 1858), 266–67; "South Carolina Institution for the Deaf, the Dumb, and the Blind," *The North Carolina Journal of Education* 2, no. 8 (August 1859), 248–51; "The Wrongs of the Deaf and Dumb; or, Ignorance and Education," *The R. I. Schoolmaster* 6 (January 1860), 9–11; "Anecdotes of the Deaf and Dumb," *The Magazine of Good News* (July 1862), 197–98; "The Arkansas Deaf-Mute Institute," *The Home Guardian* 31, no. 2 (February 1869), 39–42.

38. Clymer, "Letter from Washington," *The Deaf-Mutes' Friend* 1, no. 5 (May 1869), 156.

39. See *The Deaf-Mutes' Friend* 1, no. 9 (September 1869), 275.

40. "XIX. Pathological Researches into the Diseases of the Ear, Supplement to Seventh Series: Sebaceous Tumours in the External Auditory Meatus. By Joseph Toynbee. . . ," *Medico-Chirurgical Transactions* 47 (1864), 203–7; "The Physical, Moral and Intellectual Constitution of the Deaf and Dumb," *Athenaeum* 1878 (October 24, 1863), 537.

41. "Leaves from the Journal of an Old Doctor. Number Nineteen. The Deaf and Blind Patient," *Street & Smith's Literary Album* 1, no. 22 (May 19, 1866), 345–46.

42. Thomas Gallaudet, "Church Work among Deaf-Mutes," *The Spirit of Missions* (March 1866), 114–15; "A Deaf and Dumb Service," *Fraser's Magazine for Town and Country* 79, no. 471 (March 1869), 336–40; "A Deaf Mutes Prayer," *The Advocate of Christian Holiness* 7, no. 4 (April 1876), 118.

43. B. St. John Ackers, "Deaf, Not Dumb," *Journal of the Society of Arts* 25 (April 27, 1877), 541–49; "Deaf, Not Dumb," *The British Medical Journal* 2, no. 875 (October 6, 1877), 481.

44. *The Deaf-Mutes' Friend* 1, no. 6 (June 1869), 178.

45. Ibid.

46. "Early Teaching and Training of Deaf and Dumb Children," *The Deaf-Mutes' Friend* 1, no. 5 (May 1869), 138–40.

47. "Letter from Washington," *The Deaf-Mutes' Friend* 1, no. 4 (April 1869), 126; Edward M. Gallaudet, "Deaf-Mutism," *American Annals for the Deaf and Dumb* 20, no. 4 (October 1875), 244. As regards Patterson, see Andrew R. Dodge and Betty K. Koed, *Biographical Directory of the United States Congress, 1774–2005: The Continental Congress, September 5, 1774, to October 21, 1788, and the Congress of the United States, from the First through the One Hundred Eighth Congresses, March*

4, 1789, to January 3, 2005, inclusive, (Washington, DC: US Government Printing Office, 2005).

48. Edward J. Davenport, "Remarks upon the Deaf and Dumb," *The Boston Medical and Surgical Journal* 12, no. 16 (May 27, 1836), 246.

49. "How to Educate the Deaf and Dumb: A Short Exposition of the Proposed Plan for the Establishment of Day Schools for Teaching the Deaf and Dumb to Speak by means of Articulation and Lip-Reading, on Mr. Mary's System," *Athenaeum* 2048 (January 26, 1867), 119.

50. "Communication with and Between Deaf Mutes," *Scientific American* 21, no. 24, New Series (December 11, 1869), 372–73.

51. "Deaf-Mutes," *The Deaf-Mutes' Friend* 1, no. 3 (March 1869), 93.

52. Ibid. Emphasis in the original.

53. Ibid.

54. "Of Deaf Mutes That Talk," *New York Academy of Medicine* (October 1861), 270.

55. Harvey Peet, "Analysis of Bonet's Treatise on the Art of Teaching the Dumb to Speak," *American Annals of the Deaf and Dumb* 3, no. 4 (July 1851), 200–11, here 204–5.

56. "Letter from New York," *The Deaf-Mutes' Friend* 1, no. 1 (January 1869), 22–23.

57. Ibid., 23.

58. Ibid.

59. Ibid.

60. "Letter from New York," *The Deaf-Mutes' Friend* 1, no. 11 (November 1869), 348.

61. Babu J. N. Banerji, "Education of the Deaf in India," *Lend a Hand* 16, no. 5 (May 1896), 359–62.

62. Cuming Walters, "Deaf and Dumb Heroines in Fiction," *Athenaeum* 3570 (March 28, 1896), 414; Deas Cromarty, "Deaf and Dumb Heroines in Fiction," *Athenaeum* 3571 (April 4, 1896), 448.

63. "Education of the Deaf in the United States," *Charities Review* 7, no. 1 (September 1897), 606–10.

64. E.g., "Oral Instruction of the Deaf and Dumb," *The British Medical Journal* 2.2324 (July 15, 1905), 146.

2

"Enlightened Selfishness": Gallaudet College and Deaf Citizenship in the United States, 1864–1904

Joseph J. Murray

ON FEBRUARY 23, 1878, the president and the vice president of the United States, joined by the speaker of the House of Representatives and chief justice of the Supreme Court, as well as the secretary of war, the secretary of state, the attorney general, the postmaster general and the chair and members of the congressional committees on appropriations, accompanied by other governmental officials gathered in Washington, DC. What urgent and important occasion brought together the heads of all three branches of the United States government, members of the cabinet who headed the federal government's most important executive departments, and several powerful representatives of Congress's funding authority on behalf of the nation? The event began with a visit to a newly built gymnasium, where the most powerful politicians on the North American continent gathered to observe a group of young deaf men do athletic exercises. President Rutherford B. Hayes and the others then walked over to a chapel where they observed progress in the schoolwork of deaf children and of deaf college students. After this exhibition, the group enjoyed a pantomime performance by several of the college students.

The august visitors expressed "great delight and surprise at the progress which had been made by the pupils and students" on this occasion of the 21st anniversary of the founding of the Columbia Insti-

The author would like to thank Brian Greenwald for his detailed comments on earlier drafts of this article.

President Theodore Roosevelt at commencement on May 2, 1906. Courtesy of Gallaudet University Archives.

tution for the Deaf and Dumb, which also encompassed the National Deaf-Mute College, or what is today known as Gallaudet University.[1]

This visit by leading political figures was not a one-time occurrence. In the first decades of the college, the college often hosted politicians, justices of the Supreme Court, and noted leaders in higher education during its annual Presentation Day/Charter Day events, which served as graduation ceremonies and an occasion to demonstrate the work of the college to outsiders. In fact, every US president from Ulysses S. Grant to Theodore Roosevelt, except William McKinley, visited Gallaudet University during their term in office.[2] Some of these visitors, such as Chief Justice Salmon P. Chase, served on the institution's board of trustees as well.

Why this sustained interest in a small college serving a unique population? The college regularly graduated only a handful of students each year, with the distinguished guests above attending in a year when the graduating class at the college numbered only four students. There was no doubt a curiosity felt by outsiders toward deaf people. The exhibition of the academic accomplishments of deaf students was a long-standing tradition in the education of deaf people, and Edward Miner Gallaudet, president of the Columbia Institution for fifty-three years, and of the college for forty-six years, used exhibitions to gain support for the institution. His first exhibition of students took place in the old House of Representatives meeting chamber in the US Capitol building eight months after he moved to Washington, DC.[3] President Gallaudet was well known around Washington, DC.[4] His social connections no doubt helped raise the prominence of the college among the small group of social and political elites in the nation's capital. One political leader, James Garfield, was a longtime supporter of the college and deaf people, stemming from interest in deaf education in his home state of Ohio. Garfield was a nine-term member of the United States House of Representatives, chair of the appropriations and the ways and means committees, and, for a brief 200 days before his assassination, the twentieth president of the United States. His support was critical to the college during the annual congressional budget debates and in raising the profile of the college during his political career.[5] Garfield's steadfast support for the college was an important part of the college's prominence in its first decades. All of these played an important role in the attention the college attracted over the years.

In addition to hearing, nonsigning people's fascination with deaf education, Garfield's support, and Gallaudet's networking skills, the college attracted much interest and support from leading political and intellectual figures of the day because its supporters, both hearing and deaf, held it up as an example of America's image of itself as a nation that gave all its citizens an equal chance to succeed. The college encompassed this ideal in several ways. The benevolence encompassed in raising deaf people to the status of college graduates demonstrated the greatness of the United States in a way no other nation could claim. This benevolence was a demonstration of the country's democratic ideals. A democracy requires educated, enlightened citizens and the college served as an example of the commitment the government made to ensure all its citizens could participate in the democratic process. And finally, the college and its graduates served as an example of what Garfield called "enlightened selfishness," demonstrating the foresight of politicians in investing in people who would then be "capable of doing a great work for the country" as contributing citizens.[6]

Supporters of the college, including its graduates, used this reasoning to argue for the necessity of a college for deaf people, and held the college up as a symbol of national pride. Supporters used the accom-

James Abraham Garfield, president of the United States and supporter of the National Deaf Mute College. Courtesy of Gallaudet University Archives.

plishments of the college's graduates to show that deaf people were ready to fully participate in American society as equal citizens. An important part of this argument was a conception of citizenship that embraced sign language-using deaf people as full members of American society. This understanding of deaf people as members of the deaf community but also as full participants in larger society has earlier been referred to as the idea of "co-equality."[7]

The ways in which the college was seen in its first decades, as well as the ways in which deaf people promoted the college and their accomplishments, can be said to show how deaf people attempted to harness larger social discourses to promote equality for sign language–using deaf people. During the presidency of Edward Miner Gallaudet, however, conceptions of citizenship changed. In addition to an earlier emphasis on hard work as a path to equality, the criteria of physical fitness, including the ability to speak, became increasingly important. The college's supporters had to change their presentation of the college and its graduates in the 1880s and 1890s to fit shifting social ideologies of what it meant to be a *fit* citizen, an additional criteria from the earlier focus on *equal* citizenship. This chapter looks at how the college and its supporters presented themselves in the college's annual reports during its first four decades in existence, focusing mostly on the public lectures and presentations during the college's annual Presentation Day exercises, as well as other special public events recorded in the annual reports.

A Deaf College in a Growing Nation

James Garfield, a long-time supporter of the college, noted at the time of the founding of the college, in 1864, the United States government supported three colleges directly with federal funding, the others being the colleges of the army and the navy.[8] The founding of the Columbia Institution in 1857, historian James McPherson notes, "established a precedent for direct federal aid to education."[9] The United States later enabled the creation of institutions of higher education through the Morrill Act of 1862 (and 1890), which gave large swathes of federal lands to the states to sell and endow colleges and universities. President Gallaudet often referred to these land grant colleges as justification for federal support of Gallaudet College, saying deaf people were not able to participate in other institutions of higher education because of their deafness. Since deaf people were not numerous, the country needed a single national institution for all deaf people in the United States, a point made time and again during congressional debates over appropriations to the college.[10]

The larger point being made by federal support of education was that education was seen as a national good. Amos Kendall, who was instrumental in founding the Columbia Institution, along with Gallaudet College, was a Jacksonian democrat who had long argued for the benefits of free public education.[11] The value of education was in that it enabled people to contribute back to society. Education was held up as a means of creating successful citizens. Representative William Niblack, a congressman from Indiana and long-time member of the Gallaudet Board of Trustees, asserted that "popular education, universal education, is a necessity of our political condition."[12] By this, he meant education for all, including deaf people, was necessary for securing a fully functioning democracy. McPherson traces the impulse for education of deaf people in the United States as enabling deaf people to receive "a fair chance in the race of life" and points to Jacksonian democracy as a key "current of social and political thought," which created the conditions for the establishment of the college.[13] The college fit squarely in a white male vision of free public education shaping an egalitarian nation.

It should be noted that this US egalitarianism was accorded only to white males during the nineteenth century, as was the privilege of matriculating at the college most of that century. Historian Lindsey M. Parker writes of Edward Miner Gallaudet's long opposition to admitting women to the college. It was only after an outside women's organization, the Western Association of Collegiate Alumnae, wrote in with concerns about this, pointedly noting the college's public funding, did Edward Miner Gallaudet relent and allow the admission of women in the fall of 1887.[14] Agatha Tiegel Hanson, reminiscing on the early period of co-education at Gallaudet, said "I resented that there might be any question of the right . . . of my sisters and myself to take our places in the sun."[15] Parker notes the "bonds of maleness transcended deafness in higher education" as Gallaudet University was male-only in its early years.[16] Whiteness transcended deafness at the college for 90 years until the first black deaf person, Andrew Foster, received his bachelor's degree in 1954. While the Columbia Institution had black pupils for many years, it became segregated in 1905 when the number of black students reached 14, its' highest up to that point, and remained so for nearly fifty years.[17] For nearly the entire period covered in this chapter, the words "students" and "alumni" almost always mean white men, both deaf and hearing, and this carried with it an assumption of the privileges of white male citizenship in nineteenth-century United States.

Edward Miner Gallaudet and other supporters of the college promoted an ideal of the college as a national institution from the very start. The annual report of the Columbia Institution after the founding of the college outlined an ambition to "build up an institution which shall be truly national in its influence and relations."[18] One graduate declared the mission of the college was one that unified the country, since the college admitted students from different states and thus brought together all parts of the American nation. Noting the college was founded during the Civil War, graduate Samuel G. Davidson commented that however divided "the people's representatives from the North, South, East, and West" were on politics and policy, they were "unanimous in their response to the appeal made to their common humanity" in founding the college.[19] The college's charter called for two members of Congress to be members of the college's board of trustees and had early on sought to appoint one member from each political party, in a conscious attempt to show the college as above the partisan fray. Its supporters in Congress were eager to do the same, with a supporter warning during an annual appropriations debate "we do not want politics connected with the deaf and dumb institution."[20]

To its supporters, the college's success was a point of national prestige. An 1882 Presentation Day presenter noted ". . . it is an high honor for our country that it has led all other countries in this movement" of providing deaf people with the opportunity to go to college.[21] James Garfield and his contemporaries noted the college was founded in 1864, its charter signed by Abraham Lincoln during the Civil War. At a time of great national expenditures, the federal government nonetheless made the decision to establish a new college for deaf people. James Garfield said, "That . . . the College had its origin in the midst of exhausting civil war, that appropriations have been liberally made for its support . . . during a period when demands upon the public treasury have been heavy beyond precedent, that it stands out the first of its kind in the world, reveals lasting honor on our Government."[22]

The government enabled higher education for deaf people, and this education made deaf individuals ready to make their way into the world and therefore enhance the country's status. This is a formulation of American national power as something that was given to the country by educated, enlightened citizens. In an 1878 address at the college, Garfield reminisced about seeing the US Capitol columns being built during the final stages of the Civil War, seeing the massive building project as evidence of citizens' "unshakeable faith in the final triumph and permanency of the Union." He then drew a parallel between the construction of the Capitol building and education, saying "the work of education" was pursued during the Civil War because "our citizens saw that the safety of the nation required it." The opportunity for deaf people to enjoy "college rights and privileges equal to those not similarly afflicted" was evidence that the country saw itself as setting deaf people in a place where they should have an equal chance in the race of life, tying the education of deaf people to larger national purpose of educating citizens for democracy. Garfield ended his address saying, "And that is great. It is a great glory to our nation that she has done it; and at a time when it cost something to do it."[23] These sentiments were also voiced by William Niblack at the same event. Niblack emphasized the "magnificent generosity" of the federal government in funding the college, and considered the achievements of deaf education in the United States over the past century a signature accomplishment, leaving him with "a better opinion of our race and the civilization under which we live."[24]

To its supporters, the college was a national project, one aligned with the national goal of providing opportunities to all its citizens. Education equalized the opportunities open to white deaf people, and indeed, as Garfield stressed in an address to graduates, made them "the equal of all . . . citizens not afflicted as you are."[25] Niblack declared to students and visitors at Presentation Day in 1878, "The deaf-mutes of the country are just as much a portion of our population and as much citizens of the United States as any other portion of the community."[26] At the first and only Presentation Day exercises Garfield attended as President of the United States, which was also his last public appearance, he declared that Gallaudet College made each student "a great power; and that increased power you to-day give to the country."[27] S. M. Freeman, in a speech at the college's twenty-first anniversary in 1878, declared, with President Rutherford Hayes and Vice President William Wheeler sitting in the audience, that students and graduates of the college had a "debt of gratitude we can never repay" to the college, Congress, and the country for their education.[28]

In the case of deaf people, this need for education was even more acute than for others. In his 1878 address, James Garfield noted deaf people were "only recently regarded as an almost helpless and useless portion of our common humanity" before provisions were made for education.[29] Without education, deaf people were burdens to the nation, incapable of supporting themselves. Garfield's formulation was grounded in most hearing people's image of deaf people as unable to be educated. Deaf people who were without language, were, in antiquity, held harmless for their crimes and this image of deaf people and peoples with disabilities as incapable of assuming the rights of citizenship was still very much alive at the time.[30] The act of educating deaf people at the primary and secondary level was often justified by evoking the pitiable condition of uneducated deaf people. This point was reinforced by deaf people, including one white male graduate who declared the opportunity for education as being "an escape from the thraldom worse than slavery of the body."[31] This language was common for the times as a means of promoting the need for the education of deaf people. The college's first annual report praised the "triumph" of schools for deaf people in "open[ing] the doors of knowledge to the soul-darkened deaf-mute" and thus laying the foundation for the success of the college.[32]

The twelfth annual report of the college laid out the education of deaf people as a social science experiment involving "the transmutation of a non-productive class of persons into a producing class" and deaf education as providing successful evidence of the ability of primary education to do so.[33] This presentation of deaf education was not concerned with deaf students' physical fitness or their use of sign language but on the potential for education to give deaf people opportunities to join "the producing class," a question answered in the affirmative for deaf children.

Arguments against the college during its founding and in its early years revolved around whether deaf people could even benefit from a collegiate education. President Gallaudet admitted that "benevolent and liberal-minded people" could wonder about "the practical value of a collegiate course of study to persons who are, by reason of natural disability, debarred from entering upon the full practice of any of the learned professions."[34] The answer to this lay in the graduates themselves. Garfield's presumption that the college equipped deaf people to assume "the full responsibility of citizenship" was an argument that compelled the college and its deaf graduates to demonstrate that they could work alongside hearing people, thus fully participating in American society.[35] Being offered equality conferred on Gallaudet college's graduates the necessity to show they were willing to take advantage of the opportunities they had received. Former Secretary of State John Hay told graduates they were entering "a world . . . ready to lend a hand to those who are prepared and willing . . . to help themselves."[36] In short, their success, and by extension the college's success, rested on the willingness of the white male deaf graduates to take responsibility for themselves to join the "producing classes."[37]

A key vindication of funding for the college was the actions of its graduates. What students did after graduation while "engaged in the sterner duties of mature life," as the college put it in an 1883 pamphlet, was held up as a reason for its continued funding.[38] This issue was raised with the very first graduating class of the college, in 1869, when the annual report asked, "what can educated deaf mutes do?" The answer to this question lay in the jobs the three new graduates were to take on upon graduation. Two were to be teachers and the third attained a government job after passing a civil service examination.[39] This argument, based on examples of the college's graduates' success in their life after college, had to be made time and again, in a constant justification of deaf people's abilities. This argument rested on the idea that the college made solid national citizens of its students and that these citizens contributed back to society. The majority of graduates in its first two decades, 40 altogether by 1883, went on to become teachers at schools for deaf people across the country, evidence of the college's endeavors benefitting different states across the country. Ten others worked in the civil service, six were in journalism, including three newspaper editors, and others worked as scientists and in other professional fields.[40] Recital of graduates' accomplishments occurred regularly, with President Gallaudet, six years away from retirement, proudly presenting the occupations of the college's 280 graduates on the occasion of the college's 40th anniversary in 1904.[41] Presentation Day exercises were opportunities for students to demonstrate their fitness to enter "the battle of life." The goal of students' addresses was to portray themselves as able participants in society the same way as other male and female college graduates, and their addresses drew heavily on gendered norms of citizenship. A senior male student at the college, Samuel M. Freeman, noted in 1878 that the college showed evidence of "a vigorous life" at its twenty-first anniversary, comparing it (and by extension its students) to a "young man . . . upon the threshold of manhood . . ." prepared to enter "the world's battle-field."[42] Alumnus William L. Hill noted in 1894 that the results of the college over time could be see "in almost every State of the Union" in "young men engaging successfully in the higher pursuits of life, and nobly meeting the real test of manhood and citizenship."[43]

Agatha Tiegel, later Agatha Tiegel Hanson, the first deaf woman to receive a bachelor's degree from the college, used her platform as the valedictorian of the class of 1893 to argue that women also belonged in the ranks of the college educated. In her valedictory address, "The Intellect of Women," she presented a woman's approach, saying a woman "has her own way to make in the world" and could succeed "according as her judgement is rendered accurate, her moral nature cultivated, her thinking facilities strengthened."[44] Male graduates, however, argued in terms of fitness for the battle of life. These justifications of the college's validity via deaf people's actions evoked the discourse of co-equality in gendered ways. The graduates did not hide that they were deaf or that they used sign language. But they saw deaf education and sign language as a means by which they could participate in the larger society along the same terms as other college graduates, male and female.

An 1883 eulogy to President Garfield delivered by Robert Patterson McGregor, an alumnus and first president of the National Association of the Deaf, portrayed deaf people, not as recipients of charity, but as active, engaged citizens, furthering the claim of deaf people's right to full citizenship. In his eulogy McGregor claims three roles for deaf people. "As patriots, we are proud of the achievements of the soldier; as citizens . . . we revere the dignity of the President; but as students and alumni of this college we revere the friend who loved it."[45] McGregor thus showed deaf people as active citizens, participating in rituals of patriotism and grieving, but also, as deaf people, as having a special tie to Garfield. The college's deaf students and graduates, along with its supporters, did not want deaf people viewed as objects of charity, but as full and equal US citizens.

These positive formulations of the college and deaf people's abilities are found in the Columbia Institution's annual reports and in other documents issued by the college. These sources are valuable in discovering how supporters of the college justified its existence. It should be mentioned, however, that some politicians opposed federal appropriations to the college. Many of Gallaudet's most nerve-wracking moments came during annual appropriations debates about the college. As noted earlier, the idea of the college met with skeptics in its early years who considered deaf people as unable to benefit from higher education. Those affiliated with the college resisted attempts to portray the college as a charity. Gallaudet resisted all congressional attempts to categorize the college as a charity under the control of the Board of Charities of the District of Columbia, feeling this would reduce the prestige of the institution.[46] Instead, the college was portrayed as a national institution that was supported, as the college put it, "on the broad grounds of public good."[47] Another strand of opposition in Congress had little to do with deaf people and more with a philosophy of government. The college was incorporated as a private institution and congressional opponents revolted against the idea that the federal government was making annual appropriations to a private corporation. Proponents of the college fell back on several arguments, including that the government supported other institutions of higher education via the land-grant act. Another argument was based on inertia—the government had been funding the college all along and should not stop now. But the most prominent reasons were those given above—that the college was an institution performing an important function and this function reflected well on the United States and its form of government.

The Rise of Normalcy

The college's attempts to justify its existence via its graduates continued in a period when sign language and deaf people were seen in less positive light. In the 1880s and 1890s, the rise of an educational method promoting oralism and discouraging sign language influenced public perceptions of the college and influenced how the college presented itself to the public. Students and graduates of the college at this point were not seen as prominent symbols of American ideals but as people who were different from other, normal, Americans. James McPherson calls the spirit of the times an instance of "hearing conformity," giving name to the expectation that deaf people were to fit in, via speaking and rejecting sign language, along the lines of the "Anglo-conformity" pushed by nativist anti-immigrant movements.[48] This changing perception necessitated a change in how the college's graduates presented themselves to the public.

Presentation Day exercises during the 1890s were less regularly attended by a wide range of prominent political figures, although Gallaudet's connections were enough to ensure these visitors did not disappear altogether. Addresses by outside speakers at Presentation Day exercises begin to take a different turn in the late 1880s and into the 1890s. Instead of emphasizing a common citizenship with students, visitors remarked on the differences between themselves and deaf people. While previous visitors marvelled at the accomplishments of the deaf students before them; starting in the 1890s, guests remarked upon the strangeness of the language and students of the college even while continuing to agree to its importance for deaf people.

In 1894, Secretary of the Interior Hoke Smith told graduates at the Presentation Day ceremonies that "the language which you speak to me is as wonderful and as mysterious as the language which I speak is to you."[49] This quote contravenes the ideal of co-equality. The language that was spoken to the graduates was English, and the graduates of the college were assuredly fluent in written English, and likely also in written Latin, French and other languages they had studied in the previous years. But as people "compelled to use" sign language, as Secretary Smith stated it, they were seen as different, regardless of how many written languages they knew.[50]

At the 1893 Presentation Day exercises, Daniel C. Gilman, president of Johns Hopkins University, remarked on the oddity of speaking via a sign language interpreter. He told the audience he felt "a sort of 'dumb crambo' is going on . . . close by me in which you are much more interested in what my lips may utter."[51] "Dumb crambo" was a pantomime game similar to that of charades. Not only did Gilman portray sign language as pantomime but he also stressed a distance between the students and himself in which students were not able to access what he

had to say. D. B. Henderson, a member of the US House of Representatives, related to his audience at the 1898 Presentation Day a story of
meeting a deaf couple conversing with one another by "going on in this
peculiar way (making gestures)." He admitted not "knowing any of this
deaf and dumb business," but "understood a great deal" of the young
man's romantic overtures to the young woman. Sign language was apparently a "deaf and dumb business" but since it was just gestures,
he could understand it just the same.[52] Justice Brewer of the Supreme
Court wondered out loud at the 1902 Presentation Day ceremony if the
college students before him "went at it this way" when "making love"
and gesticulated an imitation of "manual spelling and signs" with his
hands to emphasize his point.[53]

The accounts of all these presenters reflects a shift from earlier decades where sign language was seen as crucial for deaf people in achieving equality. As historian Douglas Baynton has pointed out, this period
increasingly saw people adopt negative perceptions of sign language
as throwbacks to an earlier evolutionary era now transcended with the
adoption of speech. The unseemly musings on love and sexual activities
of the college students in a public forum is perhaps due to this perception of sign language, and those who used it, as primitive.[54]

A more skeptical tone dominated the presentations of outside
speakers in the 1890s. Deaf people were more often seen as limited or
hindered in their ability to participate in larger society. Secretary Smith
told the graduates the college "lifts you above your fellow-men" giving
"opportunities beyond those of your ordinary fellow-citizens endowed
with speech." While this is at first glance similar to earlier presentations, there is a marked difference in the emphasis on physical differences between deaf and hearing people throughout Smith's address.
He exhorted the graduates to dedicate "a large portion of your lives" to
"fulfil your duty . . . to watchfulness and care for those who must use
the same language which you are compelled to use."[55] Other presenters
also made the point that graduates of the college were most suitable to
"help every imprisoned soul bereft of any of the senses" or those forced
to use the same language, a distinction which differs from earlier praise
for the college's graduates as contributing to the national mission of
education as teachers of deaf people.[56] Now, this profession was seen
as a specialized field of care, not one that had a larger national purpose. The establishment of a Normal School, a teacher training college
in 1891, showcased this shift in thinking about deaf people. The Normal
School, open only to hearing people, conferred a postgraduate degree

as confirmation they had received professional training as teachers of deaf people. As indicated earlier, however, the college's deaf graduates could not apply.[57]

This shift also saw an increasing emphasis on the physical difference of students from the rest of society, with comparisons influenced by the spread of social Darwinist thought at the time. Beniah L. Whitman, president of Columbian College, now known as George Washington University, praised the college in his 1896 address as an example of the progress of "modern civilization" by using the analogy of a herd of deer. If one deer was "lame and weak and can't keep up . . . it falls behind and goes off alone to die" as an analogy of how human society had presumably treated its weaker members in the past. The college illustrated "the better nature of man" in that it showed "we must care for those . . . who are less fortunate than those who are able to go on in the ordinary way."[58] Whitman clearly saw the college as mitigating the extremes of social Darwinism but his primary comparison of the students to "lame and weak" animals shows that he clearly saw students as different from "those . . . able to go on in the ordinary way."[59] A similar comparison was made by Representative Henderson, who compared ancient times when "deaf people were cruelly disposed of" with the current opportunities offered by the college. Henderson admitted "pain" at seeing the students because "you are of the unfortunate of earth" because of their deafness. However, there were other unfortunates, such as those "shut out the sight of the skies and parks and fields and flowers." Despite this, the students need not "despair" because there were advantages to their physical difference, such as the fact that "something or other in your misfortune closed your eyes and sealed your lips to scandal," an observation which no doubt came as a revelation to the young college students in the audience.[60] This stress on compensation for physical deficiency was made by several presenters, but Justice Brewer noted the extra obligations presented to the graduates. Should they give up the fight, they would "sink into uselessness and loneliness far sooner" than hearing people because the deaf graduates were "deprived of much of that contact" with the "outer life" or society at large.[61]

This constant reinforcement of physical difference was used by numerous presenters to stress the differences between themselves and deaf people and consequently, sought to redefine the college's mission as alleviating students' difficulties. Ethelbert D. Warfield, president of Lafayette College, spoke to the graduates at an 1897 Presentation Day of his mother, "so shut in because she cannot hear," but he reassured them that all people have limitations and "limited as you may be, you may yet plant a little tree" which could grow to assist future generations.[62] The French ambassador noted that his country held the same views as the United States with respect to their common efforts toward the "relief of the unfortunate" in his 1898 address to students, a task that promoted "the advancement of civilization."[63] By way of contrast, former Secretary of State John Hay, who had presented the college's charter to President Abraham Lincoln in 1864, evoked an earlier era's view of the college in his 1898 presentation when he spoke of the graduates entering "a world which looks kindly on earnest, well-taught young men and women" and which would support those "willing, as these young people are, to help themselves."[64] An earlier era's view of education as providing autonomy and equal citizenship to deaf people along the lines offered other citizens had shifted to a social Darwinist view of the college as an attempt to mitigate the worst of the problems faced by people who were seen as physically deficient.

The college itself, led by Edward Miner Gallaudet, took steps to emphasize the normalcy of its graduates during this period. Annual reports in the 1890s shared accounts of speech training and Presentation Day exercises of the time showcased graduates' speaking abilities. Some deaf graduates even gave their addresses in spoken English. The stated aim of these speech demonstrations was to show that an education in sign language would not hinder the development of speech.[65] But that these demonstrations were necessary at all shows the increasing power of the pure oral movement in deaf education in claiming control over public representations of deaf people. Because oralists were publically skeptical of the college, seeing it as an "irritant" and a "stronghold" of sign language, the college felt a need to establish a department of articulation and stressed in 1893 that it would "preserve unimpaired . . . whatever powers of speech and reading" students had before entering the college.[66] While the college apparently had first seen as impractical the development of speech in students not previously using it, their views changed during this time, as shown in the 1898 annual report that noted the success of the college in speech training classes for these students.[67]

Public demonstrations of speaking abilities at Presentation Day exercises in the 1890s likely reinforced hearing people's impressions of deaf people as physically different and not quite equal to hearing people. Whitman called himself "amazed" to witness the speaking abilities of the 1893 graduates, calling it a "wonderful thing" if students could "utter with clearness even a few words to those within the sound of the voice."

Indeed, the fact that one student presenter "spoke nearly, if not quite, as distinctly and clearly, and as well as an ordinary speaker" could be considered one of the "marks of progress" that one should admire.[68] The tone of Whitman's remarks is very different from the proclamations of equal citizenship by presenters in the 1870s and 1880s.

Deaf people maintained the discourse of co-equality, but brought in discourses of normalcy to promote their ability to make their way in society as deaf people. This was also true of the college's deaf supporters. Amos Draper, a long-time professor of mathematics and intellectual leader in the American Deaf community, published a set of justifications for the college in the 1890 annual report which encapsulates this new orientation. Draper asserts the need for a college along traditional lines, noting the accomplishments of its graduates in the field of deaf education. But he also emphasized that deaf graduates also entered a wider variety of professions outside of deaf education. One was an attorney admitted to practice at the US Supreme Court, "and is reputed to command an income of $15,000 a year."[69] Another was a newspaper editor whose product "is an elevating influence even in the center of cultured Massachusetts where it is published."[70] Draper emphasized the success of graduates outside of schools for deaf people to argue that the college was able to prepare its graduates to serve as mentors to other deaf people and achieve success in larger society.

Draper also emphasized the essential biological fitness of the college's students. Only the best deaf people were admitted, and prospective students should be "endowed with talent and possessed of good character."[71] Draper stressed the necessity of a deaf-centered space to promote deaf men's development. At the time, even educators who supported the use of sign language were concerned about Deaf people forming associations. Gallaudet himself had earlier decried "clannishness" among deaf people although this did not extend to the college, rather he saw the college as educating its graduates so they could make their way in society.[72] Draper presented the interaction of the college's graduates with deaf people in schools and associations as inevitable, seeing it as an "unchangeable principle of human nature."[73] Rather than promoting clannishness, with its underlying connotations of inbreeding, Draper portrayed this deaf-centered space as a space that allowed for the promotion of biologically fit individuals. During their collegiate years, "whatever is good and strong is likely to come out and grow better and stronger; whatever is weak and mean is equally sure to be discovered and soundly snubbed, if not cured."[74] The college's strength

Gallaudet College Class of 1904. Photo in NFSD-Ida W. Roberts Collection. Courtesy of Gallaudet University Archives.

came from the "the incessant action and reaction of the students upon each other," promoting a continuous trial of strength which trained the graduates for life outside Kendall Green.[75] Upon graduation, students had "a sounder body, a quickened purpose, and an enlarged capacity."[76] Draper saw the college as a space where social Darwinist principles were successfully producing strong, physically and mentally fit individuals. Seen in this light, the college was a training ground for the new ideal of a fit individual, and Draper's formulation counters the ideas of limitations and "little trees" exemplified by outside speakers."[77] This formulation of the college refutes hearing perceptions of deaf people as physically deficient. Draper's use of this Darwinist imagery establishes the fitness of Deaf people by stressing the innate abilities of graduates who withstood a rigorous screening process and promoting the college as using competition to prepare students for the race of life. It is also an argument that uses deaf-centered spaces as an argument for deaf people's participation in society.

Arguments for Gallaudet College changed over the first four decades of its existence, reflecting dominant social discourses of the times.

The college was presented by its early supporters, including James Garfield, as a symbol of US national greatness in its early years, as an example of the nation's benevolence and the power of democracy to give all white male citizens the opportunity to succeed in the battle of life. The success of this argument can be seen in the prominence the college achieved among political and intellectual leaders in Washington, DC, in the 1870s and 1880s. Changing social discourses and the rise of Darwinist thought emphasizing physical and intellectual fitness forced the college's supporters to change their justifications for the college. In the face of public perceptions of sign language–using deaf people as different and inferior, the college's supporters justified the college as a space where deaf people were able to prepare themselves for the battle of life. The crux of the idea of co-equality was that deaf people needed deaf spaces to succeed in larger society. The arguments advanced by the college's deaf professors, students, and alumni harnessed changing social discourses over time—the value of education in promoting national citizenship, social Darwinism—to support the existence of Gallaudet College as a deaf-centered space which allowed its students the opportunity to succeed in the race of life.

Notes

1. *Twenty-first Annual Report of the Columbia Institution for the Deaf and Dumb* (Washington, DC: Columbia Institution, 1878), 7–8.

2. Eight of nine US presidents visited Gallaudet in this period. Edward Miner Gallaudet, *History of a College for the Deaf, 1857–1907* (Washington, DC: Gallaudet College Press, 1983), 203.

3. David de Lorenzo, "A Legacy of Leadership: Edward Miner Gallaudet and the Columbia Institution, 1857–1864," in *A Fair Chance in the Race of Life: The Role of Gallaudet University in Deaf History*, ed. John V. Van Cleve and Brian H. Greenwald (Washington, DC: Gallaudet University Press, 2008), 29.

4. de Lorenzo, "A Legacy of Leadership," in *A Fair Chance in the Race of Life*, 29; Maxine Tull Boatner, *Voice of the Deaf: A Biography of Edward Miner Gallaudet* (Washington, DC: Public Affairs Press, 1959), 103.

5. Edward Miner Gallaudet, *President Garfield's Connection with the National Deaf-Mute College* (Washington, DC: Gibson Brothers, 1882).

6. *Twenty-fourth Annual Report of the Columbia Institution for the Deaf and Dumb* (Washington, DC: Columbia Institution, 1881), 8.

7. Joseph J. Murray, "One Touch of Nature Makes the Whole World Kin: The Transnational Lives of Deaf Americans, 1880–1924" (PhD diss., University of Iowa, 2007).

8. Garfield's remarks in the *Twenty-first Annual Report of the Columbia Institution for the Deaf and Dumb*, 16; Howard University gained its Congressional charter in March 1867. Walter Dyson, *The Founding of Howard University By Walter Dyson* (Washington, DC: Howard University Press, 1921).

9. James McPherson, "A Fair Chance in the Race of Life: Thoughts on the 150th Anniversary of the Founding of the Columbia Institution," in *A Fair Chance in the Race of Life*, 6.

10. Boatner, *Voice of the Deaf*, 93; ". . . deaf so few," in Edward Miner Gallaudet, *History of a College for the Deaf, 1857–1907*, 91, 145.

11. Albert W. Atwood, *Gallaudet College: Its First One Hundred Years* (Lancaster, PA: Intelligencer Printing Company, 1964), 5.

12. *Twenty-first Annual Report of the Columbia Institution for the Deaf and Dumb*, 14.

13. The phrase "the race of life" was a common phrase for the time and served as the title of an edited collection on Gallaudet's history. "Current of social and political thought" in McPherson, "A Fair Chance in the Race of Life," 4.

14. Lindsey M. Parker, "The Women of Kendall Green: Co-Education at Gallaudet, 1860–1910," in *A Fair Chance in the Race of Life*, 93–5; quote on p. 94.

15. Agatha Tiegel Hanson, "The Victorian Era at Gallaudet," *The Buff and Blue* 1937, 8. Gallaudet University Archives, Biographical File "Agatha Tiegel Hanson."

16. Parker, "The Women of Kendall Green," 108.

17. Marieta Joyner, "Douglas Craig, 186?–1936," in *A Fair Chance in the Race of Life*, 81–2.

18. *Eighth Annual Report of the Columbia Institution for the Deaf and Dumb* (Washington, DC: Columbia Institution, 1865), 6.

19. *Twenty-eighth Annual Report of the Columbia Institution for the Deaf and Dumb* (Washington, DC: Columbia Institution, 1885), 7.

20. [Edward Miner Gallaudet], in *History of a College for the Deaf*, 156.

21. *Twenty-fifth Annual Report of the Columbia Institution for the Deaf and Dumb* (Washington, DC: Columbia Institution, 1882), 7.

22. As quoted in Atwood, *Gallaudet College: Its First One Hundred Years*, 20.

23. *Twenty-first Annual Report of the Columbia Institution for the Deaf and Dumb*, 15–16.

24. Ibid., 15.

25. Ibid., 16.

26. Ibid., 14.

27. *Twenty-fourth Annual Report of the Columbia Institution for the Deaf and Dumb*, 12; Atwood points out that the 1881 Presentation Day was Garfield's last public appearance in Atwood, *Gallaudet College: Its First One Hundred Years*, 20.

28. *Twenty-first Annual Report of the Columbia Institution for the Deaf and Dumb*, 8.

29. *Twenty-first Annual Report of the Columbia Institution for the Deaf and Dumb*, 16.

30. Harvey P. Peet, *On the Legal Rights and Responsibilities of the Deaf and Dumb* (Richmond, VA: C. H. Wynne's Steam-Powered Press, 1857). For an analysis of the use of legal capacity and incapacity for persons seen as disabled, see Kim Nielsen, "Property, Disability, and the Making of the Incompetent Citizen in the United States, 1860s-1940s," in *Disability Histories,* ed. Susan Burch and Michael A. Rembis (Urbana: University of Illinois Press, 2014), 308–20.

31. *Twenty-eighth Annual Report of the Columbia Institution for the Deaf and Dumb,* 8.

32. *Eighth Annual Report of the Columbia Institution for the Deaf and Dumb,* 6.

33. *Twelfth Annual Report of the Columbia Institution for the Deaf and Dumb* (Washington, DC: Columbia Institution, 1869), 5.

34. *Ninth Annual Report of the Columbia Institution for the Deaf and Dumb* (Washington, DC: Columbia Institution, 1866), 14–15.

35. *Twenty-fourth Annual Report of the Columbia Institution for the Deaf and Dumb,* 7.

36. *Forty-second Annual Report of the Columbia Institution for the Deaf and Dumb* (Washington, DC: Columbia Institution, 1899), 15.

37. *Twelfth Annual Report of the Columbia Institution for the Deaf and Dumb,* 5.

38. Announcement of the National Deaf Mute College, 1882–1883 (Washington, DC: Gibson Brothers, 1883), 18.

39. *Twelfth Annual Report of the Columbia Institution for the Deaf and Dumb,* 5.

40. *Announcement of The National Deaf Mute College,* 18.

41. *Forty-seventh Annual Report of the Columbia Institution for the Deaf and Dumb* (Washington, DC: Columbia Institution, 1904), 6–8.

42. *Twenty-first Annual Report of the Columbia Institution for the Deaf and Dumb,* 8.

43. *Thirty-seventh Annual Report of the Columbia Institution for the Deaf and Dumb* (Washington, DC: Columbia Institution, 1894), 10.

44. Agatha Tiegel Hanson, "The Intellect of Women," *Gallaudet Today,* 4:3, Spring 1974, 1–2.

45. *Twenty-sixth Annual Report of the Columbia Institution for the Deaf and Dumb* (Washington, DC: Columbia Institution, 1883), 9.

46. Gallaudet, *History of the College for the Deaf,* 197.

47. *Twenty-sixth Annual Report of the Columbia Institution for the Deaf and Dumb,* 6.

48. McPherson, "A Fair Chance in the Race of Life," 8–9.

49. *Thirty-seventh Annual Report of the Columbia Institution for the Deaf and Dumb,* 8.

50. Ibid.

51. *Thirty-sixth Annual Report of the Columbia Institution for the Deaf and Dumb* (Washington, DC: Columbia Institution, 1893), 7.

52. *Forty-first Annual Report of the Columbia Institution for the Deaf* (Washington, DC: Columbia Institution, 1898), 9.

53. The Honorable Justice Brewer concluded by saying, "It strikes me that

[signing] would take all the romance out of it." in the *Forty-fifth Annual Report of the Columbia Institution for the Deaf* (Washington, DC: Columbia Institution, 1902), 6.

54. Douglas C. Baynton, *Forbidden Signs: American Culture and the Campaign against Sign Language* (Chicago: University of Chicago Press, 1998), 36–55; Douglas Baynton, "The Curious Death of Sign Language Studies in The Nineteenth Century," in *The Study of Signed Languages: Essays in Honor of William C. Stokoe*, ed. William C. Stokoe, David F. Armstrong, Michael A. Karchmer, and John V. Van Cleve. (Washington, DC: Gallaudet University Press, 2002), 13–34.

55. *Thirty-seventh Annual Report of the Columbia Institution for the Deaf and Dumb* (Washington, DC: Columbia Institution, 1894), 8.

56. "help every imprisoned soul . . ." was uttered by Justice Brewer at the 1902 Presentation Day exercises; in the *Forty-fifth Annual Report of the Columbia Institution for the Deaf and Dumb*, 8.

57. For more on the debate over the school, see Richard Winefield, *Never the Twain Shall Meet: Bell, Gallaudet and the Communications Debate* (Washington, DC: Gallaudet University Press, 1983), 43–61. Edward Miner Gallaudet covers this in, *History of a College for the Deaf*, 182–3, 185.

58. *Thirty-ninth Annual Report of the Columbia Institution for the Deaf and Dumb* (Washington, DC: Columbia Institution, 1896), 9.

59. Ibid.

60. *Forty-first Annual Report of the Columbia Institution for the Deaf and Dumb*, 9–11.

61. *Forty-fifth Annual Report of the Columbia Institution for the Deaf and Dumb*, 7.

62. *Fortieth Annual Report of the Columbia Institution for the Deaf and Dumb* (Washington, DC: Columbia Institution, 1897), 9.

63. *Forty-first Annual Report of the Columbia Institution for the Deaf and Dumb*, 9.

64. *Forty-second Annual Report of the Columbia Institution for the Deaf and Dumb*, 15.

65. *Thirty-third Annual Report of the Columbia Institution for the Deaf and Dumb* (Washington, DC: Columbia Institution, 1893), 10.

66. Baynton, *Forbidden Signs*, 98; *Thirty-third Annual Report of the Columbia Institution for the Deaf and Dumb*, 11.

67. *Forty-first Annual Report of the Columbia Institution for the Deaf and Dumb*, 7.

68. *Thirty-third Annual Report of the Columbia Institution for the Deaf and Dumb*, 9.

69. Amos Draper, "Some Results of College Work," Appendix to the *Thirty-third Report of the Columbia Institution for the Deaf and Dumb*, 15.

70. Ibid.

71. Ibid., 17.

72. Baynton, *Forbidden Signs,* 26. Gallaudet recanted his opposition to deaf associations by the end of the nineteenth century. Edward Miner Gallaudet, "The Value of the Sign-Language to the Deaf," *American Annals of the Deaf* 32 (1887): 141–7.

73. Amos Draper, "Some Results of College Work," 17.

74. Ibid., 16.

75. Ibid., 15–16.

76. Ibid., 17.

77. "Little tree" in address by Ethelbert D. Warfield, president of Lafayette College, at an 1897 Presentation Day, *Fortieth Annual Report of the Columbia Institution for the Deaf and Dumb,* 9.

3

Citizenship and Education:
The Case of the Black Deaf Community

Carolyn McCaskill, Ceil Lucas,
Robert Bayley, and Joseph Hill

THE THIRTEENTH AMENDMENT to the US Constitution that abolished slavery was not enacted until December 6, 1865, and the Fourteenth Amendment, which defined citizenship, was enacted on July 9, 1868. The Fifteenth Amendment that prohibits denial of suffrage based on race, color, or previous conditions of servitude was enacted on February 3, 1870. Until the passage of these three amendments, Black Americans, regardless of whether they were hearing or deaf, faced severe barriers to participation in the civic life of the nation. Black Deaf Americans in particular were excluded from the educational system that is crucial to the development of a sense of citizenship and agency. Slavery, which had existed in the United States for more than two hundred years prior to the Civil War, resulted in a public policy in the South that prohibited the education of Blacks. It was illegal during that era to teach Blacks, whether slave or free, to read or write because the white power structure feared the potential influence of educated Black people. In addition, if Black people were educated, claims of inferiority would be harder to maintain. Those discovered learning to read or write were frequently severely punished.[1] Even after the Civil War ended in 1865, many Black Americans had to hide their educational aspirations. Litwack, for example, observes,

> The sight of blacks carrying books often had the same effect on whites as the sight of armed blacks, and many would have found no real distinction between the two threats. After the Civil War, in Charleston, South Carolina, black children hid their books in

market baskets until they reached the schoolhouse, fearing they would be harassed or turned back if whites thought they were going to school.[2]

After the abolishment of slavery in 1865, education was provided to freed slaves with the help of the Freedmen's Bureau during the American Reconstruction period.[3] In his recent history of African Americans, Gates notes that states, particularly southern states, spent much less on education for Black students than for White students.[4] Any ideas of citizenship or agency in the Black Deaf community, then, have no relevance until at least 1865 and in many cases until considerably later.

Education for Black Deaf Children

Publicly supported education for White deaf Americans began in 1817 in Hartford, Connecticut, with the establishment of the Connecticut Asylum for the Education and Instruction of Deaf and Dumb Persons, later renamed the American School for the Deaf (ASD).[5] In 1825, ASD admitted Black deaf students and became the first integrated school in Connecticut.[6] Following the founding of ASD, more schools were established in northern states such as New York, Pennsylvania, and Ohio,[7] and these schools had small Black populations. In the North, no separate schools for Blacks were established, but Baynton has reported that the Clarke School in Northampton, Massachusetts, which favored oral instruction, in 1908 affirmed a policy of excluding Black students.[8] However, some states did allow Black deaf students to attend classes with their White deaf counterparts.[9]

Some attempts were made to provide education exclusively for Black deaf children. In 1856 Dr. Platt H. Skinner established the P. H. Skinner School for the Deaf, Dumb, and Blind in Niagara Falls, New York. Although Skinner's background was controversial, he is still considered a pioneer. He was an abolitionist who taught fugitives and free slaves to read and write, and he was among the earliest educators to provide formal education for Black deaf students. In defending his school, Skinner wrote,

We are aware that it is a novel thing—that [it] is the first effort of its kind in the country: but why not these poor unfortunate despised African children become useful independent and happy citizens?

Why not they be producers instead of consumers? Why not they inhabit pleasant and cheerful homes of their own, instead of our poorhouses, jails, and penitentiaries, or sit upon the corners of our streets and beg? We receive and instruct those and those only who are refused admission to all other institutions, and are despised on account of their color.[10]

The School for Colored Deaf, Dumb, and Blind moved to Trenton, New Jersey, in 1860 and closed in 1866.[11]

After the Civil War, schools for Black deaf children slowly began to emerge.[12] These schools were often physically isolated, as were the residential schools for White deaf children. Separate schools, as well as so-called "Colored Departments" of White schools, were established in seventeen southern and border states. Sometimes, the "Colored Department" was on the same campus as the White school (e.g., in Kansas and Missouri), but in other states, these departments were in different parts of the state (e.g., in Georgia and Mississippi).[13] The schools were designed to house both Black deaf and Black blind students.

Most of the Colored departments and separate schools opened many years (an average of 33 years) after the White school (see table 1). Some schools accepted students from other states that did not have a separate facility for Black students. For example, Black children from Washington, DC, were sent to school in Overlea, Maryland,[14] and Black children from Louisiana went to school in Mississippi, attended public school without support services such as interpreters or note takers, or remained at home. The Black deaf schools remained open well into the twentieth century, some even after *Brown v. Board of Education*. As late as 1963, eight states still maintained separate facilities,[15] and Louisiana did not desegregate until 1978.

In addition to the Black deaf residential schools in the United States, there were several day schools and day classes for Black children enrolled in public schools. As table 2 shows, some of these classes were not established until the middle of the twentieth century.

Higher education for Black deaf students was also a challenge. Mary Herring Wright, a former student of the North Carolina State School for the Blind and Deaf (NCSSBD) recounts that she had heard about a college for the deaf in Washington, but it turned out to be only for Whites. The principal of her school discussed with her mother the possibilities of her attending a local college. In her autobiography, Wright recounts the following statements from her mother.

Table 1. Black and White Deaf Schools: Founding and Desegregation

State	White school established	Black school/ department established	Desegregation	Years between establishment of Black and White schools	Years between establishment of Black schools and desegregation
DC, KDES	1857	1857 (dept.)	1958	0	101
N. Carolina	1845	1869	1967	24	98
Maryland	1868	1872	1956	4	84
Tennessee	1845	1881 (dept.)	1965	36	84
Georgia	1846	1882	1965	36	83
Mississippi	1854	1882 (dept.)	1965	28	83
S. Carolina	1849	1883 (dept.)	1966	34	83
Kentucky	1823	1884 (dept.)	1954–60	61	70
Florida	1885	1885	1965	0	80
Texas	1857	1887	1965	30	78
Arkansas	1850	1887	1967	27	80
Alabama	1858	1892	1968	34	76
Missouri	1861	1888 (dept.)	1954	37	66
Kansas	1861	1888 (dept.)	1954 (?)	27	66
Virginia	1839	1909	1965 (2 schools)	70	56
Oklahoma	1898	1909 (dept.)	1962	11	53
Louisiana	1852	1938	1978	86	40
W. Virginia	1870	1926	1956	56	30

Note: Adapted from *American Annals of the Deaf* (1951 January); Fay (1893).

Table 2. Day Schools and Day Classes for Black Children

Day Schools and Day Classes for African American Deaf in Public Schools	Established
St. Louis, Missouri	1925
Baltimore, Maryland	1938
Kansas City, Missouri	1939
Richmond, Virginia	1939
Shreveport, Louisiana	1950
Louisville, Kentucky	1951

Note: Adapted from *American Annals of the Deaf* (1951 January)

I said he told me how smart and intelligent you are and that he hated to see your education end here. He, Miss Watford, and Mr. Mask all said they'd looked into the possibility of you going to Shaw University next year, but you'd need an interpreter for classroom work. They said the state didn't provide for that and it would be too costly.[16]

Wright graduated from the school in 1941. After graduation, she was hired as a teacher at the NCSCDB for one year. The school felt she was an excellent role model for the students. Since she did not have the necessary degree, however, she eventually left the school and moved to Washington, DC, to work at the US Department of the Navy.

William "Bill" King, a graduate of the Indiana State School for the Deaf in Indianapolis, faced a similar predicament. He was excited by the thought of attending Gallaudet College with his classmates. When he was informed that he could not attend Gallaudet because of the color of his skin, he was devastated. King applied to West Virginia State College, a historically Black college (HBCU), and after graduation, he was hired as a teacher at the West Virginia School for the Colored Deaf in the town of Institute.[17]

In addition to a number of Black deaf residential schools in the United States, there were several day schools and day classes for Black children enrolled in public schools. As table 2 shows, some of these classes were not established until the middle of the twentieth century.

Not surprisingly, Black deaf people were affected by the same racial discrimination that Black hearing people faced, as well as the same social isolation and marginalization that contributed to the development and maintenance of African American English (AAE). Racial discrimination was present in local, state, and regional organizations in the Deaf community. The National Association of the Deaf (NAD), founded in 1880, welcomed Black Deaf Americans at first. However, in 1925, the Cleveland Conference of the NAD changed its bylaws to prohibit Black people from becoming members.[18] Black people (and women of all races) had to wait until 1964 to gain the right to vote in the association.[19]

Studies of Black people in the Chicago and Washington, DC, Deaf communities in the 1980s reported that clubs and congregations were still segregated and that the races rarely intermingled.[20] Black deaf children were impacted in particular ways; for example, some states had laws requiring that Black deaf students be taught only by Black teachers.[21] Tennessee passed such a law in March 1901.[22]

Teachers, Oralism, and Language from Home

Three key issues are central to understanding the education Black deaf children received in segregated schools. First, is the teachers—Who taught at the Black schools in the South? Were they hearing or deaf, Black or White, and did they have formal training in teaching deaf children? Second, is oralism—did it have the same role in the education of Black deaf children that it did in the education of White deaf children? That is, did Black children receive instruction in signed language, or did they suffer from exclusively oral instruction? Finally, what kind of language did children from Black deaf families bring to school? Was it ASL, a distinct variety of ASL, or a system of home signs? Unfortunately, information is scarce regarding this last factor, and we only touch on it later.

The Teachers

Historically, African American educators have been the largest group of professionals to provide leadership within the community. Throughout the nineteenth century and the first half of the twentieth, African American educators in private and public schools held themselves responsible for the educational achievement of the children and adults attending their schools[23] and viewed education as the way to achieve individual enrichment, as well as social progress.[24]

In the early years of deaf education in the South, there was a mixture of Black and White and deaf and hearing teachers, at least at some schools. In North Carolina, for example, the superintendent from 1896 to 1918 was John E. Ray, a hearing advocate of deaf teachers and sign communication. He hired deaf faculty, both Black and White, including Thomas and David Tillinghast, Blanche Wilkins, and Thomas Flowers. Wilkins and Flowers were both Black and were obvious role models for the students.[25]

African American teachers were important for the children they taught because the children needed to see that teachers of color could exist and that people of color could assume leadership positions, as well as serve in many other roles.[26] Many scholars have called attention to the need for representative role models for children and youth.[27] Historically, the low academic achievement of minority students has been attributed in part to the minimal presence of minority professionals in public education,[28] thus adding a further rationale for integration to improve the self- and racial esteem of African American deaf children.

The North Carolina State School for the Blind and Deaf. Courtesy of Gallaudet University Archives.

THE TRAINING OF AFRICAN AMERICAN TEACHERS FOR THE DEAF

Many of the teachers of African American deaf children were White, despite the fact that administrators sought out better-qualified Black teachers to educate the deaf members of their own race.[29] Their number, however, was very limited.[30] In fact, White teachers were employed in several Black deaf schools, including at the Alabama School for the Negro Deaf, the Maryland School for the Colored Deaf and Blind, the Negro Department in the Kentucky School for the Deaf, and the Tennessee School for the Deaf Colored Department.[31]

Statistics regarding the work of Black teachers with Black deaf and hard of hearing students are difficult to find. Settles reported on a questionnaire that was sent to 16 institutions for the deaf that had schools or departments specifically for the Black deaf.[32] While all 16 schools replied, one school failed to give the rates of attendance. Responses from 15 schools indicated that there were 837 Black pupils (428 males and 409 females) who were taught by 81 teachers (22 males and 59 females). In addition, the questionnaire revealed that of the 81 teachers, 48 were college graduates, 18 had two years of college, and 15 were high school

Table 3. Schools for the African American Deaf and Historical Black Colleges/ Universities

Schools for the "Colored/Negro" Deaf	Historical Black Colleges/ Universities
Kendall School for the Deaf	Howard University
North Carolina State School for the Deaf and Blind	Shaw University
Alabama School for the Negro Deaf and Blind	Talladega College
Virginia School for the Colored Deaf	Hampton University
West Virginia School for the Colored Deaf	West Virginia State College
Florida State School for the Deaf	Florida A&M University
Southern State School for the Deaf	Southern State University
Mississippi School for the Negro Deaf	Jackson State University
Arkansas School for the Colored Deaf and Blind (Madison School)	Philander Smith College

graduates. Many schools recruited teachers from HBCUs. However, despite shared ethnicity, many of these teachers had little education or experience in methods of teaching deaf students.[33] Mary Herring Wright, a graduate of the North Carolina school, comments directly on this issue. She describes one teacher as "never bothering to really learn the signs. She mostly made up her own signs and her motions were quick and jerky. We had to teach all of the new teachers how to sign."[34] Ties between HBCUs and Black deaf schools were broken when desegregation resulted in the closure of the Black schools and the pupils were sent into formerly all White schools.[35] Table 3 shows the relationships between a number of HBCUs and Black deaf schools.

According to Brill, the problem was not addressed until Superintendent E. A. Gruver of the Pennsylvania School discussed it in his address as president of the Convention of American Instructors of the Deaf (CAID) at its twenty-seventh meeting in 1931.[36] He said, "The Convention should inaugurate a movement to assist the Negro teacher in receiving the benefits of the established training classes, summer schools and other activities."[37] Superintendent Gruver employed Black teachers but found it difficult to recruit Black teachers trained to work with the deaf. He urged that a program be established to provide the training teachers would need to succeed: "It seems to me that provision should be made for the systematic training of Negro young men and women in the theory and practice of the oral method of instruction as well as the general theory of teaching the deaf, so that they can train their own people later."[38]

A special training center for Black teachers of the deaf was started at West Virginia State College in Institute in 1938. In 1942 the training center for Black teachers of both the blind and the deaf was transferred to Hampton Institute in Virginia.[39] Another training class for Black teachers of the deaf was conducted at Southern University near Baton Rouge, Louisiana.[40] During the summer of 1948, 267 students were enrolled at Hampton in the curriculum for the special education of the deaf and the hard of hearing. Staff members from Gallaudet College taught during the summers of 1948 and 1949.[41] Courses were arranged over a period of several years so the students at Hampton University could earn both a bachelor's and a master's degree in special education.[42]

Even in the late twentieth century, the teaching staff in schools and programs for deaf children was still about 90 percent White.[43] In a 1993 survey of 6,043 professionals in 349 deaf education programs, Andrews and Jordan found that the number of minority teachers and professionals in deaf education was very low, constituting only about 10.4 percent of the total, and that, of those minority professionals, only 11.7 percent were deaf.[44] Redding raised the question of whether the low numbers reflect a continued resistance to change or the lack of a large pool of qualified minority candidates.[45]

The Role of Oralism

Oralism, the belief that spoken language is inherently superior to sign language, played an important role in deaf education. Even though deaf education in the United States began in 1817 with sign language as the medium of instruction, by 1880 the oral method of instruction was starting to take hold in the White schools.[46] As Burch and Joyner note, "the rise of oralism motivated schools across the country to replace deaf teachers with hearing instructors who would speak to students rather than sign with them."[47] However, oral education was not extended to Black deaf students on the same basis as it was to White deaf students. According to Settles,[48] eleven of sixteen schools or departments for Black deaf students surveyed still used an entirely manual approach (i.e., signing).[49] In 1920, three-fourths of the children at the Texas White school were being taught orally, while less than one-third of the children at the Black school were being taught orally.[50] Baynton notes: "Because of the continued use of sign language in the classroom, however, the

The Texas Asylum for Colored Deaf and Dumb and Blind
Colored Youth. Courtesy of Gallaudet University Archives.

ironic result of this policy of discrimination may have been that Southern deaf African Americans, in spite of the chronic underfunding of their
schools, received a better education than most deaf White students."[51]
Nevertheless, although some African American children received more
comprehensible instruction than White children, they were still placed
in vocational rather than academic tracks. Moreover, the facilities for
White children were far superior to those for Black children. Wright,
for example, describes a visit to the school for White blind children:
"[W]e were given a tour of their campus and the differences between
their school and ours were unbelievable. . . . [S]eeing such a difference
in how the White children were treated and how we were treated at the
Black state school left us depressed and angry."[52]

Oralism did have an impact on the education of some our study
schools who were forbidden to use ASL and forced to use speech in
the classroom even though their speech was unintelligible. The North
Carolina School for the Colored Deaf and Blind supported the oral
method, and teachers and students were forbidden to use ASL in the
classroom. This drastically hampered the students' learning and affected
their academic achievement. However, outside of the classroom, the
students continued to use ASL.[53]

Students' Early Language

The third factor concerns the language the children brought with
them to the school. There were a considerable number of Black deaf

families who used signing, and their children brought this language to school. These children no doubt served as sign models, as did White children from deaf families.[54] Most of the children, though, were from hearing nonsigning families. This area is ripe for systematic research as very little work has been done on Black deaf parents and their deaf children.

Legal Challenges to Segregation

The first challenge to the segregation of Black and White deaf children began in 1951. In *Miller v. Board of Education of the District of Columbia*, Mrs. Louise Miller, the mother of a Black deaf child, sued to overturn the District of Columbia legislation that forced Black deaf children to attend school outside the district, either the Maryland School for the Colored Deaf in Overlea or another school. Unhappy with the conditions and instruction at the Maryland school, the Millers sent their son to the Pennsylvania School for the Deaf in Philadelphia in 1949.[55] In 1952 a federal district court ruled that Black deaf children had the right to attend the Kendall School, although they remained in segregated classes there until 1958.

Two years after the Miller case was decided, on May 17, 1954, the US Supreme Court ruled in *Brown v. Board of Education* that "racially segregated schools are inherently unequal" and that segregated schools for Black and White students must be abolished.[56] The Court found support for its decision in studies that indicated that minority students learn better in racially mixed classrooms.[57] According to Frankenberg and Lee, "From the late 1960s on, some districts in all parts of the country began implementing such [desegregation] plans, although the courts made it much more difficult to win desegregation orders outside the South."[58] Opposition to *Brown* was intense in some southern states. Governor George Wallace of Alabama famously stood in a doorway at the University of Alabama, and angry Whites terrorized Blacks.[59] As we will see, this landmark decision affected not only hearing students but Deaf students also.

Reflections on Agency

In 2007, the authors of this paper began a large project to study the variety of ASL used by Black signers and known as Black ASL. An extensive videotaped corpus collected from 96 African American signers in the southern United States was created and we explored the geographical and social conditions that led to the development of a separate African American variety of ASL and documented its distinct linguistic features. We filmed 96 Black signers in six of the seventeen states that had segregated education, in free conversation and interviews and also elicited lexical items. Signers were divided into two groups, those over 55 who attended segregated schools and signers under 35 who attended integrated schools. Eight linguistic features were described.[60]

During the filmed interviews, we asked the participants specific questions about their use of language, such as when they had learned to sign, the languages they used in school, the teachers' signing skills, older signs that were unique to school and region, and their perception of the difference between Black and White signing. Overwhelmingly, the interviewees said that Black signing differs from White signing. What was very striking and unexpected were the widespread perceptions that the education for White deaf children and the signing of White deaf people were both superior to the education and the signing of Black deaf children.

Four themes emerged from the participant responses. Two of the themes clearly reflect the *lack* of a sense of agency and empowerment, the cost of from segregation and oppression. The other two themes reflect a growing sense of agency, identity, and empowerment, resulting from the end of segregated education and the rise of mainstreaming, whereby deaf children of all ethnicities can, in theory, be educated together. We say "in theory" because many schools for deaf children at this point still have largely minority populations.[61]

The First Theme: "White Deaf Education Is Better."

Many of the older signers commented that their own school was inferior to White deaf schools. They said that their schools had fewer recreational activities, sports, and materials than White schools and that their own teachers' signing skills were not as good. They also complained that they did not learn much at school. Some older signers who transferred to White schools reported that the school materials and assignments were much more difficult than the ones they had in the Black deaf schools. Also, the signers who transferred reported that White teachers' signing was so different from their own they could not understand it, and they assumed that the signing was better because it was more complex and had a more extensive vocabulary.

Even long after court-ordered desegregation following the 1954 *Brown vs. Board of Education* decision, some younger signers complained about the quality of education in their racially mixed, but formerly segregated, schools. For example, one Virginia group had a long discussion about education at their school in Hampton. They felt that the Hampton school was not as good as the Model Secondary School for the Deaf (MSSD) in Washington, DC, where they later transferred. One important difference was that they did not say that White deaf education was better; however, even though the formerly segregated school had been desegregated, in their opinion the quality of education there had not improved.

The Second Theme: "White Signing Is Better and More Advanced."

Most older signers said that White signing was better because it differed in vocabulary and complexity. One signer from Louisiana said that White signing was better because "it was difficult to understand." She was not the only person with that sentiment. Many other older signers shared this perception as well, which might be related to their perception of education: If it was challenging, then it must be superior. One Texas signer expressed the opinion that Black signing was "more gestural" and White signing was "cleaner," but she added that Black deaf people were not ashamed of their language.

The last statement was striking because all of the signers seemed willing to set aside their signing to adopt White signing. In fact, many of the older signs that they had used at the segregated school were no longer in use. A few of the younger signers believed that White signing was better than Black signing, but not for the same reasons given by the older signers. One young participant from Louisiana said that White signing was better than Black signing because Black signing had a thuggish or "street" component that would be inappropriate in some settings (e.g., WHAT'S-UP, N____?). However, another Louisiana signer disagreed and said that *both* Black and White signing—not just Black signing—had proper and improper forms. Most younger signers held a positive discussion about Black signing, which leads to the third theme.

The Third Theme: "Black Signing Is Different from White Signing Based on Style, Attitude, and Culture."

While both older and younger signers agreed that Black signing is different from White signing, the younger signers offered more positive comments about the former. A group of signers from Texas said that Black signing was more powerful in expression and movement and that it had rhythm and style, whereas White signing was more monotonic and lacking in emotion—"not fun to watch," as one of them mentioned. Also, this group said that Black deaf signers were able to show their true selves in their signing and that White signers were snobbish. It may seem that this group was critical of White signing, but one member did say that White signing was polite and courteous in comparison to Black signing.

One North Carolina signer made an interesting observation about ASL discourse. According to her, Black deaf people do not maintain eye contact with signers during a conversation. In general, eye contact is an important discourse function to maintain in a conversation between ASL signers, and breaking eye contact is considered impolite. Another North Carolina signer remarked that Black deaf signers tried to behave like Black hearing people with similar manners and expressions.

The Fourth Theme: "Younger Black Deaf Signers Sign Differently Depending on the Situation and People."

Younger signers showed an awareness of diversity in signing styles and said that they changed their register depending on the situation and the social characteristics of their interlocutors. One signer from Louisiana observed that when he socialized with older Black deaf signers, he knew that they signed differently, so he tried to accommodate to their signing; when he was with his peers, he signed like them. One Texan said that when she was at school or work, she was signing "White" to give a professional appearance (as opposed to signing "Black," which was more "street," as one Virginian remarked). A group of signers from Virginia commented that the signing at their school in Hampton was more uniform than that at the Model Secondary School for the Deaf.

Both older and younger signers agreed that a difference exists between Black signing and White signing, but they offered divergent reasons for the variation. Older signers held a negative view of Black signing because of their experience in segregated schools, where fewer activities and resources were available and their teachers had poor signing and teaching skills. Younger signers held a more positive view of Black signing as a result of their increased metalinguistic awareness and positive Black cultural expressions, but they said that Black signing was more "street" compared to White signing, which was polite and courteous (i.e., more standard). Our linguistic analyses show that, in contrast to these perceptions, Black ASL has some linguistic features that conform more closely to standard, prescriptive forms of ASL than does White signing.

In Conclusion

A lot has changed for Black Deaf Americans since the dawn of the American Reconstruction period with the provision of formal education and the eventual recognition as rightful citizens. Even though advancements have been made, poor education, underemployment, lack of professional role models, and racism are still persistent issues that are intrinsically familiar to the majority of Black Deaf Americans, despite many interventions by the outside forces. A group of Black Deaf individuals came together to find a way to combat these issues and an association created for, run by, and belonging to Black Deaf people was created: the National Black Deaf Association (NBDA). Founded in 1982, NBDA is an advocacy organization that promotes leadership, economic, and education opportunities and protects the general welfare of Black Deaf people (NBDA website). In 1987, the National Alliance of Black Interpreters (NAOBI) grew out of a workshop in an NBDA conference to take care of hearing Black interpreters who were their natural allies. NAOBI serves as a place for Black interpreters where they can go for support in their quest for excellence in their profession. NBDA and NAOBI are the powerful instances of human agency present in Black Deaf individuals who have had their fill of injustice and inequality and have pressed on with the determination to take care of themselves with their culture, their sense of identity, their education, and their language intact.

Endnotes

1. Nancy Boyd-Franklin and A. J. Franklin, *Boys into Men: Raising our African American Teenage Sons* (New York: Dutton, 2000).

2. Leon F. Litwack, Trouble in Mind: Black Southerners in the Age of Jim Crow (New York: Alfred A. Knopf, 1998), 87.

3. Eric Foner, *Reconstruction: American's Unfinished Revolution, 1863–1877* (New York: Harper Perennial Modern Classics, 1988).

4. Louis Henry Gates, *Life Upon These Shores: Looking at African American History 1513–2008* (New York: Alfred A. Knopf, 2011).

5. John V. Van Cleve and Barry A. Crouch, *A Place of Their Own: Creating the Deaf Community in America* (Washington, DC: Gallaudet University Press, 1989).

6. Gary Wait, "The Hartford Connection." (Hartford, CT: Hartford History Center, 2008).

7. Donald Moores, *Educating the Deaf: Psychology, Principles, and Practices* (Boston: Houghton Mifflin, 1987).

8. Douglas Baynton, *Forbidden Signs: American Culture and the Campaign against Sign Language* (Chicago: University of Chicago Press, 1996).

9. R. G. Brill, "The Training of Academic Teachers of the Deaf," *American Annals of the Deaf* 96 (1951): 282–87.

10. P. H. Skinner, *The Mute and the Blind* (Niagara City, NY: Author, 1959), 117.

11. Lindsay Dunn, "Education, Culture, and Community: The Black Deaf Experience," in *Deafness, Life and Culture II: A Deaf American Monograph,* vol. 45 (Silver Spring, MD: National Association of the Deaf, 1995), 37–41; E. A. Fay, *Histories of American Schools for the Deaf, 1817–1893* (Washington, DC: Volta Bureau, 1893).

12. Fay, *Histories;* Jack R. Gannon, *Deaf Heritage: A Narrative History of Deaf America* (Silver Spring, MD: National Association of the Deaf, 1981).

13. Baynton, *Forbidden Signs.*

14. Sandra Jowers, "Ending the Educational Exile of Black Deaf Children from Washington, DC: *Miller v. Board of Education of the District of Columbia*" (PhD diss., Howard University, 2005).

15. Ernest Hairston and Linwood Smith, *Black and Deaf in America: Are We that Different?* (Silver Spring, MD: TJ Publishers, 1983).

16. Mary Herring Wright, *Sounds Like Home: Growing Up Black and Deaf in the South* (Washington, DC: Gallaudet University Press, 1999), 248.

17. J. Vale, "Review of Little Paper Family for 1947–1948," *American Annals of the Deaf* 93 (1948): 511–62.

18. Susan Burch, *Signs of Resistance: American Deaf Cultural History 1900–1942* (Chapel Hill: University of North Carolina Press, 2007); John Tabak, *Significant Gestures: A History of ASL* (Westport, CT: Praeger, 2006).

19. Burch, *Signs of Resistance.*

20. Aramburo, "Sociolinguistic Aspects"; Paul Higgins, *Outsiders in a Hearing World: A Sociology of Deafness* (Beverly Hills: Sage, 1987).

21. Powrie V. Doctor, "Deaf Negroes Get a Break in Education," *The Silent Worker* (November 1948).

22. *History of the Negro Department at the Tennessee School for the Deaf.* 100th Anniversary of the History of the Tennessee School, 1845–1945 (Tennessee School for the Deaf, 1945); Gannon, *Deaf Heritage.*

23. V. P. Franklin, "They Rose and Fell Together: African-American Educators and Community Leadership, 1795–1954," *Journal of Education* 172 (1990): 39–64; Cynthia Neverdon-Morton, *Afro-American Women of the South and the Advancement of the Race, 1895–1925* (Knoxville: University of Tennessee Press, 1989).

24. Kathleen Weiler, "The School at Allensworth," *Journal of Education* 172 (1990): 9–38.

25. Susan Burch and Hannah Joyner, *Unspeakable: The Story of Junius Wilson* (Chapel Hill: University of North Carolina Press, 2007), 20–21.

26. Sabrina Hope King, "The Limited Presence of African American Teachers," *Review of Education Research* 63 (1993): 115–49.

27. See, for example, Alvis A. Adair, *Desegregation: The Illusion of Black Progress* (Lanham, MD: University Press of America, 1984); P. A. Graham, "Black Teachers: A Drastically Scarce Resource," *Phi Delta Kappan* 68 (1987): 598–605; Joseph Stewart, Jr, Kenneth J. Meier, and Robert E. England, "In Quest of Role Models: Change in Black Teacher Representation in Urban School Districts, 1968–1986," *Journal of Negro Education* 58 (1989): 140–52.

28. J. Andrews and D. Jordan, "Minority and Minority Deaf Professionals," *American Annals of the Deaf* 138 (1993): 388–96; Hairston and Smith, *Black and Deaf in America.*

29. Doctor, "Deaf Negroes Get a Break."

30. Jowers, "Ending the Educational Exile."

31. F. C. Higgins and Powrie V. Doctor, "Tabular Statement of American Schools for the Deaf, Oct. 31, 1950. A.: Public Residential Schools in the United States," *American Annals of the Deaf* 96 (1951): 191–95.

32. C. J. Settles, "Normal Training for Colored Teachers," *American Annals of the Deaf* 85 (1940): 209–15.

33. T. Flowers, "Education of the Colored Deaf," in *Proceedings of the Twentieth Convention of American Instructors of the Deaf, 1914* (Washington, DC: US Government Printing Office, 1915).

34. Wright, *Sounds Like Home,* 211.

35. Harlan Lane, Robert Hoffmeister, and Benjamin Bahan, *Journey into the* DEAF^WORLD (San Diego, CA: DawnSign Press, 1996).

36. Brill, "The Training of Academic Teachers of the Deaf."

37. Ibid., 91.

38. E. A. Gruver, "President's Address," *American Annals of the Deaf* 76 (September 1931): 367–68.

39. Doctor, "Deaf Negroes Get a Break"; I. S. Fusfield, "Summer Courses for Teachers of the Deaf in Louisiana," *American Annals of the Deaf* 86 (1941): 385.

40. S. L. Netterville, "The New State School for Negro Deaf in Louisiana," *American Annals of the Deaf* 38 (1938): 448–49.

41. Vale, "Review of Little Paper Family."

42. Brill, "The Training of Academic Teachers of the Deaf."

43. Andrews and Jordan, "Minority and Minority Deaf Professionals"; Oscar P. Cohen, John Fischgrund, and Reginald Redding, "Deaf Children from Ethnic Linguistic and Racial Minority Backgrounds," *American Annals of the Deaf* 135 (1990): 67–73; Robert Mobley, "Deaf Teachers of the Deaf," paper presented at the Conference of the Association of College Educators in Hearing Impairment, Jekyll Island, GA, February 1991.

44. Andrews and Jordan, "Minority and Minority Deaf Professionals."

45. Reginald Redding, "Changing Times, Changing Society: Implications for Professionals in Deaf Education," *American Annals of the Deaf* 142 (1997): 83–85.

46. Lane, Hoffmeister, and Bahan, *Journey into the* DEAF^WORLD.

47. Burch and Joyner, *Unspeakable,* 21.

48. Settles, "Normal Training for Colored Teachers."

49. Baynton, *Forbidden Signs.*

50. Ibid., 46.

51. Ibid., 180.

52. Wright, *Sounds Like Home,* 179–80.

53. Carolyn McCaskill, Ceil Lucas, Robert Bayley, and Joseph Hill, *The Hidden Treasure of Black ASL: Its History and Structure* (Washington, DC: Gallaudet University Press, 2011).

54. Lane, Hoffmeister, and Bahan, *Journey into the* DEAF^WORLD.

55. Jowers, "Ending the Educational Exile"; Sandy White, "Papers of Sandy White's Project on Black Deaf." Gallaudet University Archives, research materials: MS118 Box 1, Folder 2, 1990.

56. Erica Frankenberg and Chungmei Lee, *Race in American Public Schools: Rapidly Resegregating School Districts* (2002). Available from http://civilrightsproject .ucla.edu/research/k-12-education/integgration-and diversity/race-in-american -public-schools-rapidly-resegregating-school-districts (accessed November 22, 2010).

57. C. V. Willie, "The Future of School Desegregation," in *The State of Black America, 1987,* ed. J. Dewart (New York: National Urban League, 1987), 37–47.

58. Frankenberg and Lee, *Race in American Public Schools,* 2.

59. Paul Finkelman, *Segregation in the United States* (2002). Retrieved from https://web.archive.org/web/20011108164506/http://africana.com/Articles /tt_928.htm.

60. See McCaskill et al., *Hidden Treasure of Black ASL.*

61. Arthur N. Schildroth and Michael A. Karchmer, eds., *Deaf Children in America* (San Diego: College-Hill Press, 1986).

References

Adair, A.V. *Desegregation: The Illusion of Black Progress.* Lanham, MD: University Press of America, 1984.

Andrews, J., and D. Jordan. "Minority and Minority Deaf Professionals. *American Annals of the Deaf* 138(1993): 388–96.

Aramburo, Anthony. "Sociolinguistic Aspects of the Black Deaf Community." In *The Sociolinguistics of the Deaf Community,* ed. Ceil Lucas, 103–22. New York: Academic Press, 1989.

Baynton, Douglas C. *Forbidden Signs: American Culture and the Campaign against Sign Language.* Chicago: University of Chicago Press, 1996.

Boyd-Franklin, Nancy, and A. J. Franklin. *Boys into Men: Raising our African American Teenage Sons.* New York: Dutton, 2000

Brill, R. G. "The Training of Academic Teachers of the Deaf." *American Annals of the Deaf* 96 (1951): 282–87.

Brown vs. Board of Education of Topeka, Kansas, 347 US 583 (1954).

Burch, Susan. *Signs of Resistance: American Deaf Cultural History 1900–1942.* New York: New York University Press, 2002.

Burch, Susan, and Hannah Joyner. *Unspeakable: The Story of Junius Wilson.* Chapel Hill: University of North Carolina Press, 2007.

Cohen, Oscar P., John Fischgrund, and Reginald Redding. "Deaf Children from Ethnic Linguistic and Racial Minority Backgrounds." *American Annals of the Deaf* 135 (1990): 67–73.

Doctor, Powrie V. "Deaf Negroes Get a Break in Education." *The Silent Worker* (November, 1948).

Fay, E. A. *Histories of American Schools for the Deaf, 1817–1893.* Washington, DC: Volta Bureau, 1893.

Finkelman, Paul. *Segregation in the United States.* Retrieved from https://web.archive .org/web/20011108164506/http://africana.com/Articles/tt_928.htm, 2002.

Flowers, T. "Education of the Colored Deaf." In *Proceedings of the Twentieth Convention of American Instructors of the Deaf, 1914.* Washington, DC: US Government Printing Office, 1915.

Foner, E. *Reconstruction: America's Unfinished Revolution, 1863–1877.* New York: Harper Perennial Modern Classics, 1988.

Frankenburg, Erika, and C. Lee. *Race in American Public Schools: Rapidly Resegregating School Districts.* http://civilrightsproject.ucla.edu/research /k-12-education/integgration-and diversity/race-in-american-public -schools-rapidly-resegregating-school-districts (accessed November 22, 2010), 2002.

Franklin, V. P. "They Rose and Fell Together: African-American Educators and Community Leadership, 1795–1954." *Journal of Education* 172 (1990): 39–64.

Fusfeld, I. S. "Summer Courses for Teachers of the Deaf in Louisiana." *American Annals of the Deaf* 86 (1941): 385.

Gannon, Jack R. *Deaf Heritage: A Narrative History of Deaf America.* Silver Spring, MD: National Association of the Deaf, 1981.

Gates, Louis Henry. *Life Upon These Shores: Looking at African American History 1513–2008.* New York: Alfred A. Knopf, 2011.

Graham, P. A. "Black Teachers: A Drastically Scarce Resource. *Phi Delta Kappan* 68 (1987): 598–605.

Gruver, E. A. "President's Address." *American Annals of the Deaf* 76 (September 1931): 367–68.

Hairston, Ernest, and Linwood Smith. *Black and Deaf in America: Are We that Different?* Silver Spring, MD: TJ Publishers, 1983.

Higgins, F. C., and Powrie V. Doctor. "Tabular Statement of American Schools for the Deaf, Oct. 31, 1950. A.: Public Residential Schools in the United States." *American Annals of the Deaf* 96 (1951): 191–95.

Higgins, P. *Outsiders in a Hearing World: A Sociology of Deafness.* Beverly Hills: Sage, 1987.

Jowers, Sandra. "Ending the Educational Exile of Black Deaf Children from Washington, DC: *Miller v. Board of Education of the District of Columbia.*" PhD diss., Howard University, 2005.

King, S. H. "The Limited Presence of African American Teachers." *Review of Educational Research* 63 (1993): 115–49.

Lane, Harlan, Robert Hoffmeister, and Benjamin Bahan. *Journey into the DEAF^WORLD.* San Diego, CA: DawnSign Press, 1996.

Litwack, Leon F. *Trouble in Mind: Black Southerners in the Age of Jim Crow.* New York: Alfred A. Knopf, 1998.

McCaskill, Carolyn, Ceil Lucas, Robert Bayley, and Joseph Hill. *The Hidden Treasure of Black ASL: Its History and Structure.* Washington, DC: Gallaudet University Press, 2011.

Mobley, Robert. "Deaf Teachers of the Deaf." Paper presented at the Conference of the Association of College Educators in Hearing Impairment, Jekyll Island, GA, February 1991.

Moores, Donald. *Educating the Deaf: Psychology, Principles, and Practices.* Boston, MA: Houghton Mifflin, 1987.

Netterville, S. L. "The New State School for Negro Deaf in Louisiana." *American Annals of the Deaf* 38 (1938): 448–49.

Neverdon-Morton, C. *Afro-American Women of the South and the Advancement of the Race, 1895–1925.* Knoxville: University of Tennessee Press, 1989.

Redding, Reginald. "Changing Times, Changing Society: Implications for Professionals in Deaf Education." *American Annals of the Deaf* 142 (1997): 83–85.

Schildroth, Arthur N., and Michael A. Karchmer, eds. *Deaf Children in America.* San Diego: College-Hill Press, 1986.

Settles, C. J. "Normal Training for Colored Teachers." *American Annals of the Deaf* 85 (1940): 209–15.

Skinner, P. H. *The Mute and the Blind.* Niagara City, NY: Author, 1859.

Stewart, J., K. J. Meier, R. M. LaFollette, and R. E. England. "In Quest of Role Models: Change in Black Teacher Representation in Urban School Districts, 1968–1986. *Journal of Negro Education* 58 (1989): 140–52.

Tabak, J. *Significant Gestures: A History of ASL.* Westport, CT: Praeger, 2006.

Vale, J. "Review of Little Paper Family for 1947–1948." *American Annals of the Deaf* 93 (1948): 511–62.

Van Cleve, John V., and Barry A. Crouch. *A Place of Their Own: Creating the Deaf Community in America.* Washington, DC: Gallaudet University Press, 1989.

Wait, Gary. "The Hartford Connection." Hartford, CT: Hartford History Center, 2008.

Weiler, Kathleen. "The School at Allensworth." *Journal of Education* 172 (1990): 9–38.

White, Sandy. "Papers of Sandy White's Project on Black Deaf." Gallaudet University Archives, research materials: MS118 Box 1, Folder 2, 1990.

Willie, C. V. "The Future of School Desegregation." In *The State of Black America, 1987,* ed. J. Dewart, 37–47. New York: National Urban League, 1987.

Wright, Mary Herring. *Sounds Like Home: Growing Up Black and Deaf in the South.* Washington, DC: Gallaudet University Press, 1999.

4

From Deaf Autonomy to Parent Autonomy in the Chicago Public Day Schools, 1874–1920

Motoko Kimura

Day schools for deaf children in the United States started at the end of 1860s as an alternative to residential schools for deaf children. These schools were classrooms within public schools in cities and large towns, and mostly consisted of a small group of children of mixed ages. The deaf students spent most of the day in this class and some of them were mixed with hearing students only during recess, art, and other nonacademic subjects. These day schools had a twofold purpose — to keep children in their homes with their families and to integrate deaf and hearing children in order for deaf children to become familiar with the hearing world.[1]

Most of day schools were established as oral method schools by hearing people. However, there were schools founded by deaf people as sign method schools, such as the Chicago School, the Cincinnati School, and the Evansville School.[2] They were mostly established before the day school movement began to gain ground in the 1880s, choosing the oral method of teaching its students. In these schools deaf people had a voice and became involved in decision making regarding quality day school education for deaf children. These schools initiated by deaf people, however, gradually disappeared or shifted to oral schools, and deaf autonomy in advancing opinions and making decision began to be restricted.

This failure of these schools and deaf autonomy should not be understood only as problems within deaf education. The development of

This study was supported by JSPS KAKENHI Grant Number 21730724. I am indebted to Mickey Jones for his assistance in reading the draft.

day schools for deaf children coincided with the development of city public school systems near the beginning of the twentieth century; therefore, day schools cannot be discussed separately without analyzing why the development of public school systems occurred. Chicago was the fourth largest city in the United States, and, like other cities, it was forced to solve various social problems by implementing public school education. Therefore, Chicago is a good example for examining day schools with regard to how its public school system attempted to resolve social problems through education.

Deaf Initiatives in Founding Day Schools in Chicago during the 1870s

The first institution for deaf children in Illinois was established in 1846 in Jacksonville. Like other state-supported residential schools, it received state funds and was expected to accept all deaf children residing in the state. However, as the population of Illinois and, commensurately, the number of deaf children, increased in the late nineteenth century, especially in Chicago, the largest city in the state, the Illinois Institution became too crowded to accommodate all the deaf pupils. At the same time, many parents were unwilling to send their deaf children to the institution because of its long distance from their homes. For example, it was approximately 230 miles from Chicago. Furthermore, some parents wanted to avoid the non-denominational education at the institution. Additionally, poor parents could not afford to pay for their child's travel back and forth between home and the institution. If they wanted to get support for its transportation fees, they had to receive poor certification from the county.[3] For these reasons, at least 141 deaf children were uneducated in Illinois in the early 1870s.[4]

This lack of educational opportunity prompted the Chicago Deaf-Mute Society, founded in 1874 by deaf people, pushed for the establishment of day schools in Chicago.[5] In their petition to the Chicago Board of Education, that appeared in an *American Annals of the Deaf* [hereafter AAD] article, the society claimed that day schools could bring deaf children, their parents, and communities together. It would allow parents to teach their children their own trade, for the children to contribute to work in the home, provide religious education for them, and place their deaf children in school before the age of ten.[6] In addition, the society reported that many teachers preferred small schools. They also emphasized the economic merits of day school—parents would not have to bear travel costs from home to Jacksonville, and the state could manage the schools at a much lower cost than could the state institution.[7] Thus, the society provided a brand-new rationale for establishing day schools, which the editor of the *AAD* found to be made "more fully and forcibly than we have seen them stated before."[8]

Through this movement, deaf people in the society were not excluded from decision making with regard to deaf education because they were deaf. On the contrary, their deafness favorably affected the success of the movement. The society members were graduates of the state residential school in Jacksonville or in other states, and they were employed. In addition, they gave speeches via sign language and showed that education empowered deaf people to be contributing members of society. Thus, they impressed the members of the Chicago Board of Education and proved they deserved to express their opinions. In brief, society members demonstrated the desirable results of deaf education.

Moreover, there seemed to be another reason why the board favorably received the society's petition. The Illinois compulsory education system was not yet successfully developed in the 1870s.[9] The board had tried resolving the problem of increasing numbers of truant and uneducated children. The list of uneducated deaf children in Chicago prepared by the society may have persuaded the board to support their petition, which offered a solution to these problems with regard to deaf children.

In planning for the new schools, the city's board of education anticipated that members of the society would be employed as teachers because some of them had teaching experience. Since the members used sign language at the time of the proposed petition, it seems, then, that the board was not initially concerned about the schools' communication methods in instructing their students. There is evidence to support this. State authorities also did not demonstrate a keen interest in the teaching method of the day schools. There was no discussion about it in the state biennial reports from around 1875 until 1882. Instead, the state seemed more interested in establishing another residential school in the northern part of the state.[10] The 1874 petition of the Chicago Deaf-Mute Society was favorably received because the city board of education and state authorities initially saw day schools as a temporary solution to the problem of overcrowding in Jacksonville.

Philip A. Emery, principal of the first day
school in Chicago. From *Landscapes of History:
A Manual Explanatory of Chart, Religion and
Science, and the Twelve Axioms of History,* 1875.
Courtesy of Gallaudet University Archives.

Day School Education during the First Twenty Years and Deaf Movements against Low Quality Education

The first day school for the deaf in Chicago opened in January 1875
within the Jones public school, with Philip Emery as its principal.[11] The
school faced a number of problems in its early years. The biggest problem was poor attendance, caused by a number of factors, such as the
board of education's repeated relocation of the day school classroom
to different schools due to overcrowding in the public schools,[12] young
children having difficulty traveling alone in the city to get to school,
indigent pupils who could not afford train fares and, as a result, usually walked to school (and did not attend in inclement weather), and
some indigent pupils not having appropriate school clothing.[13] As a re-

sult, irregular attendance led to ineffective teaching. Some pupils did attend school regularly and some often were absent from school, but the teachers were forced to teach all pupils at the same time and in the same classroom.

Emery tried to enforce the state law to promote students' regular attendance. When the Committee on Text Books and Course of Instruction within the Chicago Board of Education decided to found the first day school for the deaf in Chicago, the committee also suggested that committee members compose a memorandum to the state legislature asking for funding of the Chicago day school.[14] During this process, Emery worked with Martin A. DeLany, the senator who represented the North Chicago district. In 1879, the state legislature retroactively appropriated $15,000 for the school years 1874–75 to 1878–79, and continued to support $5,000 per year until the school year 1881–82.[15] Owing to the appropriations, the number of day schools increased from one to five. This state support played an important role in the management of Chicago day schools during their early years. The reason why the state approved the support may lie in the fact that they expected the day schools to complement deaf education that the state institution could not provide at the time until a second institution could be established in the future.[16]

The new schools were located in three divisions of the city: north, south, and west. Until the academic year 1891–1892, each school had one teacher and enrolled approximately ten pupils. Emery became the principal of all the schools, and he employed one articulation teacher for all the schools' pupils. Though the number of schools increased, state law did not permit the schools to use its funding for commuting fares or boarding even though some parents living in Chicago suburbs wanted to enroll their children.[17] Consequently, Emery accommodated some of his pupils at his own home, and he and other teachers including deaf teachers sometimes paid train fares for their pupils, but this did not solve the attendance problems.[18] In an effort to increase the school enrollment, Emery walked through the city after school to seek out deaf pupils and persuade their parents to send them to day schools.[19] Despite these efforts, the enrollment in the day schools did not increase at all, and the quality of education in them did not improve until the 1890s.

The Chicago Board of Education wanted permanent state funding for the day schools because the board could not afford to finance the maintenance of these schools.[20] However, the state aid lasted only until 1881–1882, despite the fact that the state shifted its policy to support the day schools rather than build a new residential school.

Table 1. The Outline of Chicago Day Schools for the Deaf, 1875–1917

Year	Funding Source	Number of Schools	Number of Pupils	Principal	Communication Mode
1875	City	1	20 to 40	Philip Alfred Emery	Sign
1880	State	4–5 small schools	About 50	Philip Alfred Emery	Sign
1886–1894	City	4–5 small schools	About 50	Philip Alfred Emery, until 1891	From sign to combined and oral
1895–1896	City	4–5 small schools	60–70	Lawrence Oscar Vaught; Henry C. Hammond	From sign to combined and oral
1897–1912	City and State	9–13 small to medium-size schools	100–250	Mary McCowen	Combined to oral
1912–1917	City and State	4 large center schools	250–300	Mary McCowen	Combined; oral

Note: The author compiled the data from the *AAD* and the *ARBEC*. The number of students shows the enrollment, not the actual attendance.

The students enrolled in the day schools were highly diverse in terms of former schooling, age, gender, ethnicity, family economic status, and hearing conditions, (e.g., congenitally deaf, semi-deaf,[21] and late deafened people). During the schools' first twenty years, teachers used the manual method because it proved to be the most efficient teaching method. Emery, who was deaf, strongly believed in the manual method over the oral method, which needed more individualized instruction. He gave higher priority to the development of students' reading and writing skills over speech skills in the early grades. Perhaps for this reason, many of the teachers were deaf or semi-deaf, and some of them had been residential school students. Between 1875 and 1896, the Chicago day schools had approximately twenty teachers, including deaf and semi-deaf teachers; Emery, his wife Mary, James E. Gallagher, Webster D. George, and Lars M. Larson, and Mary Griswold.[22]

The day schools were expected to improve the old curriculum of the residential institutions and introduce a curriculum similar to that used in the public schools. While the common public school curriculum was partially adapted for the day schools, there was no demand to meet the public school grade system and standards.[23] After all, day schools could not provide an education that enabled deaf children to acquire the skills and knowledge they needed, which was the aim of the petition launched by the deaf-mute society in 1874. No records exist regarding students' educational success, such as measures of the number of graduates working in different occupations, how many became responsible citizens (i.e., taxpayers), or how many eventually enrolled in hearing high schools.[24] Further, *The Deaf-Mute Advance*, a newspaper published by the Illinois Institution, does not contain any articles on day school graduates getting jobs, although there are numerous records indicating that Illinois School alumni acquired jobs in Chicago. In addition to the low quality education, the early public day schools, unlike the residential institution, did not offer industrial education, and it was not required for deaf day school teachers to get the same teacher certification as that required for public school teachers in the nineteenth century.[25] Therefore, deaf teachers could become day school teachers, if they had teaching experiences in the institutions and could sign. The explanations given above may have affected the low quality of education in deaf day schools.

Even though Chicago's population increased, school enrollment did not, remaining at approximately 50 pupils in all five schools until the early 1890s. Parents' disappointment over the educational quality led them to transfer their children to private deaf schools. A number of poor immigrant parents enrolled their children in a Catholic school, the Ephepheta School for the Deaf, which was founded in 1884. Through charitable donations from friends of the parish, Ephepheta supplied boarding accommodations.[26] Other parents, who wanted their young children to learn through the oral method, transferred them to a private school in the suburbs, the McCowen Oral School for Young Deaf Children founded by Mary McCowen in 1883.[27]

In addition to the Deaf-Mute Society, the deaf community formed another organization in Chicago, the Pas-a-Pas Club, in the early 1880s. The members disagreed with Emery about the cause of the problems experienced by the day schools. Their views were published in *The Deaf-Mute Advance* as original articles as well as reprints of articles from general newspapers and other deaf newspapers. According to those articles, the Chicago day schools received warm praise from *The Deaf-Mute Advance* editors until 1884, when the schools began to be criticized for their management. The next year, *The Deaf-Mute Advance* reprinted an article from *The Texas Mute Ranger* in which M. A. Martindale investigated the Chicago schools and concluded that there were five day schools with a total of six teachers and 57 enrolled pupils (according to *AAD*), but only 23 pupils in actual attendance.[28] The issues regarding cost effectiveness were also known to the members of the Chicago Board of Education. The 1884–85 proceedings of the board reported that T. Brenan, the chairman of the Committee on Deaf-Mute Schools and a supporter of Emery, asked for more time to communicate with Martindale regarding the management of the day schools.[29]

In 1890, *The Deaf-Mute Advance* editor wrote that the citizens of Chicago had reason to be embarrassed by the continued mismanagement of their day schools for the deaf. He referred to an article in *The Silent World*, the newspaper of the Pennsylvania Institution, in which the correspondent severely chastised the management about the fact that the annual appropriation of $4,500 was much more than the appropriation received by day schools in other cities, and yet Chicago schools ranked the lowest of all. The correspondent further criticized principal Emery, noting that "while the attendance at each school was not more than two or three, Emery received much salary." He also mentioned that deaf people in Chicago had made another united attempt to break up the "Emery Family Trust."[30] The issue of day schools thus reached the city council.[31] It was suggested that an outside expert be appointed to investigate the functioning of the schools.[32] In fact, the "Emery Family," namely, Mary Emery, Emery's wife, and Grace Emery, their daughter, had been employed as teachers at the Chicago day schools since their foundation. Deaf people of Chicago were especially critical of this fact, and sarcastically referred to the schools as a "family trust."

The Pas-a-Pas Club seemed to agree with the criticisms that appeared in *The Deaf-Mute Advance* and it began efforts to improve the undesirable situation in day schools. Ethelbert D. Hunter, a leading member of the Pas-a-Pas Club since its formation, who was educated in Kentucky, pointed out that two of the day school teachers did not know sign and insisted that they were incompetent. He was convinced that under Emery's leadership the Chicago schools were poorly managed and that Emery should be removed as superintendent.[33] He believed that a deaf superintendent could not judge whether a teacher of articulation was competent or not. Furthermore, other articles showed that Emery was too old to breathe new life into the schools.[34] The Club suggested that outside experts be brought in to investigate the day schools' management and that Philip G. Gillett, superintendent of the residential school in Jacksonville, and John W. Swiler, the superintendent of the Wisconsin School, were qualified for such roles.[35]

In 1892, the Pas-a-Pas Club finally succeeded in forcing Emery to resign. Lawrence Oscar Vaught, a hearing, former boys' supervisor at the Illinois Institution became the new principal.[36] The Pas-a-Pas Club took pride in accomplishing their goal, and they were pleased with the choice of Albert G. Lane as Chicago's new public school superintendent, as well as several members of the school board, who had expressed interest in the schools for the deaf.[37]

One possible explanation for the success of the Pas-a-Pas Club's efforts may be the diversity within Chicago's deaf community. Namely, a diversity of deaf people's views could disclose the problems in the day schools. Chicago had a large deaf population[38] and a number of deaf organizations, including the Pas-a-Pas Club, the Chicago Deaf-Mute Society, the Chicago Mute Circle, and the Chicago Young Men's Christian Association.[39] Like the larger hearing community, deaf people held a multiplicity of views, and they did not accept certain opinions simply because they were expressed by other deaf people. For example, one might believe that all deaf people at this time favored the sign system; however, a number of deaf Chicagoans objected to the day schools' educational policy of not teaching via the oral method as other schools did.[40] Such independent thinking within the deaf community seems to imply that the Chicago deaf community was not homogenous, and it challenges our preconceptions of deaf people's attitudes toward deaf education.[41]

Of course, we cannot entirely attribute Emery's resignation to the Pas-a-Pas Club. We also must consider the influence that Alexander Graham Bell [hereafter Bell] had on the day school movement. Bell was a strong proponent of the oral method, and he believed that deaf students should be integrated as much as possible into hearing society, especially in school. He visited many states in the 1880s and 1890s and was instrumental in convincing the state of Wisconsin to fund day schools throughout the state.[42] In 1884, the Illinois Board of State Commissioners of Public Charities invited Bell to Springfield, the state capital, to speak on the merits of day schools and the oral method, and Frederick H. Wines, secretary of the state board, recommended that he also address the Chicago Board of Education, which he did in July 1884. His address greatly had impressed the trend of day schools and the oral method for deaf education on both the municipal and state boards. After that, the commissioners came to be interested in the day school education and its method, and clearly endorsed maintaining day schools as an alternative to building another residential school in the state.[43] Thus, after 1885, hearing people gained more influence over the decision-making in education for deaf students.

A Shift from Deaf Autonomy to Increased Parental Autonomy

The Pas-a-Pas Club's efforts to reform the day schools did not end with the resignation of Emery. In 1893, the club formed a subcommittee of graduates from the Illinois Institution, the Chicago day schools, the Clarke Institution in Massachusetts, the Lexington Institution in New York, and the Missouri Institution to investigate the issues involved in building another residential school in northern Illinois. This subcommittee suggested that one central school with boarding facilities would be more effective than the several day schools scattered throughout the city and it recommended funding be secured by private, city, or state aid. Because the Illinois Institution was too crowded to handle the growing number of deaf children in the state, this proposed centralized school could form graded classes and provide instruction throughout the day for deaf children who needed individualized attention and extracurricular learning. In addition, since the school would be in Chicago, deaf children could go home every weekend. It means that the school would not deprive deaf children of their parents' attention and affections.[44]

The Chicago Board of Education initially agreed with this plan. According to the board's proceedings, it discussed whether a recommendation should be made for a legislative bill that would restructure the day schools into one centralized deaf school with boarding facilities. They believed that this would solve the day school attendance issues for many children who were too poor to go to school by public transportation or too young to travel in the streets by themselves. The recommendations of residential facilities also aimed to increase the enrollment of uneducated deaf children; consequently, the board thoroughly investigated daily school attendance, and wrote letters to parents of deaf day school pupils to ask their opinion of the new plan for one centralized day school. The board received approvals from most parents.[45] Additionally, they sent letters to a number of graduates from the Illinois School to request an opinion about the plan for a centralized school and they received letters from former pupils of the Chicago day schools who favored the plan.[46] The members of the Pas-a-Pas Club might have been among the people who sent out these letters. Despite these actions, the board decided to postpone its recommendation for the legislative bill.[47] The reasons for this are discussed later in this chapter.

Another group became active in the Chicago school reform movement in the mid-1890s — the Chicago Association of Parents of Deaf Children, organized in 1895 to promote the education and welfare of deaf children. The association sent an open letter to the state legislature in which they proposed a bill to establish and maintain one or more day schools that would have an average attendance of not less than three pupils in cities throughout Illinois.[48] This bill passed in 1897, after this more day schools were added, resulting in a total of 13 schools, until these were finally merged into four schools in 1913. In the end, the Chicago day schools adopted the small school system recommended by the parents' association rather than the centralized school plans the Pas-a-Pas Club and the board of education had originally endorsed.[49]

The identity of the parents' association members and their educational philosophy may explain why the board rejected the centralized school plan in favor of the small school plan. Most association members were middle class, and they included Chicago businessmen, philanthropists, progressive educators, a teacher at the Hull House, oralist deaf educators, Chicago day school teachers, the McCowen School teachers, and deaf teachers who were former Chicago day school teachers or still taught at the day schools (see table 2). Most of them were a part of the progressive movement of the late nineteenth century that advocated the improvement of society on all levels, including education. They believed in equal treatment and economic and educational opportunity for all people including minority groups and disabled children. Therefore, they could not agree with the boarding plan because it would compel deaf children to be separated from hearing communities and homes that they would have been able to participate in if they could hear. In other words, the plan for a centralized school was rejected not because it was presented by deaf people, but because the progressivists in Chicago at the time—including the Chicago board of education members—did not agree with it.

Many prominent Chicagoans were active in the progressive movement. Mary McCowen herself, who established the McCowen Oral School, was a key figure in the Chicago day school reforms, and had strong ties with Chicago progressivists. John Dewey, the progressive educator, was a member of the Board of Trustees of the McCowen Oral School. Other members of McCowen's Board of Trustees were spouses of Chicago's prominent education reformers. Mrs. Martin Ryerson, whose husband was president of the Board of Trustees of the University of Chicago and president of the McCowen Oral School Board of Trustees; Mrs. Charles L. Hutchinson, whose husband was president of the Art Institute of Chicago, was one of the board members. Cornelia Smith Crane, president of the parents' association, who was married to a prominent benefactor who was instrumental in establishing manual training in Chicago public schools. He himself was associated with Dewey. Cornelia Crane, was president of the parents' association not only because her husband was a philanthropist but also because their daughter, Mary Josephine Crane, had become deaf in early childhood. The fact that such people were leading members of the parents' association and the day school movement is one reason for their success. In addition they corresponded with Bell, well-known for his oralist views on deaf education.[50]

Bell's influence in Chicago cannot be ignored. The Chicago Association of Parents of Deaf Children's open letter contained many references to Bell's opinion about day schools, the use of the oral system, and the Wisconsin Plan that Bell had promoted.[51] The Chicago progressivists believed all Chicago residents deserved to be educated in public schools within their own communities, and many parents of deaf children, association members, and the Chicago board of education members agreed.[52]

Table 2. Deaf Educators and Prominent Members of the Parents' Association

Name	
Philip G. Gillett	The ex-superintendent of the Illinois Institution
Alexander G. Bell	A national leader of the day school movement
Caroline Yale	A principal of the Clarke Institution
Sarah Fuller	A principal of the Boston day school
Mary McCowen	The founder of the McCowen School and a principal of the Chicago day schools
Robert C. Spencer Charles N. Haskins Dora Montgomery Fannie Williams James E. Gallagher	The first president of the board of directors of the Wisconsin Phonological Institute for Deaf Mutes Teacher at the Chicago day schools
Albert G. Lane	The superintendent of the Chicago public schools
Ella Flagg Young	The president of the Chicago Normal College, the superintendent of the Chicago public schools from 1909, a progressive educator
Mr. and Mrs. Charles Richard Crane	A Chicago businessman, a philanthropist, a leader to introduce the manual training in Chicago public schools, parents of a deaf daughter
Col. And Mrs. Francis W. Parker	The founder of the Parker Practice School and the Francis Parker School, "a father of progressive education"
Dr. Frank Billings	The founder of the Institute of Medicine of Chicago in 1915
Mrs. John Dewey	A wife of a national progressive educator, the founder of the Chicago Practice School
Dr. John W. Streeter	The president of the board of trustees of the McCowen School when the school was incorporated in 1890
Mrs. Marion F. Washburne	A lecturer of the Chicago Froebel Association
Mary McDowell	A teacher of kindergarten at the Hull House
Mr. and Mrs. Orville T. Bright	The founder of the Orville T. Bright School
Mr. and Mrs. Sidney O. Blair	The secretary of the board of trustees of the McCowen School when the school was incorporated in 1890

Source: The Chicago Association of Parents of Deaf Children, *Public school classes for deaf children: An open letter*, 1897, 15–16.

Moreover, it is important to note that several deaf people approved of the aims of the parents' association and enrolled as members. They included Gallagher, Philip Hasenstab, and Mary Griswold, who all had teaching experience in the Chicago day schools or connections with the Chicago day schools. Gallagher had taught at least from 1878–79 to 1899–1900.[53] Hasenstab was a graduate of the Illinois Institution and became a teacher there; he led the Chicago Mission for the Deaf for a long time and became a special substitute teacher candidate of the Chicago day schools in 1894.[54] Griswold was a semi-deaf teacher with a long teaching career at the Chicago day schools.[55] The fact that some deaf people initiated the foundation of the northern Illinois Institution, while others supported the small day school plan in Chicago, once again demonstrates the complexity of the Chicago deaf community's views on this issue.

We cannot explain the Chicago Association of Parents' success in the day school reform movement without pointing out that teacher-parent cooperation became an important part of Chicago public schools from the late 1890s onward because it was believed to improve overall educational efficacy.[56] The Chicago Association of Parents' success in the day school reform movement, therefore, did not originate only from the progressive notions such as equal treatment for all people that were preferred by Chicago and state education authorities. The expansion of parents' roles in public school education similarly encouraged its success.

However, the question remains of why the board of education rejected the plan for a centralized boarding school. Many parents approved of the plan proposed by the board and the Pas-a-Pas Club. To thoroughly understand this issue, we must consider that parents of deaf children can be classified into two groups—middle-class parents, such as members of the parents' association, and working- and lower-class parents, such as those who could not afford to have their children attend school regularly. A considerable number of parents could not afford good care for their children. That is, they could not afford to pay attention to the fact of their children's school attendance and punctuality, to feed and clothe their children properly, and make their homes an effective place for their children's developing speech skills, because poor parents were living on the subsistence level. The Chicago School Board should have encouraged the latter parents to become interested in the day schools, but because this was not the case, middle-class parents were expected to be more involved in school affairs, with support from upper-class Chicago citizens. Still, no single cause for the rejection of the boarding school plan can be determined. Nevertheless, the powerful effect of the progressive surge toward "normalcy," expressed by day schools and oralism, cannot be ignored. The Chicago Association of Parents especially emphasized their merits, and thus influenced the course of Chicago day school reforms.

Educating Citizens through the Oral Method and Producing "False Positive" Subnormal Children

The day school reform movement came to fruition through the 1897 state law authorizing school districts to establish and maintain classes for the deaf in the public schools by State common school funds. As a result, day schools changed in various ways. First, the number of schools increased from five to nine and eventually to thirteen by 1912. Thus, the Ephepheta School, for example, which provided residential facilities and was supported by private donations, experienced a decrease in pupils after the law was enforced, while the Chicago public day schools experienced a significant increase in pupils.[57] Second, travel conditions improved; the increased number of schools placed throughout the city made them more accessible from the children's homes. Moreover, financial support for transportation fees contributed positively to school attendance rates in that enrollment increased to 100, and then steadily up to 300 by the 1910s. Third, four new teachers were hired.[58] After Emery resigned as principal in 1891, three new principals were appointed in succession;[59] then, in January 1896 the board selected a hearing principal, Mary McCowen.[60]

McCowen instituted changes that aimed to make deaf education equal to that in the public schools, and, as a result, the notion of citizenship in Chicago day schools began to change. Whereas Emery had focused on literacy and work skills, McCowen insisted that all children in the day schools must be educated through the same eight-grade system that the public schools employed for hearing children. The curriculum had a strongly defined structure that distinguished it from the eclectic curricula of Emery's tenure. McCowen believed that no child, at any grade, could be promoted until he or she fulfilled all grade requirements. Furthermore, to follow the public school course of study, she suggested that all subjects should be taught. She believed that, if they could complete such a full course of study, deaf children would be prepared for high school. In other words, McCowen asserted that all deaf children with an appropriate education could become Chicago citizens equal to hearing citizens or even excelling more than hearing people. It is especially significant that she presented an example as a model citizen, which children could become, as a benefactor. Such citizenship was, of course, far removed from the defective classes, and only attainable for middle- or upper-class citizens.[61] In brief, McCowen's model aimed for a type of citizenship that was equal to that of the middle-class parents who that had advocated for their children through the parents association for the deaf. Therefore, it appears that citizenship advocated by McCowen was tied to these parents' demands. To this end, she introduced the oral method more strongly than Emery had done, even though combined method schools and oral method schools both operated in the city until the early 1900s.[62] In 1910, a local newspaper reported that two deaf pupils were preparing to enter regular high school the next fall.[63] In the 1920s, many graduates had entered general or technical high schools;[64] one female pupil had entered a business college.[65]

The Chicago Board of Education generously allowed parents to choose a school based on its communication method; however, all deaf children were generally taught via the oral method since the 1910s. The day schools made significant efforts to classify the deaf children objectively according to auditory characteristics, language, speech, and intellectual abilities, believing that this would contribute to a better, and more appropriate, education for the pupils.[66]

Chicago established a Department of Child Study in 1899 to promote the scientific analyses of all children in Chicago public schools.[67] The analysts originally thought that the percentage of "true" subnormal (i.e., low or borderline mental ability) deaf children should be the same as the percentage of subnormal hearing children, but the results from 1912 and 1913 showed a higher percentage of deaf children classified as subnormal (see table 3).[68] Teachers assumed the cause of this higher percentage was not a problem of mental ability but was due to the method of instruction associated with deaf education, and they tried to improve instructional methods for language acquisition, namely, the oral method. Despite their efforts, many deaf students did not complete the deaf school curriculum and grade system and they left school without sufficient language ability, academic knowledge, and social skills to function as useful Chicago citizens. Most of these pupils were born deaf.[69]

Although an oral day school education for Chicago's deaf children was declared equal to the education for hearing children, it excluded

Table 3. Mentality of the Pupils in the Day School for the Deaf

Mentality	Pupil				
	1912		1913	
	Persons	%	Persons	%
Normal	183	71.5	206	79.8
Slightly subnormal	42	16.4	34	13.2
Distinctly subnormal	20	7.8	14	5.4
Very low mentality	11	4.3	4	1.6
Total	**256**	**100**	**258**	**100**

Source: Ella Flagg Young, "Report of the Superintendent of Schools," *ARBEC* 58, (1911–12):246; Young, "Report of the Superintendent of Schools," *ARBEC* 59, 1912–13:338.

certain deaf students who failed to learn for various reasons. Thus, the Chicago day schools produced "false positive" subnormal children who failed to acquire the skills and knowledge required to practice citizenship.

Strong Parental Support for Children's Success

We cannot acquire a comprehensive understanding of the outcomes of the Chicago day schools following the overall introduction of the oral method without considering the changing societal trends at the turn of the century. Chicago, like other growing American cities, experienced profound social change in several ways. With the development of Chicago's rail system, numerous industries relocated to the city and attracted millions of people from other states and countries seeking jobs. Employment opportunities shifted to factory work that rewarded efficiency and mass production.[70] These jobs required abilities quite different from those needed in the workshops staffed by a foreman and artisans before industrialization swept across the nation at the turn of the century.

City public schools across the country were expected to produce citizens suited for this new capitalistic society. Furthermore, the schools were faced with the challenge of educating children from different countries. Thus, the function of public schools changed; they now were driven to mold all students into American citizens.

As a result of Chicago's growing population, the number of pupils increased in all the day schools, and though parents could choose between combined method and oral method schools, most parents sent their deaf children to oral schools. Table 4 compares the number of pupils in schools using the combined method with those using the oral method in the years 1899 and 1900. The most noticeable difference lies in student attendance between the two types of schools. In clear contrast, the largest number of students in attendance for the schools using the combined method was under six months, while that of the oral schools was over nine months. In brief, the Chicago day schools were supported by parents who understood the importance of education, made their children attend school every day, and were willing to cooperate with teachers for educational improvement.

Positive educational results depended not only on the pupils' abilities but also on a strong cooperation between parents and schools. Pupils in residential schools could attend their classes without any difficulties or travel, however, pupils in day schools did not have that advantage. Therefore, the efforts undertaken by parents to ensure their children's regular school attendance was crucial for the day school pupils' educational results. To develop parent-school cooperation, Mary McCowen organized Mother's Study Clubs within the first solely oral method schools. The Yale School organized such a club immediately following its opening, which was promptly followed by similar clubs at the Lyman Trumbull and Prescott Schools. These parents were actively involved in their children's education; for instance, weekly study meetings were held that might have improved parents' understanding of the importance of regular attendance.[71]

As more pupils attended the oral method schools, more parents chose the oral schools; in brief, a virtual circle was created. The schools with enough pupils to form graded classes could maintain better student classifications, which led to better results.

McCowen fulfilled the needs of middle-class parents; however, she could not respond well to the needs of other parents. Educational success presupposes regular school attendance, and despite receiving additional train fare support, some parents including indigent parents could not force their children attend school regularly, as table 4 implies. This was problematic because the oral method required more instruction time than did the sign or combined methods. Pupils whose parents could not afford to have their children attend school regularly or could not provide support of their children's education at home became

Table 4. Comparison of the Number of Pupils between the Combined Method Schools and Oral Method Schools (School Year 1899–1900)

		Combined Method Schools				Oral Method Schools				Pupils (persons)
		Boy	Girl	Total	%*	Boy	Girl	Total	%*	
Total (persons)	June, 1899	35	27	62	38.0	60	41	101	61.9	163
	June, 1900	43	18	61	32.4	76	51	127	67.5	188
	Down/up			▼1	▼5.6			▲26	▲5.6	▲25
Attendance for the school year (persons)	Over 9 months	14	4	18	29.5	45	31	76	59.8	94
	6–9 months	12	5	17	27.8	21	15	36	28.3	53
	Under 6 months	17	9	26	42.6	10	5	15	11.8	41

*The second decimal place was disregarded. ▼ = down; ▲ = up.
Source: McCowen, "Report on the Day Schools for the Deaf 1899–1900," *ARBEC*, 46(1889/1900): 248–49.

increasingly disadvantaged over time. Consequently, these pupils had difficulty achieving good results and fell easily into backward or sub-normal categories. Furthermore, it was particularly difficult for children born deaf to succeed in an oral-only environment, regardless of their socioeconomic class. Day schools were *public* schools, so their prom-ise should have led to success for every deaf child. Nevertheless, day schools were much more affected by parental support or the economic situation of their pupils' parents than were the residential schools. The result was that deaf children whose home situations were not ideal might not be adequately prepared to practice citizenship.

A Manifest Restriction of Deaf Autonomy in the 1900s

After McCowen adopted the oral method in the day schools, deaf people tried to offer their opinions on some deaf education of the day schools. However, the Chicago Board of Education would not allow them to address the board because they were not parents of deaf children and they were denied any say in how the schools functioned.[72] Middle-class parents were increasingly seen as having more of a legitimate voice in the board's decision-making process. Poorer parents, however, had no influence on school board decisions, because they were preoccupied with making a living and could therefore not afford autonomy.

One of the most interesting characteristics of the Chicago public schools, including day schools for deaf children, was the fact that edu-cational problems were strongly connected with problems in the larger society. This was one of the reasons why noneducators, such as business-men, could become involved in educational issues. People like this who could solve social problems were considered stakeholders. As a result, not only parents, but middle- and upper-class citizens also were encour-aged to become advocates of public school education. As such, middle-class parents who were members of the Chicago Association of Parents of Deaf Children had greater autonomy in determining their children's education. These parents had a louder voice because they could solve the educational problems connected with social problems by becoming involved both in the schools and with their children at home, and by forming connections with other middle- or upper-class Chicago citizens who were interested in social problems. Lower-class parents had no say in how their children's low achievement levels might improve. More-over, their children were not adequately prepared to become productive and autonomous citizens due to sporadic school attendance and low school achievement levels. Once oralism came to dominate educational philosophy in the Chicago day schools, deaf people who had once been seen as the experts in deaf education and who had exercised greater autonomy during the late nineteenth century, consequently, were left out of discussions regarding deaf education.

We have seen how day schools prevailed through the dominance of oralism and the influence of Bell. The restriction of deaf autonomy during this period has been regarded as an increased manifestation of hearing people's views on deaf education versus those of deaf people or, alternatively, a debate about whether oralism or manualism was the most effective way of educating deaf children. However, we cannot overlook the prevailing attitude of public school education at that time; namely, the emphasis on parent involvement as a means to improve city public school education. This philosophy had a profound effect on deaf people's influence in the day schools.

Conclusion

Deaf people in Chicago had opinions and took action against Chicago day school education before the end of the nineteenth century. At times they opposed the Chicago Board of Education, while at others they cooperated with the board. Deaf graduates of residential institutions were the primary participants in the movement against day school education for deaf children. Because deaf people from different states moved to Chicago, they formed a variety of deafness-related groups and also expressed different opinions about deaf education. Though the Illinois Institution newspaper articles demonstrates that deaf people generally felt positive about other deaf people's work near the turn of the century, Chicago deaf communities criticized deaf teachers working in Chicago public schools. The varied views of Chicago deaf communities could reveal that the quality of education in Chicago day schools for deaf children was low during the initial twenty years because of problems such as inconvenient school locations for some students, transportation issues, low or sporadic school attendance, economic differences existing between students' parents and the effects of this on educational quality and school mismanagement.

Deaf people initially enjoyed autonomy regarding the education of deaf children even though the board of education did not pay enough attention to day schools for deaf children. Deaf people's autonomy was restricted after the Chicago School Board recognized that day schools could possibly solve educational and social problems within Chicago's society by making deaf students part of the public school system. While deaf people's autonomy regarding deaf education became curtailed, parents in general gained a greater ability to express their opinions about education to the Chicago Board of Education. The board began to regard parent-school cooperation as crucial for the improvement of schools. However, parents occupied two different economic strata, namely, the middle and the indigent classes. The former group had a stronger voice because upper-class citizens and progressivists supported these middle-class parents in their goal of having deaf children educated in more of a normal, (i.e., hearing school) environment. From the 1890s, middle-class parents helped facilitate the success of Chicago day schools for deaf children under McCowen's superintendency. Her influence, along with that of others, led to these schools employing the oral method.

One of the most interesting characteristics of the city public schools was the fact that the educational problems were strongly connected to the social problems inherent in the public school system. This was one of the reasons why people who were not educators, such as business-men, could get involved in educational issues. Such people, who could solve social problems through public school education, were considered stakeholders. As a result, in addition to parents, middle- and upper-class citizens were also encouraged to become stakeholders and advocates of public school education. As such, middle-class parents of students in the Chicago public school system came to have a greater say in their children's education over time while deaf people's autonomy became diminished at the same time. If deaf people wished to have a continuing influence on the direction of deaf education, they should have presented effective solutions to these social problems, cooperated more with mid-dle- and upper-class citizens and parents, and they might have achieved accomplishments more in line with their views. However, the fact that deaf people did not pursue these strategies, may help explain how their autonomy and influence on deaf education waned during this period.

Notes

1. John V. Van Cleve and Barry A. Crouch, *A Place of Their Own: Creating the Deaf Community in America* (Washington, DC: Gallaudet University Press, 1989), 117–19. See also Robert L. Osgood, "The Horace Mann School for the Deaf," in *For "Children Who Vary from the Normal Type": Special Education in Boston, 1838–1930*, (Washington, DC: Gallaudet University Press, 2000), 93–117, about the Horace Mann School in Boston.

2. Michael A. Reis, "A Tale of Two Schools: The Indiana Institution and the Evansville Day School, 1879–1912," in *The Deaf History Reader,* ed. John V. Van Cleve (Washington, DC: Gallaudet University Press, 2007), 85–115, about the Evansville Day School.

3. "Terms of Admission," *Annual Report of the Illinois Institution for the Education of the Deaf and Dumb, Located at Jacksonville* [hereafter ARIIDD] 34, (1873–74):61. Some of these impoverished parents hesitated to send their children to the institution because of wishing to avoid the stigma of poverty which was associated with receiving certification as poor.

4. Since young deaf children, impoverished children, and other children with various reasons had difficulties in enrolling in the Institution, at least 141 uneducated children existed in the state. In Phillip G. Gillett, "Report of the Principal," *Biennial Report of the Illinois Institution for the Education of the Deaf and Dumb* [hereafter BRIIDD] 32, (1871–72):15. The Chicago day schools were expected to promote such uneducated deaf children in Chicago to receive education. See "Arguments for A Day-School," *American Annals of the Deaf and Dumb* [hereafter AAD] 20, no.1 (January 1875):36.

5. Ibid., 34–6.

6. The Illinois Institution did not allow children under 10 years old to enroll. "Terms of Admission," *ARIIDD* 34, (1873–74):60.

7. "Argument for A Day-School," *AAD* 20, no.1 (January 1875):34–6.

8. Ibid.

9. Although the first compulsory education law in Illinois was passed in 1883, the free school system has been already made by the 1870s. However, the problems of truancy and non-attendance were recognized by the state superintendent of Public Instruction of Illinois. Edith Abbot and Sophonisba P. Breckinridge, *Truancy and Non-Attendance in the Chicago Schools: A Study of the Social Aspects of the Compulsory Education and Child Labor Legislation of Illinois* (Chicago: The University of Chicago Press, 1917), 47.

10. The bill to establish the second state institution in the northern Illinois was presented to both the Senate and the House in 1879 and 1881. See *Journal of the Senate of the General Assembly of the State of Illinois: Regular Biennial Session,* 31st Leg., 1879, 372 and 32nd Leg., 1881, 271, about the Senate Bill no. 363 of 1879, and no. 243 of 1881; and the *Journal of the House of Representatives of the General Assembly of the State of Illinois: Regular Biennial Session,* 32nd Leg., 1881, 424, about the House Bill no. 579.

11. Lawrence O. Vaught, "Short Sketch of the Chicago Day Schools for the Deaf, 1870–1893," in *Histories of American Schools for the Deaf, 1817–1893,* ed. Edward A. Fay (Washington, DC: Volta Bureau, 1893), 2:629–30.

12. The public schools were extremely overcrowded. For instance, 1,088 pupils were accommodated in rented classrooms, and no less than 12,919 pupils were half-day pupils who attended the morning or afternoon classes because of classroom shortages in 1882–83. See Norman Bridge, "Report of the President,"

Annual Report of the Board of Education of the City of Chicago [hereafter ARBEC] 29, (1882–83):13. Therefore the day schools for deaf children suffered from frequent relocations. For example, the Third Avenue School in the south division of the Chicago School District changed its location to the Archer Avenue School in 1885–86, the Twenty First Street in 1886–87, the Heaven School in 1892–93, and the old high school building on the west division in 1893–94. As the school in the south division became the school in the west division, another school was established on the south division. It was first located at the Doolittle School, then at the Melville W. Fuller School during the same school year, then it was moved to the Hartigan School in 1895–96. Peter Conlan, Thomas Brenan, and Rudolf Brand, "Report of Committee on Deaf Mute Schools," *ARBEC* 32, (1885–86):131–2; T. Brenan, M. B. Hereley, and Frank H. Collier, "Report of the Committee on Deaf Mute Schools," *ARBEC* 33, (1886–87):161; Severt T. Gunderson, Lucy L. Flower, M. J. Keane, John J. Badenoch, and Patrick H. Duggan, "Report on Committee on Special Funds," *ARBEC* 39, (1892–93):169; Henry C. Hammond, "Report on the Committee on Special Funds," *ARBEC* 40, (1893–94):168; Albert G. Lane, "Report of the Superintendent," *ARBEC* 42(1895–96):63.

13. Brenan, Stensland, and Bridge, "Report of Committee on Deaf Mute Schools," *ARBEC 28*, (1881–82):98; Conlan, Brenan, and Brand, "Report of Committee on Deaf Mute Schools," *ARBEC* 32, (1885–86):132.

14. S. Johnston, "School for instruction of deaf mutes," *Proceedings of the Board of Education of the city of Chicago* [hereafter PBEC], (December 29, 1874):44.

15. DeLany became a member of the city board of education and subsequently the president. He also was the first chairman of the first regularly organized Committee of Deaf Mute Schools. See P. A. Emery, *A Brief Historical Sketch of the Chicago Deaf Mute Day Schools* (Chicago: n.p. 1886):10. The appropriations were used for maintaining the schools from the school years 1878–79 to 1884–85.

16. The plan of establishing the second institution for the deaf had been discussed in the legislature until 1881.

17. The appropriation was not permitted for paying students' boarding fees, even though the Board received several applicants from parents living in Chicago suburbs. M. A. DeLany, E. G. Keith, and P. O. Stensland, "Report of Committee on Deaf Mute Schools," *ARBEC* 26, (1879–80):76.

18. Brenan, Stensland, and Bridge, "Report of Committee on Deaf Mute Schools," *ARBEC* 28, (1881–82):97, about Emery's support for accommodation. See Philip A. Emery, "Report of Principal of the Deaf Mute Day Schools," *ARBEC* 37, (1890–91):169–70, about teachers' financial support for train fares.

19. DeLany, Keith, and Stensland, "Report of Committee on Deaf Mute Schools," *ARBEC* 26, (1879–80):74–5. On the other hand, Emery began to have ideas regarding establishment of a residential school with cottages to secure homely care during this period. See J. R. Freeman, "Chicago," *The Deaf-Mute Advance* 11, no.25 (January 19, 1880):2, about his plan.

20. The board discussed about closing the day schools because the state appropriations stopped. "Continuance of Day Schools for Deaf Mutes," *PBEC*, (August 1, 1887):284.

21. It means hard of hearing.

22. Emery, *A Brief Historical Sketch of the Chicago Deaf Mute Day Schools, from June, 1874 to June, 1886, Including Some Remarks on Such Schools, and the Best Medium of Instruction* (Chicago: n.p. 1886), 5–6; "Assignment of Additional Teachers in West Division High Schools, with Salary, Also Salaries of Teachers of Deaf Mutes," *PBEC* (September 11, 1879):7–8, about Emery, his wife and Gallagher; "Election of Teachers of Deaf Mutes," *PBEC*, (June 30, 1882):181, about George; "Resignation of Teacher of Deaf Mutes," *PBEC*, (July 21, 1884):228, about Larson; "Resignation of Teachers of Deaf Mute School and Vacancy Filled," *PBEC* (September 6, 1888):19, about Griswold, a semi-deaf teacher. See also Jack R. Gannon, *Deaf Heritage: A Narrative History of Deaf America* (Silver Spring, MD: The National Association of the Deaf, 1981), 62–3.

23. Mary McCowen as a principal of the day schools indicated that the problems of day schools until the end of the nineteenth century was that deaf day schools didn't follow a regular course of study. Mary McCowen, "Report of the committee on special funds," *ARBEC* 43, (1896–97):134–5.

24. It was similar to the result of the Boston day school, one of the successful day schools. Osgood wrote that the Board of Boston Public Schools had not provided any specific data regarding the success or failure of the Horace Mann School for the Deaf graduates, which was also true with respect to exact figures on post-school activity or employment. See Osgood, *For "Children Who Vary from the Normal Type,"* 111, about pupils' careers after leaving the Horace Mann School for the Deaf.

25. A teacher certification or specific instructions in teaching experience deaf students for a terms of at least one year was required by the state law supporting to maintain deaf classes in the cities enforced in 1897. See Lane, "Report of the Superintendent," *ARBCE* 43, (1986–97):50–51. The new department for the deaf oral teacher training was added in the Normal College. See Edwin G. Cooley, "Report of the Superintendent," *ARBEC* 51, (1904–05):131.

26. The Ephepheta Society, *Annual Report of the Ephepheta Society for the Improved Instruction of Deaf-Mutes, Chicago* 2 (1886):8; Mary C. Hendrick, "The Ephepheta School for the Deaf, Chicago, Illinois, 1884–1893," in *Histories of American Schools for the Deaf, 1817–1893*, ed. Edward A. Fay (Washington, DC: The Volta Bureau, 1893), 3:3–4. Not only pupils of day schools but also those of the Illinois Institution transferred to the Ephepheta School. See "Tattle," *The Deaf-Mute Advance* 19, no. 42 (October 13, 1888):3.

27. Mary McCowen, 'The McCowen Oral School for Young Deaf Children. Chicago: 1883–1893," in *Histories of American Schools for the Deaf, 1817–1893*, ed. E. A. Fay (Washington, DC: The Volta Bureau, 1893), 3:3.

28. "Day Schools vs. Boarding Schools," *The Deaf-Mute Advance* 16, no.15 (April 11, 1885):2.

29. "Further Time to Report on Deaf Mute Schools," *PBEC* (February 11, 1885):107; "Communications in Reference to Management of Deaf Mute Schools," *PBEC* (April 22, 1885):154.

30. "Notes," *The Deaf-Mute Advance* 21, no.40 (October 11, 1890):2.

31. Brenan presented a report of the Committee on Deaf Mute Schools, stating that the Committee had considered communications from Martindale. "Communication in Reference to Management of Deaf Mute Schools," *PBEC*, (April 22, 1885):154.

32. A reprint from *The Wisconsin Times*, *The Deaf-Mute Advance* 22, no.2 (January 10, 1891):2, and a reprint article from the *Chicago Daily News*, "May Call Experts to Decide," *The Deaf-Mute Advance* 22, no.2 (January 10, 1891):4.

33. Ibid., 3.

34. "Our Chicago Letter," *The Deaf-Mute Advance* 23, no.47 (November 19, 1892):3.

35. However, the editor of *The Advance* cited an opinion from the article of *The Deaf Mute Hawkeye*, which insisted that external experts should not be people who previously worked in the same school. The editor of *The Advance* recommended the superintendent of the Iowa Institution as an outside investigator. See *The Deaf-Mute Advance* 22, no.2 (January 10, 1891):2.

36. Vaught was a young hearing man, who served three years as a boy's supervisor at the Illinois Institution, and subsequently attended the normal department of the National Deaf Mute College for one term. "Our Chicago Letter," *The Deaf-Mute Advance* 23, no.47 (November 19, 1892):3.

37. Ibid.

38. The School Committee of the Pas-a-Pas Club estimated that there were not less than 600 deaf people under 21 years old in Chicago because the city had 471 deaf people according to the census of 1890. See O. H. Regensburg, C. C. Codman, F. P. Gibson, J. J. Killinghams, B. Frank, and G. T. Daugherty, "Report of the School Committee of the Pas-a-Pas Club," *The Deaf-Mute Advance* 24, no.11 (March 18, 1893):2.

39. *The Deaf-Mute Advance* 13, no.50 (December 16, 1882):2.

40. There were some pupils who transferred from Chicago day schools to the Illinois Institution because the institution made more efforts to adopt the oral method. See "Teaching Deaf Mutes" from *The Chicago Tribune*. *The Deaf-Mute Advance* 17, no.7 (February 13, 1886):3. In fact, the Illinois Institution was one of the earliest institutions that had adopted the oral method.

41. Sometimes deaf community members argued because many deaf people came into a big city like Chicago from other states and these diverse people had various opinions. In 1877, the editor of *The Deaf-Mute Advance* strictly accused a certain person who "killed" the House bill to establish the Chicago

Institution for the Deaf. See "The Lost Bill," *The Deaf-Mute Advance* 8, no. 21 (May 26, 1877):2. In 1880, another argument began in the deaf community about Christian work for the deaf in Chicago. See "The Deaf Mutes of Chicago" reprinted from *The Chicago Tribune* Jan. 29, n.y. *The Deaf-Mute Advance* 11, no.6, (February 7, 1880):3.

42. Van Cleve and Crouch, *A Place of Their Own*, 118–19.

43. "The Education of the Deaf and Dumb," *Biennial Report of the Board of State Commissioners of Public Charities of the State of Illinois* 8, (1882–84):145–61; "Invite Pro. Bell of Washington, D.C., to Address a Public Meeting on Matter of Education of Deaf Mutes," *PBEC*, (May 29, 1884):167.

44. Regensburg, Codman, Gibson, Killinghams, Frank, and Daugherty, "Report of the School Committee of the Pas-a-Pas Club," *The Deaf-Mute Advance* 24, no.11 (March 18, 1893):2.

45. "Report of Committee on Special Funds and Prizes," *ARBEC* 41, (1894–95):233–40.

46. Ibid., 241.

47. Theodore J. Bluthardt, a member of the Chicago board of education, suggested this. See "Board and Lodging for Pupils Attending Deaf Mute Day Schools," *PBEC*, (November 7, 1894):218–19.

48. The Chicago Association of Parents of Deaf Children, *Public School Classes for Deaf Children: An Open Letter to the Fourtieth General Assembly of the State of Illinois from the Chicago Association of Parents of Deaf Children* (Wm. C. Hoolister & Bro., Printers, Chicago, 1897):12–13.

49. Ibid., 9–10, about the small school plan.

50. See Harriet H. Louthan, "McCowen Oral School for Young Deaf Children," *The New Era* 29, no.13 (March 27, 1898):11, about the connection between McCowen and the progressivists. See Norman E. Saul, *The Life and Times of Charles R. Crane, 1858–1939: American Businessman, Philanthropist, and a Founder of Russian Studies in America*, (Lanham: Lexington Books, 2012):26, about Charles Richard Crane's family.

51. The Chicago Association of Parents of Deaf Children, *Public School Classes for Deaf Children*, 1–14.

52. The Parents' association claimed that public schools for deaf children should equally apply the same day school system as public schools for hearing children, which were established as close proximity to the homes of the pupils as possible. See ibid., 2.

53. "Assignment of Additional Teachers in West Division High Schools, with Salary, Also Salaries of Teachers of Deaf Mutes," *PBEC*, (September 11, 1879):7–8; "Schools for the Deaf," *PBEC*, (June 27, 1900):299.

54. He was a special substitute candidate, but it was deferred. See "Appointment of Substitute for Deaf Mute Day Schools Deferred," *PBEC*, (November 7, 1894):218.

55. Griswold had taught at least from 1889 to 1900. See S. Johnston, "Resignation of Teacher of Deaf Mute School and Vacancy Filled," *PBEC*, (September 6, 1888):19 and "Election of Teachers," *PBEC*, (June 27, 1900):499.

56. Lane, the superintendent of the Chicago Public Schools, reported that numerous lectures for the Chicago citizens were given in the public school buildings during 1896–98. He wrote it would lead to a better knowledge of the work of the schools and make schools and parents closer. He added "Parents' Meetings" at the school house was another movement to make the relations of the home and school closer and the teacher's effectiveness in instructing would be greatly enhanced by the better mental attitude of the children, which was produced by the favorable home influences. See Lane, "The School House an Educational Center for the People," *ARBEC* 44, (1897–98):96–109.

57. The number of students in Chicago schools; 61 in November 1895, 95 in November 1896, 110 in November 1897, and 196 in November 1898. On the contrary, the number of students in Ephepheta School—98 in 1895, 103 in 1896, 110 in 1897, and 68 in 1898. See "Tabular Statement of American Schools for the Deaf," *AAD* 41, no.1 (January 1896): 45; ibid., *AAD* 42, no.1 (January 1897):47; ibid., *AAD* 43, no.1 (January 1898):53, 56; ibid., *AAD* 44, no.1 (January 1899):61, 64.

58. However two deaf teachers continued to be employed, since combined method schools were maintained. Four new teachers were employed because of the increased number of schools that year. See "Elections of Teachers," *PBEC*, (June 17, 1896):460.

59. Vaught was the principal for only one year. Although there is no record regarding the reasons for his resignation, it likely caused his immature career. "Our Chicago Letter," *The Deaf-Mute Advance* 23, no.47 (November 19, 1892):3. After he resigned, Henry C. Hammond succeeded him, who had a long teaching experience at deaf schools and was welcomed by the Illinois deaf community. However, he also left his superintendency only after two years because he accepted a more remunerative position as a superintendent at the Kansas Institution. Louthan, "Chicago Day Schools for the Deaf," *The New Era* 29, no.13, (March 27, 1898):12.

60. McCowen was elected in January 1896 and became a principal in September 1896.

61. McCowen, "Report of the Committee on Special Funds," *ARBEC* 43, (1896–97):133–35.

62. After the initiation of the first strictly oral method school, the Yale School in January 1896, more oral schools were added every year, and the number of pupils in these oral method schools kept increasing. Lane, "Report of the Superintendent," *ARBEC* 44, (1897–98):64–65; McCowen, "Report of the Day Schools for the Deaf, 1899–1900," *ARBEC* 46, (1899–1900):248–49.

63. "Deaf Mute Learns to Speak," *Chicago Daily Tribune,* (January 22, 1910):11.

64. We can hardly conclude that this result was only from day school education in the 1910s, because support teachers assisted day school children when they were partially integrated in hearing classes during the 1920s. It could be thought that deaf children could follow regular school curriculum with the help of such support teachers.

65. The public school education of the time generally appreciated the subjects connected with the business world more than academic subjects. Therefore, entering technical school and business college was an admirable choice after leaving grammar school both for hearing children and deaf children. Mary J. Herrick, *The Chicago Schools: A Social and Political History* (Beverly Hills, CA: Sage Publications, 1971):58–9, about the educational policy of the Chicago public schools.

66. Ibid., 82.

67. W. M. Christopher, "Report on Child Study," *ARBEC* 45, (1898–99):27; Ella F. Young, "Report of the Superintendent of Schools," *ARBEC* 57, (1910–11):168. The Department also examined and classified blind (or defective vision), deaf (or defective hearing), crippled, truant, tuberculosis, defective in speech, subnormal, feeble mind, epileptics, backward, children with constitutional depletion, and other special cases such as unusually bright children.

68. John D. Shoop, "Report of the Superintendent," *ARBEC* 64, (1917–18):81.

69. Ibid., 80.

70. Van Cleve and Crouch, *A Place of Their Own*, 155–6.

71. These mother's meetings were held to form a connecting link between home and school, ensuring mother and teacher communication, enabling each to profit by the experience of the other, and working together for the best interest of the child. See Louthan, "Chicago Day Schools for the Deaf," *The New Era* 29, no. 13, (March 27, 1898):13.

72. The Chicago Board of Education refused to permit a group of Deaf adults to address them about the city's day schools in 1904. John V. Van Cleve, "The Academic Integration of Deaf Children: A Historical Perspective," in *Looking back: A Reader of the History of Deaf Communities and Their Sign Languages*, ed. Harlan Lane and Renate Fischer (Hamburg: Signum Press, 1993), 342.

5

"Are We Not as Much Citizens as Any Body?" Alice Taylor Terry and Deaf Citizenship in the Early Twentieth Century[1]

Kati Morton Mitchell

ALICE TAYLOR TERRY WAS a prominent advocate for deaf people in the United States during the early twentieth century. During that era, several movements came into vogue that threatened the rights of those who were deaf, such as oralism and eugenics. Terry, through her writing and leadership, challenged the hegemony of these philosophies and affirmed the citizenship of deaf people in America. A close study of her writings shows Alice Terry's belief that deaf people had a place in society, leading her to challenge false perceptions perpetuated by the press and advocate on behalf of the deaf community regarding eugenics, oralism, and deaf organizations.

Alice Taylor was born in Missouri in 1878 and became deaf when she was nine years old.[2] She learned sign language at the Missouri School for the Deaf in Fulton, which she attended for five years beginning at age 12.[3] She enrolled at Gallaudet College for one year, where she met Howard L. Terry, whom she married in 1901. In the early years of their married life, Howard and Alice Terry lived on a farm in southwest Missouri.[4] During their first nine years of marriage, Howard and Alice had three children: Catherine Basset, born November 25, 1902, Howard Terry Jr., born December 18, 1905, and Victor T. Terry born January 3, 1910.[5] Despite the daily pressures of running a farm and raising children, Alice Terry found time to write. Her husband Howard Terry noted: "During these years on the Missouri farm, and at Carthage, Alice was writing for the old *Silent Worker*, winning friends thereby all over the nation. She became more and more interested in the education of deaf children, and in the welfare of the deaf generally."[6] After farming in Missouri, the family moved to California in 1910.[7] They moved multiple times while living in California, eventually settling in Hollywood where they lived for 30 years.[8] In California, Alice Terry continued her advocacy work for the deaf community. Her husband noted that "here Alice's real work for the deaf began."[9]

Once in California, Terry became actively involved in deaf organizations. In 1914, she worked within the California Association of the Deaf (CAD) and was also involved with its parent organization, the National Association of the Deaf (NAD).[10] Terry became the first female president of the California Association of the Deaf in 1923 and was also president of the Los Angeles Silent Club.[11] Furthermore, Terry was also a writer, with more than 130 known articles penned in publications including *The Silent Worker, The Jewish Deaf, The Deaf Mutes Journal* and the *Los Angeles Times*. In addition to her extensive activities and efforts on behalf of the deaf community, Terry was also a wife, mother, and grandmother, showing that she was a multifaceted woman, focusing on both her family as well as advocacy outside the home.

Terry's advocacy work puts her firmly within the ranks of other female political activists and reformers of the time. This group, however, was relatively small, with women's activities largely devoted to the domestic sphere during the late nineteenth and early twentieth centuries.[12] Women, particularly married white women, did not participate in the paid labor force in large numbers during that period. In 1920, only 6.5% of European American women who were married held paid employment.[13] While Terry's advocacy was volunteer work, she was active outside of the home during a time when it was not commonplace. While her work does fall within the tradition of female activism, her advocacy for deaf people also puts her squarely in the political sphere, particularly as she was an active leader in the CAD, a state-wide political association, as well as its national parent organization, the NAD.[14]

Terry's advocacy on behalf of the deaf community often incorporated discourse on citizenship. "Are we not as much citizens as any body?" she inquired in a 1920 book review.[15] Terry argued that deaf people were citizens and deserved equal treatment in society. Terry openly criticized the misrepresentation of deaf people by news media: "As usual the newspapers think our side of the matter, that is our sacred rights of citizenship, would not sufficiently interest the reading public, so do not encourage us for copy."[16] In this quote, Terry was commenting on the rights of deaf people to drive automobiles, which was a pressing issue at that time. Multiple states passed laws in 1923 that forbade deaf people from driving.[17] According to historian Susan Burch, automobiles were a vital resource for deaf people because they provided employment opportunities. They were also one of the few remaining contemporary technologies that were open to the deaf community during an age that saw the popularization of the radio, telephone, and movies, audio-dependent forms of entertainment that excluded deaf people from their benefits. Driving restrictions thus fueled a "passionate self-defense" from the deaf community.[18] Terry believed the deaf viewpoint regarding driving rights did not receive adequate attention from the press and that this omission threatened deaf people's "sacred rights of citizenship."

Such media misconceptions and misrepresentation inspired Terry to write about deaf issues in order to correct erroneous information, and she believed other deaf people should do the same. "So . . . long as our rights and liberties are threatened by an unsympathetic public which has been wrongly educated concerning us, then, and so long have we got to chronicle the sordid truth."[19] A lack of accurate information about the deaf population in the media put their rights at risk, and Terry believed it important to document and disseminate facts from the deaf perspective. To do so, Terry invoked the founding of the United States to inspire deaf writers in their duty to protect citizenship. "If we do not do this, we are not men and women—we are cowards and shirkers; and as such we are unworthy our proud boast of ancestry, we are unworthy even the memory of our forefathers who fought and bled and died that America might forever be the home of the free and the land of the brave."[20] According to Terry, as America citizens, deaf people had a responsibility and obligation to defend their rights.

Terry did not shirk from the responsibility of teaching the public about the deaf community. In 1926, while president of the CAD, she conducted an experiment with radio. "Notices" were sent to thousands of deaf and hard of hearing people, requesting that they listen to the radio on a designated night, and then report what they could understand from the broadcast by answering a series of questions.[21] However, while this test was aimed at studying whether deaf people could use the radio, part of the program was a message written by Terry where she argued that deaf people had much in common with their hearing counterparts and lived similarly to them:

We have lived and worked for a full rounded education, with the necessary initiative to mark the successful individual, the good cit-

izen. That is what we are asking of our schools for the deaf today. . .
We deaf and hard of hearing, live in widely scattered communities
of the city and country. We are just like our neighbor—the only
difference being that they can hear and we cannot. We go about
our daily tasks, work and take pride in the growth and progress
of our communities. We rear and educate our children, offspring
as a rule more fortunate than their parents, in that they have full
possession of all their faculties. We drive our own automobiles and
we do it as well or better than the hearing fellow, for the deaf are
necessarily more acutely trained on vision than any other class of
people. Nothing escapes our observation.

   I cannot resist this opportunity to speak to you who are not
deaf. We want no favors or charity. All that we want is a chance.
Given employment that suits us, whether it be in the field of industry, art or the professions, we are sure to make good.[22]

   The radio was a means of reaching a broader audience. Terry knew
hearing people would be listening that night and her address touted the
qualities of deaf people as productive: they worked, raised families, and
lived in their communities. According to Terry, all deaf people wanted
was equal opportunity. Interestingly, she used the radio, a forum largely
inaccessible to the deaf community at that time, in order to spread her
message of citizenship. Terry was a prolific writer, but broadcasting on
the radio provided an opportunity to potentially reach a population that
her articles did not.

   While Terry took advantage of technology such as the radio, her
frequent publications were a primary and essential part of her advocacy.
She typically focused on matters relevant to deaf people at the time, one
of which was eugenics. Eugenics was a popular movement in mainstream America during Terry's lifetime. The term was coined by Francis
Galton in 1883 and was essentially the promotion of "better breeding."[23]
Galton described eugenics as "the science which deals with all influences that improve the inborn qualities of a race; also with those that
develop them to the utmost advantage."[24] In essence, eugenics sought
to advance the human race through selective breeding while also discouraging (potentially forcibly through sterilization and other means)
those who carried undesirable traits from reproducing.

   Deaf people did not escape the purview of eugenicists; deaf marriages were one target, and Alexander Graham Bell discouraged these
unions. Bell did not want marriages banned by law, but rather sought

to disassociate deaf people from each other by placing deaf children in day schools and encouraging them to speak English and lipread instead of using sign language.[25] Terry's writings on eugenics counter the false perceptions held by many hearing people, and demanded that deaf people be treated equally.

Terry stood in strong support of deaf marriages. However, she too called on deaf people to do their part as citizens and not perpetuate genetic deafness through their children. This seemingly contradicted her argument that deaf people had a place in the world. This inconsistency however seems to come not from a belief that deaf people were inherently inferior, but rather that they were misunderstood by society.

Some members of the American deaf community acquiesced to the pressure of the larger society, believing that deaf people who might possibly pass their deafness to the next generation should avoid marrying one another. The NAD passed a resolution to this effect in 1920: "Resolved, That the National Association of the Deaf go on record as viewing such marriages with disapproval and earnestly urge the deaf to avoid such union if possible."[26] While the NAD openly discouraged these marriages, Terry was strongly opposed to restrictions on deaf unions.

> I read the above resolution with surprise—and disapproval. The NAD knows that deaf-mutes as a class have no place in the ranks of the undesirables that people the earth. On the contrary, the NAD, through intimate association, knows that deaf-mutes are educated, sensible, hard-working and law-abiding citizens. They are an asset, not a liability to the communities in which they live."[27]

Terry argued against the resolution, restating that deaf people were contributors, and thus they should not be barred from marrying one another. Terry warned deaf people to be wary of those who attempted to deny their right to marry. "Herein may lie a tale—and the deaf better take warning. Let them be sure that they are not unawares (sic) accepting flattery and favors from a clique of men whose ultimate motive may be only to rob them of their greatest and most sacred happiness— marriage and a home!"[28] Terry implored deaf people to zealously guard their right to marry and not unwittingly assist those who attempted to regulate deaf marriages.

Terry published an extensive article in *The Silent Worker* that is particularly revealing of her complex views regarding eugenics and deaf people. Published in 1918, two years before her criticism of the NAD's rejection of deaf-deaf marriages, she opined that while deaf people should be allowed to marry one another, those with a genetic predisposition to deaf offspring should refrain from childbearing. "Should the deaf marry? Yes. Should they intermarry? Yes . . . Should all the deaf who marry have children? No. No. Here it is necessary to discriminate."[29] She believed that deaf people with the possibility of having offspring like themselves should refrain from having children. However, as she further expounded on this idea, she indicated that the reason for this attitude was primarily due to American society's negative treatment of deaf people:

> All that the deaf need is enlightenment. Ever desirous of being a useful asset to society, I know that they will welcome a practical knowledge of genetics or the science of heredity. Once they fully realize that they as a class are not properly appreciated or understood, that instead they are classed with the unfit, the insane, the feeble-minded, the diseased, the criminal, etc., they will then naturally wish to avoid bringing into the world possibly more deaf children to share the same unkind fate. We do not fully appreciate the fact that the world looks upon deafness as a very great misfortune, much greater than we ourselves realize.[30]

She believed that deaf people had a responsibility, as citizens, to not bear deaf children. In this vein, Terry narrowly defined and interpreted principles of marriage. Deaf people faced the scorn of society during this time, and their future children should not have to suffer the same fate. In essence, Terry proposed that to be good citizens, deaf people could and should marry, but should refrain from reproducing if hereditary deafness was a likely outcome. According to Terry's views, members of the deaf community needed to conduct themselves in a certain manner in order to maintain their role as citizens. The above quote from her piece reveals the complexity of Terry's eugenic beliefs.

Besides eugenics, oralism—the philosophy that deaf children should be taught through "the *exclusive* [emphasis Baynton's] use of lip-reading and speech"—had a major impact on deaf education and the deaf community during the early twentieth century. By the early 1900s, eighty percent of deaf students in the United States were taught via oralism; contrasting with just seven and one-half percent in 1882, and forty percent at the end of the nineteenth century.[31] Oralism was a common target of Terry's vitriol, as she lambasted the method through her writing, often using passionate descriptors such as "the oral evil is the one-legged lie" and "that this evil, the Pure Oral Fad, is **the biggest fallacy in the whole educational world** [emphasis Terry's]." She referred to it as "an arrest of natural mental growth," as well as "sickening" and "misleading." She equated it to "propaganda" and its group of supporters an "oral clique." Furthermore, she viewed it as an "unnatural, narrow exclusive method" and simply: "rot."[32]

In contrast, given her clear contempt for oralism and its monopolization of the deaf education system, Terry believed in the combined system and the importance of sign language in the lives of deaf people and the education of deaf children. The combined system had multiple meanings, from using both sign language and oral approaches in the classroom, (this was the approach most closely aligned with Terry's beliefs) to starting children on an oral track and then, if they did not succeed, moving them to classes that used manual communication.[33] She believed there was liberating power in using sign language and it was the means by which deaf people could thrive. She stated quite simply that "the sign language, is our chief source of success and happiness in life!"[34] Sign language would grant deaf people success in their education, whereas the oral system would obstruct their future opportunities.

Additionally, Terry argued that sign language could be used as a way to help returning WWI soldiers who had become deaf or hard of hearing adjust to their new life circumstances. "We are here reminded of a speech Perry E. Seely made recently in Los Angeles, that our deaf soldiers need first of all to be taught **how to be deaf**, [emphasis Terry's], in other words how to be happy and useful in spite of that dreadful handicap . . . We want Congress to know that this sign language fills a vital need in the lives of the deaf."[35] For newly deafened veterans to be "happy" and "useful," and become active citizens again, they would need to learn additional skills, which included a new way of communicating. Terry urged the United States Congress to recognize the importance of sign language for returning war veterans who had been deafened.

In her support for the combined method, Alice Terry did not hold back in her contempt for those who encouraged oralism.

> We all know that the extremists, the hearing oral advocates, are working over time in an effort to destroy the great and good Abbé de l'Epée's priceless gift to mankind, the sign language. They do

not know this method of communication themselves and out of purest selfishness, ignorance, and intolerance they do not want to know. And yet they expect to be called friends and benefactors of the deaf! They should be classed as among the most ignorant of mortals."[36]

Sign language was a valuable gift, and oralists' attempts to squelch sign language met the wrath of Terry's pen.

Proper education was key to protecting the rights of the deaf population in promoting their citizenship. In a 1916 article, Terry wrote, "I will repeat what I firmly believe is the present tendency of the Pure Oral Evil and the Imposter Evil; namely, to rob future generations of the deaf of the right of citizenship entirely, which is, to throw them back into that life of torture which they endured before the days of Abbé De l'Epée."[37] Terry believed that denying deaf children access to sign language as part of their education, would have deleterious effects on their basic rights as American citizens. She noted that "fifty years ago, let's say, parents could send their deaf children off to school with every assurance that they would be educated and moulded (sic) into useful citizens;"[38] She thought that parents could no longer trust that the education system for their deaf children would make them full members of society.

According to Terry, the oral system hampered the potential of deaf children. If they did not have access to an appropriate education, their ability to exercise autonomy was compromised. Terry's writing reflected a belief that the children who were products of oralism were not successfully educated. "In place of the old-time promising, capable graduate of the Combined System schools we now have the timid, blanked-faced oral graduate, who alas! in too many cases answer accurately to the description of 'respectable idiot.'"[39] Terry believed that deaf students coming from the oral schools were incompetent since a great deal of time was focused on learning speech and comprehending spoken content. Prior to oralism, graduates of deaf education programs were "capable" but oralism had turned them into "idiots."

In addition to her publications, Terry participated in the legislative process to defend the rights of deaf people. At a March 1927 CAD meeting, Terry described multiple bills that were before the California legislature, including one that would sell the California School for the Deaf at Berkeley, another that would create more day schools, and a third bill that would require deaf children to attend the day school closest to where they lived. It was believed this would be detrimental to the combined system as day schools in California increasingly used the oral method. Terry disapproved of these bills, and she voiced her displeasure in a letter to the *Los Angeles Times*. She described how the bill to sell the deaf school at Berkeley was too ambiguous and that a new school would not be as successful as the current institution. Additionally, she invoked the harm to taxpayers if the legislation became law. "Great and unnecessary burdens are going to be heaped upon taxpayers if such outsiders and propagandists are going to dictate the education of the physically handicapped, especially deaf children" [40] Terry believed that these bills, if passed, would cause harm to deaf children, as well as negatively affect taxpayers. Given that there were multiple bills in which the deaf people of California were stakeholders, the CAD became an active participant in the law-making process. By collaborating with hearing legislators, the CAD successfully halted the sale of the Berkeley school in March of 1927. Furthermore, one of the proposed bills regarding the use of an oral system was changed by the CAD in order to make it acceptable to that organization (Terry's article about this event, however, does not provide specifics on what that bill entailed).[41] Terry and the CAD were active participants in the legislative process. Terry reported that "the California Association of the Deaf made a fine record at the recent legislature. We introduced bills, we amended bills, we defeated bills."[42] In cooperation with hearing people, the deaf community invoked their rights as citizens by influencing the legislative process that would impact the lives of deaf people in California. This was a tangible victory for Terry's advocacy; she believed certain government actions would harm her community and she successfully fought against them.

In addition to opposing eugenics and oralism, Terry published extensively on the activities of deaf organizations. She actively encouraged deaf people to exercise their citizenship by being proactive and supporting such groups. The NAD was a frequent subject in her publications and she prodded deaf people to be more involved in the NAD. "The N.A.D. needs you, and it needs me, as it has before and always needed thousands of others like us."[43] She believed that being active in the NAD's efforts was one way to counteract the societal difficulties deaf people experienced. One such effort was to ensure that the NAD Endowment Fund had adequate principal (Terry suggested $100,000). If that was accomplished, "then shall we be able effectively to combat the evils which have always threatened us—educational, industrial, social—and which shall continue to menace us in ever-growing measure until we are strong enough financially to defend ourselves."[44] She openly wrote of her own twenty-five dollar donation to the NAD, a donation that secured her lifetime membership with the NAD, and encouraged others to follow her example.[45] "Above all remember that your money goes to help YOUR CAUSE. It is no concern of your family, or your relatives, or your friends, or the public—for it is yours, and yours only. Just how far your cause advances, or how far it recedes depends, as it has always depended, upon YOU [emphasis Terry's]."[46] The responsibility of securing citizenship rested with the members of the deaf community themselves. Terry argued that becoming members of large-scale organizations, such as the NAD, allowed deaf people to stand as a group rather than individually. This would grant them more collective power to challenge issues of the era that impacted their autonomy and bring about change.

In the subsequent decades, Terry became discouraged by a lack of united support from deaf people. "The NAD should mean *everything* [emphasis Terry's] to all the deaf. It seeks to protect them as citizens— helping them in school, in society, in industry. What a pity that all cannot see it this way."[47] Terry believed in the power of organizations to advocate for deaf people and desired everyone in the deaf community to understand the type of protection that the NAD could provide for their rights.

Additionally, Terry argued that deaf people should also form alliances with the American Federation of the Physically Handicapped (AFPH). The AFPH organization was founded in 1942 by Paul Strachan;[48] a late-deafened man who had become frustrated with the NAD's then-president Thomas Anderson because he had different goals for the deaf community.[49] For Strachan, membership in the AFPH would link deaf citizens with individuals with other disabilities. However, the NAD's leadership wanted to disassociate from such groups, and remain an autonomous organization limited only to deaf people. Contrary to that stance, Terry supported the advocacy efforts of both the AFPH and the NAD. She felt that the AFPH was doing "a great work,"[50] and that creating ties with their larger network would ultimately facilitate better treatment for deaf people. By 1945, her writings argued that deaf people should unite with AFPH in order to have more political clout:

> One little group alone cannot accomplish much. It is too firmly fixed in the public mind that we are allied to other groups. As we see it, the AFPH has only humanitarian principles; it deserves the support of all right thinking people. But if the deaf prefer to stand

alone, a mere minority group, they will accomplish no more in the future than they have in the past, in the matter of employment and liberal education for all. Didn't the NAD fight the oral evil for 60 years? Look at the oral status today—worse than ever![51]

Given Terry's stance on education, that students taught by the combined system would lead to their exercising full citizenship, the ever-present oral system in deaf education threatened deaf rights. However, despite the NAD's ongoing efforts, deaf people still found themselves in a losing battle against oralists. According to Terry, aligning political capital and resources with the AFPH would give the deaf community a more powerful voice. Terry believed that the AFPH wanted to work with various groups of people and "to fight for him, for his rights as a citizen, and his rights to earn a living."[52] Contrary to her wishes, however, the NAD never did affiliate with the AFPH.

Alice Terry continued to work on behalf of deaf people until her death in 1950. Throughout her life, she seized every opportunity to counter the pressures from society at large and showcase deaf people as productive citizens who worked and lived, just as hearing people did. During the late nineteenth and early twentieth centuries, there were multiple movements that threatened the autonomy of deaf people, such as restrictions on driving and marriage. Additionally, the oral education system in vogue during that era was, to Terry, devastatingly damaging to the deaf community. She fought back through multiple mediums, including copious writing, active involvement in deaf organizations, the use of technology such as the radio, and involvement with the legislative process in California, in order to spread her message that deaf people deserved to be treated fairly. She also encouraged others who were deaf to advocate for their rights. Alice Terry's life-long activism defending the deaf community answered her inquiry, "Are we not as much citizens as any body?" with a resounding affirmation that, yes, deaf people belonged and contributed to society.

Notes

1. Portions were presented at the following academic conferences: "Alice Taylor Terry: Deaf Leader, Writer, and Advocate, 1878–1950." *Deaf Studies Today!* conference. Utah Valley University. Orem, Utah, April 2012. "Alice Taylor Terry: A Deaf Female Advocate." *Deaf History International* conference. Toronto, Canada, July 2012.

2. For location and date of birth, see Terry, H., "The Book of Alice Taylor Terry." n.d. For a description of becoming deaf, see Terry, A., "An Autobiography of My Childhood," 48.

3. Terry, A., "An Autobiography of My Childhood," 47–49.

4. "Join Marjorie Klugman," 3.

5. Terry, A., "My Dear Mrs. Fawkes," 2.

6. Terry, H., "Alice in Silentland," 4. *The Silent Worker* disbanded in 1929 and was revived in 1929, hence why Howard Terry referred to it as "old." See Buchanan, "Silent Worker Newspaper," in *Deaf History Unveiled*, ed. Van Cleve, 172–97.

7. Terry, A., "My dear Mrs. Fawkes," 1.

8. For details on the Terrys moves throughout California see ibid., "Moving Experiences," *The Silent Worker*. For the source on them living in Hollywood for 30 years, see Join Marjorie Klugman, 4–5.

9. Terry, H., "Alice in Silentland," 5.

10. Terry, A., "California-1915!," 3.

11. For the source on A. Terry as president of the CAD, see Runde, "Here and There," 4; For the Los Angeles Silent Club, see "Mrs. Terry President," 8.

12. For the Progressive Era, see Smith, "New Paths to Power," 364; For the 1920s, see Drowne and Huber, *The 1920s*, 17.

13. Amott, *Race, Gender, and Work*, 301.

14. Terry, H., "Alice in Silentland," 3–5.

15. Terry, A., "A Friendly Criticism," 183.

16. Ibid., "Let Us Have the Truth," 32.

17. Burch, *Signs of Resistance*, 159.

18. Ibid., 156–57.

19. Terry, A., "Let Us Have the Truth," 30.

20. Ibid.

21. Howson, "The Argonaut," 249.

22. Ibid., 250.

23. Stern, *Eugenic Nation*, 11.

24. Ibid.

25. Murray, "'True Love and Sympathy'," 43.

26. "Resolutions Adopted at the Convention," 1.

27. Terry, A. T., "Some N.A.D. Resolutions," *The Jewish Deaf*, 7.

28. Ibid., "Propaganda by Stealth," 7–8.

29. Ibid., "Eugenics," 96.

30. Ibid.

31. Baynton, *Forbidden Signs*, 4, 25; Van Cleve and Crouch, *A Place of Their Own*, 122.

32. Terry, A., "Our Mutual Forum," May 1916, 144. Terry also refers to oralism as a fallacy in "A Visit to Angie Fuller Fischer," March 1921, 194; Ibid., "Our

Mutual Forum," July 1916, 190; Ibid., "Our Mutual Forum," January 1916, 65; Ibid., "Future Goodyear Times in Los Angeles," May 1920, 206; Ibid., "Let Us Have the Truth," February 1923 30; "Fundamentals," February 1924, 38; Ibid., "Our Mutual Forum," July 1916, 190.

33. Baynton, *Forbidden Signs*, 69.

34. Terry, A., "Tragic Loneliness," 20.

35. Ibid., "A.F.P.H. Goes Ahead," 2.

36. Terry, Mrs. H., "The Rights of the Deaf," 3.

37. Terry, A., "Our Mutual Forum," January 1916, 65. (Abbé De l'Epée is written as Terry wrote it, with the D capitalized.) The "Imposter Evil" referred to hearing people pretending to be deaf in order to beg for money. Abbé de l'Épeé established the first deaf school in France and sign language was used there, not the oral method (see Van Cleve and Crouch, *A Place of Their Own*, 107).

38. Terry, A., "Other Days...," 3.

39. Ibid., "Funds and Funds," 136.

40. Terry, Mrs. H., "Care of the Deaf," A4.

41. Barrett, "Angelenograms," June 1927, 330.

42. Terry, A., "The Rights of the Deaf," 3.

43. Ibid., "Your Cause," 31.

44. Ibid., 32.

45. Ibid., 31.

46. Ibid., 32.

47. Ibid., "The N.A.D. Shall Not Die," 4.

48. Buchanan, *Illusions of Equality*, 114.

49. Ibid., 104–107.

50. Terry, A., "A.F.P.H. Goes Ahead," 2.

51. Ibid., "Why Stand Alone?," 2.

52. Ibid.

References

Amott, Teresa L. *Race, Gender, and Work: A Multi-Cultural Economic History of Women in the United States*. Rev. ed. Boston, MA: South End Press, 1996.

Barrett, Augusta K. "Angelenograms." *The Silent Worker*. vol. 39, no. 8, May 1927.

———. "Angelenograms." *The Silent Worker*. vol. 39, no. 9, June 1927.

Baynton, Douglas C. *Forbidden Signs: American Culture and the Campaign Against Sign Language*. Chicago: University of Chicago Press, 1996.

Buchanan, Robert. "The Silent Worker Newspaper and the Building of a Deaf Community: 1890-1929." In *Deaf History Unveiled: Interpretations from the New Scholarship*, edited by John Vickrey Van Cleve, 172–97. Washington, DC: Gallaudet University Press, 1993.

Buchanan, Robert M. *Illusions of Equality: Deaf Americans in School and Factory, 1850–1950*. Washington, DC: Gallaudet University Press, 1999.

Burch, Susan. *Signs of Resistance: American Deaf Cultural History, 1900 to World War II*. New York: New York University Press, 2004.

Drowne, Kathleen, and Patrick Huber. *The 1920s*. Westport, CT: Greenwood Press, 2004.

Howson, J.W. "The Argonaut." *The Silent Worker*. vol. 38, no. 6, March 1926.

"Join Marjorie Klugman in an Interview with Howard L. Terry: One of America's Foremost Authors." *The Silent Worker*. vol. 2, no. 9, May 1950.

Meagher, J. Frederick. "Los Angeles." *Deaf-Mutes' Journal*. vol. 45, no. 44, November 2, 1916.

Morton, Kati. "The Life and Writings of Alice Taylor Terry: 1878–1950." Gallaudet University, 2011.

"Mrs. Terry President of Los Angeles Silent Club." *The Jewish Deaf* VI, no. 2, March 1920.

Murray, Joseph J. "'True Love and Sympathy.'" In *Genetics, Disability, and Deafness*. Edited by John Vickrey Van Cleve. Washington, DC: Gallaudet University Press, 2004.

"Resolutions Adopted at the Convention of the National Association of the Deaf." *The Oregon Outlook*. vol. 29, no. 3, December 18, 1920.

Runde, Winfield S. "Here and There." *The California News*. vol. 39, no. 1, September 1923.

Smith, Karen Manners. "New Paths to Power: 1890–1920." In *No Small Courage: A History of Women in the United States*. Edited by Nancy F. Cott. New York: Oxford University Press, 2000.

Stern, Alexandra Minna. *Eugenic Nation: Faults and Frontiers of Better Breeding in Modern America*. Berkeley: University of California Press, 2005.

Terry, Alice T. "A.F.P.H. Goes Ahead." *Silent Broadcaster*. March 1945.

———. "An Autobiography of My Childhood." *The Silent Worker*. vol. 33, no. 2, November 1920.

———. "A Friendly Criticism of Arnold Payne's Book 'King Silence.'" *The Silent Worker*. vol. 32, no. 7, April 1920.

———. "California-1915!" *Deaf-Mutes' Journal*, June 25, 1914.

———. "Eugenics." *The Silent Worker*. vol. 30, no. 6, March 1918.

———. "Fundamentals." *The Jewish Deaf* 10, no. 1, February 1924.

———. "Funds and Funds: Funds for Everything but the Right Thing." *The Silent Worker*. vol. 30, no. 8, May 1918.

———. "Future Goodyear Times in Los Angeles." *The Silent Worker*. vol. 32, no. 8, May 1920.

———. "Let Us Have the Truth." *The Jewish Deaf* IX. no. 1, February 1923.

———. "Moving Experiences." *The Silent Worker*. vol. 32, no. 6, March 1920.

———. Letter titled "My Dear Mrs. Fawkes." [Gallaudet University Library Deaf Collections & Archives], August 21, 1945.

———. "The N.A.D. Shall Not Die." *New York Journal of the Deaf*, July 18, 1940.

———. "Other Days . . ." *Silent Broadcaster*. vol. 7, no. 11, December 1941.

——. "Our Mutual Forum." *The Silent Worker*. vol. 28, no. 4, January 1916.

——. "Our Mutual Forum." *The Silent Worker*. vol. 28, no. 8, May 1916.

——. "Our Mutual Forum." *The Silent Worker*. vol. 28, no. 10, July 1916.

——. "Propaganda by Stealth." *The Jewish Deaf* vol. 9. no. 8, November 1923.

——. "Some N.A.D. Resolutions." *The Jewish Deaf* vol. 6, no. 8, December 1920.

——. "Tragic Loneliness." *The Jewish Deaf* vol. 8, no. 1, February 1922.

——. "A Visit to Angie Fuller Fischer." *The Silent Worker*. vol. 33, no. 6, March 1921.

——. "Why Stand Alone?" *Silent Broadcaster*. June 1945.

——. "Your Cause." *The Jewish Deaf* VI. no. 4, May 1920.

Terry, Howard L. "Alice in Silentland." *The Silent Worker*. vol. 3, no. 3, November 1950.

——. "The Book of Alice Taylor Terry." [Gallaudet University Library Deaf Collections & Archives], n.d.

Terry, Mrs. Howard L. "Care of the Deaf." *Los Angeles Times*. March 23, 1927.

——. "The Rights of the Deaf." *Deaf-Mutes' Journal*, June 2, 1927.

Van Cleve, John Vickrey, and Barry A. Crouch. *A Place of Their Own: Creating the Deaf Community in America*. Washington, DC: Gallaudet University Press, 1989.

6

Unchurched, Unchampioned, and Undone: The St. Ann's Church Controversy, 1894–1897

Jannelle Legg

The deaf-mutes woke up one day to find that a plan had been proposed, considered and adopted by the vestry, which would leave them without a church and without a penny . . . and had it not been for the sturdy integrity of Mr. Comer, the senior warden, the deaf-mutes would have found themselves unchurched, unchampioned and undone. . . . Let all remember that 'thrice armed are they whose cause is just,' and keep up the fight until the enemy shall capitulate.

—Edwin A. Hodgson, *Deaf-Mutes' Journal*,
June 24, 1897

ON OCTOBER 17, 1897, Judge Charles H. Truax of the New York Supreme Court signed the Court Order for Union and Consolidation that legally merged the church and holdings of St. Ann's Church for Deaf-Mutes and St. Matthew's Church in New York City. From the time the St. Ann's Church buildings were sold in 1894, the deaf and hearing congregation of St. Ann's had been engaged in a growing dispute over their church's future. The resistance from key members of the deaf community has been unexamined in deaf history despite the significance of the church as the social welfare and cultural center of the New York deaf community during the second half of the nineteenth century. Through the deaf members' struggle against the consolidation of their church, major cultural issues were thrown into stark contrast, highlighting the interconnected relationship of agency and space, and the paternalistic attitudes toward deaf people in the nineteenth century. Further, the unique nature of the combined efforts of Edwin A. Hodgson, a deaf leader and editor of the *Deaf-Mutes' Journal* (hereafter DMJ), and John Comer, the hearing nonsigning senior warden of St. Ann's Church, in resisting consolidation represents an important and complicated layer in the deaf church members' struggle for autonomy. This work will revisit the church's history, examine its importance in the deaf community, and focus on the events between 1894 and 1897 in exploring this important and complicated controversy.

New York City, in the last decade of the nineteenth century, had at least 600 churches at work within city limits and steadfast church attendance was a part of life for its citizens.[1] While churches in the city provided a space where one could observe religious rituals, many also served a number of other social functions. For New York's elite, the chosen place of worship reflected one's place in society, provided the opportunity to demonstrate wealth, and reinforced social networks.[2] For the working-class denizens who labored in the city's ports and factories, the local parish provided aid and encouraged a sense of community.[3] For deaf people, St. Ann's, an Episcopal Church on West Eighteenth Street, was "the center of most of New York's activities so far as the deaf were concerned."[4] It provided them with a central social and cultural gathering site.

St. Ann's Church for Deaf-Mutes was a prominent religious institution in New York, partially, it would seem, due to the novelty of the church structure and congregation.[5] Founded in 1852 by the Reverend Dr. Thomas Gallaudet, it created a context for adult deaf social interaction through worship in sign language; social services, including employment services, financial aid, and educational opportunities; and a physical space for the community. Reverend Gallaudet was the son of Thomas Hopkins Gallaudet, a key participant in the founding of the American School for the Deaf in Hartford, Connecticut. The Reverend Gallaudet held two services each Sunday, a "service with the voice, that the parents, children, other relatives and friends of deaf mutes, may have the opportunity of joining with them in forming one parish" and a second service in the afternoon delivered in sign language for deaf congregants.[6] This formula satisfied Gallaudet in two ways; divided services eased his concerns about separating deaf and hearing family members and friends in their faith, and enabled the church to maintain a continued relationship with wealthy hearing benefactors that supported the church's endeavors.[7] Over the next four decades, the shape and practice of church work at St. Ann's changed. A number of connected religious organizations that met deaf people's needs grew from the weekly services.[8] In order to meet the many demands this work required, Gallaudet took on a number of assistants.[9] The Reverends John Chamberlain and Edward H. Krans worked at St. Ann's for the longest period and were in service at the time of the controversy. Krans served the hearing congregation, while Chamberlain worked with the deaf congregants.[10] Upon his retirement as rector in 1892, Gallaudet appointed Krans as his replacement.[11] Gallaudet maintained a close relationship with the church as Rector Emeritus and, at the end of the controversy, returned as rector of the new St. Ann's.

St. Ann's Church was founded and grew to prominence during a century when America was in the midst of great economic change, shifting attitudes toward reform and social welfare, an increasing social influence of Darwinian ideology, and lack of access to religion and education for deaf people in many parts of the country.[12] In the face of resistance from members of the wider Episcopal church and despite enormous financial barriers, St. Ann's not only came into being, it also challenged these ideas and endeavored to spread religion, education, and community.

St. Ann's Church played a multifaceted role in the lives of its communicants. It provided support for parish members through the provision of interpreting services, employment, financial aid, and housing accommodations for those in need. Further still, it played an important role in legitimizing its deaf members as citizens of the city. In the New York City of the second half of the nineteenth century, middle- and working-class leisure activities were structured around community institutions such as, "fraternal orders, benevolent societies, political and social clubs, militias and rifle clubs, unions, churches and family groups."[13] For deaf community church members who lived in the city, St. Ann's Church satisfied an important function. In 1875, Gallaudet noted that deaf people often struggled to receive admission to local social and cultural societies and were denied membership in social and cultural organizations in the same way that insurance companies refused to "issue policies on their lives."[14] At St. Ann's, deaf church members would not be denied and the church "would not reject their applications."[15] Involvement at St. Ann's enabled deaf members to perform the duties of citizenship through participation in social organizations linked to the church and fostered relationships between deaf and hearing congregants, while simultaneously enabling members to observe systems of self-governance, cultivate leadership skills as lay readers or organizational leaders, and utilize church as a place for the development of agency and autonomy.[16]

For the deaf community in New York, the Bible study and lecture rooms at St. Ann's generated the space for organizations, such as the Manhattan Literary Association and the Silent Worker's Guild, and, in turn, these organizations gave hearing and deaf participants a place to interact with one another toward the goal of elevating the position of deaf people in the community. Activities held in the church's basement rooms enriched the lives of deaf participants of different denominations by allowing them to interact and work together.[17] A number of New York deaf organizations were "outgrowths of gatherings at St. Ann's."[18] These organizations provided participation on an equal basis and generated the social and political space for collaboration and community building. In this way the church generated a place for deaf people to begin working together for one another's mutual interests.

It was this valuable function of St. Ann's Church that was threatened by institutional reorganization and consolidation in the 1890s. The church had weathered the extreme volatility of the New York City economy for over forty years, and though St. Ann's had steadily grown in size and prominence, it remained in debt and faced increasingly untenable circumstances at the beginning of the decade. The 1890s began with a series of disastrous economic downturns in New York, and for an institution that relied wholly on benevolent donations of its parishioners, St. Ann's came under growing pressure to support an expanding church mission.[19] From the 1850s onward, the space around St. Ann's, the city's southern and western neighborhoods began to change from residential areas to industrial and financial districts.[20] The surrounding community gradually transformed as residents were replaced by businesses and storefronts.[21] At the same time, the buildings that housed St. Ann's became increasingly undesirable. St. Ann's role as a social center for the New York deaf community had expanded while available physical space had not. Deaf congregants, in particular, expressed dissatisfaction with the buildings and the church remained unable to undergo renovations that would create above-ground work and meeting rooms.[22] The confluence of these issues drastically impacted the church's ability to do its work and, at the same time, a sale of the buildings was enticing, both in terms of financial returns and the church's ability to better serve its congregation.

Though the property was not desirable for the church, it was highly marketable as a commercial property.[23] As news spread about the possible relocation of St. Ann's, a number of early offers for consolidation with churches in the city were quickly debated and quietly rejected by the church's clergy and vestry.[24] On October 30, 1894, the buildings were sold for $192,000 to a manufacturing firm, with the condition that church parishioners would continue to use the buildings until the following spring.[25] Efforts to relocate St. Ann's Church and its congregation to available uptown properties began immediately. A clear and viable option was swiftly found at 148th Street. There lay a grouping of five lots, covering nearly an entire city block upon which they could build. The proposed location had the additional benefit of being within walking distance of the New York Institute for the Deaf at Fanwood, with which the Church already had close affiliation.[26] At the end of November 1894, the search committee purchased the lots with the intention of building a new edifice to house the church and its works. [27]

The first of many setbacks appeared immediately. Though the search committee appeared to have received approval from Bishop Potter and the standing committee of the diocese for settling there, by January 1895 each of the Episcopal churches surrounding the proposed site had issued letters of formal opposition. In Episcopal Church structures, churches are organized into dioceses. Just as a church is led by a priest, a diocese is overseen by a bishop. Both the bishop and a standing committee, composed of clergy and laity, make decisions for each diocese. Upon receiving letters of opposition, the bishop and standing committee of New York prevented St. Ann's from building on the site.[28] The other churches' opposition reflected their concern that as a free-church, one that did not charge "pew-rent" from adherents, the new St. Ann's Church would present an attractive option to current and new residents of upper Manhattan and the surrounding churches would lose their congregants. After two months of deliberation and attempts by St. Ann's clergy to convert their opponents, the city's standing committee formally rejected St. Ann's petition to relocate to 148th Street.[29] As the deadline to vacate their buildings steadily approached, the possibility of merging with another church was again circulated and rejected by St. Ann's vestry.[30] On April 21, 1895, the last services were held at St. Ann's on West Eighteenth Street. Temporary services to be held at the Church of St. John the Evangelist were scheduled to begin on April 28, 1895.[31] In May 1895, St. Ann's Church buildings were demolished.[32]

For the next two years, the future of St. Ann's grew increasingly unclear and community members felt greater anxiety about this, most clearly opined by Edwin A. Hodgson of the *Deaf-Mutes' Journal* and

Edwin Hodgson, editor of the *Deaf-Mutes' Journal*. Courtesy of Gallaudet University Archives.

Robert Maynard in the *Silent Worker*. Though working steadily toward locating a new site for the church, it appears that church action toward this was sluggish and communication between the vestry and the laity was lacking. An uneasy discord grew between members of the laity and the vestry of St. Ann's, while the congregation and community waited for progress.

Throughout this time, deaf members of the congregation sent letters and published articles expressing their concerns and desires. The writings of Maynard and Hodgson provided a clear insight into the anxiety of deaf community members and also highlighted a uniquely deaf perspective throughout the controversy. Their articles included frequent references to new buildings with designs attuned to the needs of deaf congregants, concern over funds and a lack of clear information, and concern over the negative impact of the exhaustive search on deaf community organizations.[33] Unfortunately, the long-standing organizations that had been housed at St. Ann's had lost most of their membership throughout the controversy. Hodgson directly linked the diminished attendance to the lack of suitable available space. Keenly aware of the impact this had on the social life of the New York City deaf community, Hodgson proclaimed that the solution could only be found in the establishment of a separate parish building for deaf communicants. Criticism from deaf writers increased through the fall and winter of 1895 and 1896, despite attempts by the church clergy to quell deaf people's concerns.[34]

By March 1897, the efforts to relocate St. Ann's Church erupted in public and volatile dissent marked by the abrupt resignation of John H. Comer, the church's senior warden. Comer, a hearing man, had served as a member of the vestry and as trustee of the church's endowment society for a number of years.[35] In his letter of resignation, Comer indicated that the sole reason for his departure was due to the vestry's decision to merge St. Ann's Church with St. Matthew's. The laity of St. Matthew's found themselves in a similarly difficult position. Their rector had opted for an abrupt retirement and the congregation was soon to be without a religious leader. Further, their church buildings were still under mortgage in the amount of $54,000.[36] The merger would combine St. Ann's and St. Matthew's congregations in worship at the existing St. Matthew's church building, and create a combined endowment of $82,000 after the former's debt was paid. The new St. Matthew's, it was promised, would "build and maintain St. Ann's Church for Deaf-Mutes whose members will be parishioners of St. Matthew's Parish."[37]

Opposition to this merger formed quickly; however, even though members of the congregation formed alliances in this effort, they had disparate motivations for their collaboration. In a letter published in the *Deaf-Mutes' Journal*, Comer made his motivations for resisting consolidation clear.[38] His major objections centered on two issues—the consolidation of St. Ann's with a pew-renting church located far uptown, and the transfer of nearly $200,000 to St. Matthew's. As part of the merger, all monies that St. Ann's held would become shared with St. Matthew's. These funds, he believed, had been expressly collected for a free church, without the benefit of consistent dues. Though Comer and other hearing members resisted the merger, their resistance to the consolidation of the two churches presented primarily financial and ecclesiastical concerns. Hodgson and the deaf community, however, framed this debate in terms of deaf community space and autonomy.

Deaf community members publicly indicated dissent in the pages of the deaf press. Hodgson was critical of the decision to turn over the namesake and funds of St. Ann's Church to St. Matthew's and was increasingly concerned with the lack of representation for deaf congregants as the combined church formed a new vestry. Hodgson asserted that any funds raised in the name of St. Ann's Church for Deaf-Mutes belonged to its namesake—the deaf community. For decades funds had been donated to the only church for deaf people in the city. These funds had enabled the purchase of the buildings on West Eighteenth Street, the sale of which had netted the church a significant amount of money. The merger proposed to turn the money over to a hearing, pew-renting church and Hodgson had serious doubts that the promises made to deaf congregants for their own building would come to fruition. Highlighting the paternalism that permeated the merger, Hodgson noted that deaf people throughout New York were "indigant [*sic*]" and "angry" about the purported attempts to deny funding to the deaf church.[39] He stressed that deaf people of St. Ann's Church were entitled to a clergyman who understood them and the funds and buildings he believed were rightfully theirs. He unabashedly directed his critique toward the nonsigning Rector Krans. Hodgson stated that he was "assured that no steps would be taken without due consideration, and that opportunity would be afforded the deaf to express opinion on any proposed change."[40] He, however, maintained that the vestry continued to operate as if deaf members of the congregation were "not to be considered as having any rights in the matter."[41] In essence, Hodgson called attention to a lack of deaf agency regarding St. Ann's and the disregard for any input from deaf congregants by the vestry and clergy.

In the first sign of collaboration between deaf and hearing members of St. Ann's Church, deaf members of the vestry, William O. Fitzgerald, Henry J. Haight, and Albert A. Barnes, joined Comer in signing a petition of formal protest against the proposed merger.[42] The petition emphasized that the total amount of St. Ann's funds had been raised for the purpose of use by "St. Ann's Church for Deaf-Mutes and should be used for no other purpose."[43] It indicated that they felt that they had voted in favor of the consolidation "under a misapprehension." They stated that if they "had understood the matter in all its bearings, we would not have voted in favor of the union of the two churches."[44]

Despite public dissent from voting members of the vestry, it seemed that the merger would be approved. A meeting of the vestry was quickly convened and, without a full representation of its members, a vote was called and again those present were unable to come to a consensus. Upon the tied votes, Krans cast the deciding vote in favor, rather than recalling the vestry with the missing members.[45] Those critical of the merger were quick to note that Krans stood to benefit greatly as the new rector of St. Matthew's, a pew-renting church that was soon to have a comfortable endowment and steady flow of congregants.[46] Despite continued discord, it would appear that care was taken to publicly quell concerns. A *New York Times* article appearing a few days later recounted the events of the vestry meeting and instead of noting a deadlocked vote, the article indicated that eleven of twelve vestrymen were present and the vote in favor of consolidation was passed "ten to two in favor."[47] The article also claimed that talk of "dissatisfaction" with regard to the merger was "groundless."[48]

Collaboration between Comer and Hodgson began in earnest in April 1897, shortly after Comer's public protest. Evidence of their correspondence indicated that Comer sought to form allies amongst deaf congregants who opposed the merger. In his initial letter to Hodgson, Comer asked him for back issues of the *DMJ* and following this exchange, the men appear to have shared information with one another in a concerted effort toward ending the merger between St. Matthew's and St. Ann's.[49] The content of Comer's letters indicated that he followed Hodgson's editorials with interest and shared them with other members of the hearing congregation.[50] Pointedly, Comer informed Hodgson of an upcoming opportunity to elect new members of the vestry and that he was encouraging members of the deaf congregation to "vote to sustain those who are fighting for them and theirs."[51] Hodgson included these insights in his columns, circulating them throughout the deaf community.

National awareness of the controversy spread as it grew in intensity.[52] This pressure prompted attempts by members of the clergy to meet with congregants.[53] The clergy's objectives in these meetings were to clarify the efforts and proposed impact of the merger; however, they had the opposite of their intended effect. Rather, they solidified an awareness of the inequalities of the proposal. In the pages of the *DMJ*, Hodgson wrote of these events in great detail. Chief amongst his complaints was that the consolidation agreement compelled St. Matthew's "in an indefinite way, to continue the special work of St. Ann's among deaf-mutes" in exchange for nearly $200,000.[54]

Although members of the vestry had clearly announced their opposition and despite explicit objections by deaf members of the congregation, the vestry of St. Ann's Church met with the vestry of St. Matthew's Church and an agreement of consolidation was drawn up and signed by the rectors, vestrymen, and church wardens of both churches.[55] In compliance with church regulations, the document was then sent to Bishop Potter and the Standing Committee for their approval.[56] Though this initial document was rejected by the committee and returned to the vestries for modification, it was clear that the vestrymen would not be swayed by public opinion.

In May of the same year, Comer and Hodgson believed that their efforts had achieved some measure of success as the standing committee had blocked the merger of St. Ann's and St. Matthew's.[57] Hodgson believed that the consolidation plan was doomed to failure because in order to merge the two churches, a justice from the New York State Supreme Court would have to approve the transfer of funds and property. He believed that when presented for approval, the judge would "repudiate it on the ground that it [lacked] equity and [was] unreasonably unjust."[58] Given the delay and the absence of the bishop on a trip to Europe, they thought they had a momentary reprieve in their struggle.[59]

An important and demonstrative event came at the end of June 1897 in the form of a public meeting held in the basement rooms of St. John the Evangelist Church, where St. Ann's members were temporarily worshipping. The episode took place shortly after Comer announced that he had uncovered a loss of roughly $17,000 in an investigation of the endowment fund of St. Ann's Church.[60] Furthering distrust in the clergy and vestry of the church, Comer indicated that a former treasurer of the fund had "borrow[ed] the funds intrusted [sic] to him until the amount reached some $17,000 which he could not pay" and that members of the church had, out of respect for the man's family, concealed the crime.[61] Two public meetings were called for the night of June 18, 1897. The first was scheduled to ratify the revised agreement between St. Ann's and St. Matthew's. The second was intended to allow members of the opposition the opportunity to discuss the proposed consolidation. Two differing accounts of these meetings exist; one was published in the *New*

York Times, the other described in a letter between Comer and Hodgson, which was later recounted in the pages of the *DMJ.*

That evening, Krans addressed the attendees and the details of the redrafted consolidation agreement were read and discussed. Gallaudet served as interpreter for both the deaf and hearing parishioners.[62] The meeting closed with a vote by members of the laity in support of the revised consolidation agreement. The *New York Times* reported that a motion was put for adjournment and suddenly a "small-sized riot" broke out.[63] Accounts published in the *DMJ,* by Hodgson and Theo Lounsbary, and those disclosed in a private letter from Comer to Hodgson, indicated that the events had unraveled earlier, during the vote. These suggest that an interpreted message was misunderstood and that it was unclear that a vote was taking place. Further, they disputed that the vote reflected a true sense of the congregation and suggested that the process had not followed appropriate procedures.[64] Both accounts noted that at the close of the first meeting, a person began to extinguish the lamps that lit the room and he was immediately stopped and removed from the premises. The *New York Times* account included a dash of sensationalism, describing him as "struck" by a deaf person and then "captured by the group and thrown down the stairs."[65] Comer indicated that he was the one who escorted the man out; Comer then returned to the hall, where the second meeting commenced. A second vote was held with a unanimous fifty-five votes against.[66] Comer recognized later that the public had received a far different version of events through the *New York Times* article and though he had sent a correction, "the papers did not publish it."[67]

The collaboration between Comer and Hodgson continued through the summer and despite repeated attempts to meet with Potter or the Standing Committee of New York, they were unable to have their case heard. By October 7, 1897, Comer and Hodgson had yet to receive a definitive answer from the bishop or the standing committee. Shortly after his return from Europe, Bishop Potter received the modified consolidation agreement and gave it his consent.[68] Without meeting with the opposition, the standing committee considered the agreement and voted in favor of consolidation. Members of the committee declared, "[t]hose opposed to the consolidation (few in number) presented several legal objections, which were examined by the Standing Committee and found by them to be of no weight."[69] Despite having filed a complaint with Archdeacon Tiffany and scheduling a meeting to dispute the proposed merger, the consolidation document was passed to the New York

Rev. Thomas Gallaudet. Courtesy of Gallaudet University Archives.

State Supreme Court. Unbeknownst to the opposition, Judge Truax of the state supreme court ruled in favor of the petitions from both St. Matthew's and St. Ann's for consolidation.[70] This ruling enabled these two large church corporations to be legally joined in the state of New York and though Comer and Hodgson attempted to pursue legal avenues to challenge the merger, they were unsuccessful.[71]

Beginning in April 1898, the commitment to build a church exclusively for deaf congregants began to see progress, and by August, the cornerstone was laid at the site of the new St. Ann's Church.[72] Two months later, the finished building opened for services.[73] Though the trustees of the combined churches maintained the stipulations of the consolidation agreement and a chapel was immediately completed on the 148th Street property, the controversy had a marked impact on those involved. The congregants of the new St. Ann's Church lacked direct financial and institutional control of the church or church funds. However, in the years that followed, the church buildings, specifically designed for the sensibilities of deaf congregants, once again came to provide space for deaf community organizations.[74] For a few short years Gallaudet returned as rector and following his death, Chamberlain took his place. Chamberlain was then assisted by a deaf lay-reader.[75] In turn, John H. Keiser (later Kent), became ordained and replaced Chamberlain upon his death in 1908, beginning the line of deaf priests at St. Ann's Church.[76]

Though the controversy at St. Ann's can be framed in terms of religious institutional dispute, in the history of the American deaf community these events remain significant in the unique expression of agency that they engendered. Not only is attention called to the role of the deaf press in creating and maintaining resistance to paternalism, it highlights the important ways in which deaf citizenship was constructed at the end of the nineteenth century. The dual mission of the church satisfied the larger cultural desire to assimilate deaf people into hearing social institutions.[77] Gallaudet had created the church because he "felt that the greatest good would be accomplished by associating the deaf-mutes with their hearing friends."[78] In uniting the hearing and deaf congregations under one edifice, Gallaudet, consciously or unconsciously, simultaneously reinforced both the paternalistic nationalism that underlay nineteenth-century thinking and undercut the burgeoning agency and autonomy of New York deaf community members.

Through membership in culturally relevant social institutions, deaf community members maintained their status as American citizens.[79] Housed at St. Ann's Church, the community members could rely upon their steady access to the building's Bible study and lecture rooms that ensured them the space for culturally appropriate expression of language and community and enabled community members to develop skills for self-support.

These processes were further reinforced by the church. Outside of the social programs generally associated with churches at this time, the

St. Ann's Free Church
For Deaf Mutes,
18th STREET, near FIFTH AVE,
Rev. THOMAS GALLAUDET, D. D., Rector.

Frontispiece of the first Report of the Church Mutes shows location at West 18th
Street. Courtesy of Gallaudet University Archives.

clergy of St. Ann's extended their influence into "all the organizations
that aimed to promote the welfare of the deaf."[80] They came to provide
legal and interpreting services, employment assistance, educational
opportunities, housing accommodations, as well as financial aid for
those in need of support. These efforts created a bridge between public
and institutional spaces, fostering a relationship between secular and
non-secular services and organizations. The frequent entertainments of
the deaf community—balls, strawberry festivals, and holiday events—
would appear to hearing congregants to serve the same purpose as other
local community events. In these cases, however, events of this nature
brought members of the entire New York deaf community together and
enabled its leaders to develop the skills needed for community building.

The 1897 controversy at St. Ann's Church represented a danger to
this social center and threatened to disrupt the small amount of agency
deaf leaders had obtained in these spaces. Beginning in 1894, the deaf
community began to struggle with the realization that the locality that

housed and supported them might be lost.[81] Throughout the three-year search for a new location for their church, members of this community's primary concern was the repossession of this physical and social space. Though their collaboration grew out of mutual respect and resistance to the consolidation, Comer's and Hodgson's motivations for protest were divergent. Comer lamented the loss of the name, St. Ann's, resisted relocation uptown and protested on the basis of obligation to the donors, who had given funds in support of a free church.[82] For Hodgson, resistance focused on a lack of autonomy for deaf members. He highlighted the inequality of such a merger; the limitations placed on deaf participation in church governance, and disparaged the church for utilizing deaf congregants in the solicitation of donations. Finally, he called, directly, for a separate church building adapted to the needs of the deaf community. Despite this disparity, Comer and Hodgson came to reinforce one another's position in an effort to block the consolidation.

The role that this, and other events, played in the development of a deaf community in the United States in the face of various pressures is a vast untapped resource for identifying the myriad ways that deaf people responded to the tensions in community institutions which operated with paternalistic attitudes, reflected in their actions and motives. At the end of the controversy, a beleaguered Maynard wrote that the deaf community would never "live long enough to ever forget the loss of their church."[83] This has proven false, however. The exploration of this important and complicated controversy calls attention to the interconnected relationship of agency and space and the paternalistic attitudes of the nineteenth century and represents an important and complicated layer in the deaf community's struggle for autonomy.

Notes

1. King, *King's Handbook*, 335.
2. Beckert, *Monied Metropolis*, 59.
3. Burrows and Wallace, *Gotham*, 1171, 1175.
4. Pach, "St. Ann's Bulletin."
5. Manson, "Work of the Protestant Churches 1815–1949, 1," 265–79; Ibid., "Work of the Protestant Churches 1815–1949, 2," 387–433; Ibid., "Work of the Protestant Churches 1815–1949, 3," 461–85; Ibid., "Work of the Protestant Churches 1815–1949, 4," 363–81; Berg and Buzzard, *Missionary Chronicle*; Ibid., *Thomas Gallaudet*; Olney, "Religion and the American Deaf Community;" Burch, *Signs of Resistance*, 46–52, 84; Edwards, *Words Made Flesh*, 104, 107–9.
6. "Church for the Deaf and Dumb," 171.

7. Gallaudet, "St. Ann's Church," 160; Ibid., "Sketch of My Life," 9.

8. This included several Sunday schools, the Mission House, the Gallaudet Home for Aged and Infirm, the Sisterhood of the Good Shepherd and the Church Mission to Deaf-Mutes. Gallaudet, "Sketch of My Life," 31–32.

9. Reverends George C. Pennell, F. C. Ewer, F. D. Cagan, E. Benjamin, Stephen F. Holmes, and H. H. Cole served as assistant ministers. Gallaudet, "History," *Sacramental Register*, vol. 1; Ibid., "History," *Sacramental Register*, vol. 2; Ibid., "History," *Sacramental Register*, vol. 3.

10. Gallaudet, *Sacramental Register* vol. 3, 6.

11. Gallaudet's reasons for selecting Krans as Rector of St. Ann's remains uncertain. It should be noted, however, Chamberlain had worked at St. Ann's for a longer period than Krans, beginning in 1872, while Krans joined in 1874. "Dr. Gallaudet's Farewell."

12. Beckert, *Monied Metropolis*, 75, 212, 216, 217; Burrows and Wallace, *Gotham*, 734, 976, 1030, 1031, 1044, 1159, 1160; Abzug, *Cosmos Crumbling*, 31; Van Cleve and Crouch, *Place of Their Own*; Walters, n.t., 199, 200, 209.

13. Burrows and Wallace, *Gotham*, 993.

14. Rider, "Religious Service In Mexico," 2.

15. Ibid.

16. Positions within the Episcopal Church structure, including lay-readers and ordained clergy, provide further examples of organizational leadership for deaf men. For a further examination of the role of religious institutions in this capacity, see Burch, *Signs of Resistance*, 52; Legg, "Not Consolidation but Absorption."

17. Pach, "St. Ann's Bulletin"; Van Cleve and Crouch, *Place of Their Own*, 97.

18. Pach, "St. Ann's Bulletin"; Ted, "New York," *Deaf-Mutes' Journal* 23, no. 43, 3.

19. The relationship between The Church Mission to Deaf Mutes and St. Ann's was ambiguous and mutually dependent. It is unclear how donations to the church were divided between organizations. The role of the church in providing basic welfare to parishioners in need certainly increased as the city faced high unemployment rates. Hodgson, "Editor's Column," *Deaf-Mutes' Journal* 25, no. 35, 2; Ibid., "Editor's Column," *Deaf-Mutes' Journal* 25, no. 52, 2.

20. Burrows and Wallace, *Gotham*, 663, 948.

21. *New York Times.* "Last Services in St. Ann's," April 22, 1895; Burrows and Wallace, *Gotham*, 663.

22. *New York Times*, "Last Services in St. Ann's," April 22, 1895; Hodgson, "Editor's Column," *Deaf-Mutes' Journal* 22, no. 44, 2.

23. Burrows and Wallace, *Gotham*, 948.

24. Tigg, "New York," *Deaf-Mutes' Journal* 22, no. 20, 3; Seabury, "Memorandum"; Murray, "Copy of Minutes"; Hodgson, "Editor's Column," *Deaf-Mutes' Journal* 26, no. 10, 2; Ibid., "Editor's Column," *Deaf-Mutes' Journal* 24, no. 21, 2.

25. "In the Real Estate Field"; Gallaudet, "Sketch of My Life," 44.

26. Edward Krans, "Correspondence, Krans to Bishop Potter," 3.

27. Hodgson's writing in the *DMJ* indicated that the purchase was made in November, 1894. In *A Sketch of My Life,* Gallaudet stated that it occurred in March 1895. Gallaudet, "Sketch of My Life," 45. Though it is possible that the information published in the *DMJ* was preemptive, it is more likely that in the process of recording the events of these years Gallaudet simply incorrectly noted the date.

28. Patey, "Correspondence," 2; Many, "Correspondence"; Fouls, "Correspondence," 3.

29. Krans, "Correspondence, Krans to Secretary"; Satterlee, "Correspondence," 1.

30. Hodgson, "Editor's Column," *Deaf Mutes' Journal* 24, no. 9, 2.

31. *New York Times,* "Last Services in St. Ann's, April 22, 1895"; *New York Times,* "St. Ann's Church for Deaf-Mutes," *Deaf-Mutes' Journal.*

32. A Quad, "New York," 12.

33. Hodgson, "Editor's Column," *Deaf-Mutes' Journal* 23, no. 48, 2; Ibid., "Editor's Column," *Deaf-Mutes' Journal* 24, no. 9, 2 (February 28, 1895); Ibid., "Editor's Column," *Deaf-Mutes' Journal* 24, no. 14, 2; Ibid., "Editor's Column," *Deaf-Mutes' Journal* 24, no. 17, 3; A Quad, "New York," 12; Hodgson, "Editor's Column," *Deaf-Mutes' Journal* 24, no. 39, 2; Maynard, "Deaf of New York," 12.

34. Maynard, "Deaf of New York"; Ibid., "New York Letter," 13. *New York Times* "Last Sermon in St. Ann's, April 22, 1895," and Hodgson, Edwin, "Editor's Column," *Deaf-Mutes' Journal* 24, no. 21, 2.

35. Despite this letter, it appears that Comer maintained his position within the Vestry until he was not reelected as treasurer and his term ended in October 1898. *New York Times,* "Churchwardens and Vestrymen"; Comer, "Correspondence, Comer to Hodgson, November 30, 1897."

36. Chamberlaine, "Correspondence."

37. Gallaudet, "Correspondence."

38. Hodgson, "Editor's Column: St. Ann's Church for Deaf-Mutes," *Deaf-Mutes' Journal* 26, no. 14, 3.

39. Ibid., *Deaf-Mutes' Journal,* 2.

40. Ibid., *Deaf-Mutes' Journal.*

41. Ibid., *Deaf-Mutes' Journal.*

42. Comer, "Correspondence, Comer to Hodgson, April 12, 1897."

43. Ibid.

44. Ibid.

45. Maynard, "Greater New York," *The Silent Worker* 9, no. 10, 160.

46. Comer, "Correspondence, Comer to Hodgson, April 12, 1897."

47. *New York Times,* "Church Consolidation."

48. Ibid., *New York Times.*

49. Comer, "Correspondence, Comer to Hodgson, April 12, 1897."

50. Ibid., "Correspondence, Comer to Hodgson, April 24, 1897."

51. Ibid., "Correspondence, Comer to Hodgson, April 13, 1897."

52. Maynard, "Greater New York," 160.

53. Gallaudet, "Correspondence"; Ted, "New York," *Deaf-Mutes' Journal* 26, no. 16, 2; Hodgson, "Editor's Column," *Deaf-Mutes' Journal* 26, no. 16, 2.

54. Ted, "New York," *Deaf-Mutes' Journal* 26, no. 16, 3.

55. "Agreement."

56. Ibid.

57. *New York Times.* "Church Merging Blocked."

58. Ted, "New York," *Deaf-Mutes' Journal* 26, no. 16, 3.

59. Hodgson, "Editor's Column," *Deaf-Mutes' Journal* 26, no. 19, 2.

60. Comer, "Correspondence, Comer to Hodgson, November 1, 1897."

61. Ted, "New York: St. Ann's-St. Matthew's," *Deaf-Mutes' Journal* 26, no. 25, 2.

62. Ibid., *Deaf-Mutes' Journal.*

63. *New York Times* "Nearly a Riot in Church."

64. Comer and Hodgson indicate that the *New York Times* article also misrepresented the number of people present. It is also significant to note, that while women were present, they were prohibited from voting. Comer, "Correspondence, Comer to Hodgson, June 22, 1897"; Hodgson, "Editor's Column," *Deaf-Mutes' Journal* 26, no. 25, 2.

65. *New York Times,* "Nearly a Riot in Church."

66. Hodgson, "Editor's Column," *Deaf-Mutes' Journal* 26, no. 25, 2; Comer, "Correspondence, Comer to Hodgson, June 22, 1897."

67. Comer, "Correspondence, Comer to Hodgson, June 22, 1897."

68. Ibid., "Correspondence, Comer to Hodgson, October 27, 1897."

69. Chamberlaine, "Statement of Consolidation."

70. Truax, "Supreme Court Order."

71. Comer, "Correspondence, Comer to Hodgson, October 30, 1897"; Ibid., "Correspondence, Comer to Hodgson, November 9, 1897."

72. *Silent Worker.* "The New St. Ann's Church," 37.

73. Ibid., *The Silent Worker* 11, no. 4, 54.

74. Pach, "Greater New York."

75. Berg and Buzzard, *Missionary Chronicle,* 92.

76. Whiting, "Brief History." St. Ann's Church is still operational today, having relocated from 148th Street, it is currently housed at St. George's Church in New York City. The parish of St. Ann's Church moved into St. George's Church at 7 Rutherford Place, in New York City in 1978. "St. Ann's Church for the Deaf."

77. Baynton, *Forbidden Signs,* 34–35.

78. Gallaudet, "Sketch of My Life," 9.

79. Burch, *Signs of Resistance,* 16.

80. Manson, "Work of the Protestant Churches 1815–1949, 2," 388.

81. Tigg, "New York," *Deaf-Mutes' Journal* 27, no. 19, 3.

82. Comer, "Correspondence, Comer to the Rector."

83. Maynard, "Greater New York," *The Silent Worker* 10, no. 6, 92.

References

Abzug, Robert H. *Cosmos Crumbling: American Reform and the Religious Imagination*. New York: Oxford University Press, 1994.

"Agreement between St. Matthew's and St. Ann's, April 24 1897." Box #45, File 9. Archives of the Episcopal Diocese of New York.

American Annals of the Deaf. "Church for the Deaf and Dumb." *American Annals of the Deaf* 5, no. 3 (April 1853): 169–81.

A Quad. "New York." *The Silent Worker* 7, no. 9 (May 1895): 12.

Baynton, Douglas C. *Forbidden Signs: American Culture and the Campaign Against Sign Language*. Chicago: University of Chicago Press, 1996.

Beckert, Sven. *The Monied Metropolis: New York City and the Consolidation of the American Bourgeoisie, 1850–1896*. Illustrated edition. New York: Cambridge University Press, 2001.

Berg, Otto Benjamin, and Henry L. Buzzard. *A Missionary Chronicle: Being a History of the Ministry to the Deaf in the Episcopal Church, 1850–1980*. Hollywood, MD: St. Mary's Press, 1984.

———. *Thomas Gallaudet, Apostle to the Deaf*. New York: St. Ann's Church For the Deaf, 1989.

Burch, Susan. *Signs of Resistance: American Deaf Cultural History, 1900 to World War II*. New York: New York University Press, 2004.

Burrows, Edwin G., and Mike Wallace. *Gotham: A History of New York City to 1898*. New York: Oxford University Press, 1999.

Chamberlaine, Henry. "Correspondence: St. Matthew's to the Standing Committee, May 29, 1897." Box #45, File 9. Archives of the Episcopal Diocese of New York.

———. "Statement of Consolidation, October 7, 1897." Box #44, File 12. Archives of the Episcopal Diocese of New York.

Comer, John H. "Correspondence: Comer to Hodgson, April 12, 1897." Box #44, File 12. Archives of the Episcopal Diocese of New York.

———. "Correspondence: Comer to Hodgson, April 13, 1897." Box #44, File 12. Archives of the Episcopal Diocese of New York.

———. "Correspondence: Comer to Hodgson, April 24, 1897." Box #44, File 12. Archives of the Episcopal Diocese of New York.

———. "Correspondence: Comer to Hodgson, June 22, 1897." Box #44, File 12. Archives of the Episcopal Diocese of New York.

———. "Correspondence: Comer to Hodgson, October 27, 1897." Box #44, File 12. Archives of the Episcopal Diocese of New York.

———. "Correspondence: Comer to Hodgson, October 30, 1897." Manhattan St. Ann's Box #44, File 12. Archives of the Episcopal Diocese of New York.

———. "Correspondence: Comer to Hodgson, November 1, 1897." Manhattan St. Ann's Box #44, File 12. Archives of the Episcopal Diocese of New York.

———. "Correspondence: Comer to Hodgson, November 9, 1897." Manhattan St. Ann's Box #44, File 12. Archives of the Episcopal Diocese of New York.

——. "Correspondence: Comer to Hodgson, November 30, 1897." Box #44, File 12. Archives of the Episcopal Diocese of New York.

——. "Correspondence: Comer to the Rector and Vestry of St. Ann's, March 30, 1897." Box #44, File 12. Archives of the Episcopal Diocese of New York.

Edwards, R. A. R. *Words Made Flesh: Nineteenth-Century Deaf Education and the Growth of Deaf Culture*. New York: NYU Press, 2012.

Fouls, Henry Dixon. "Correspondence: Rector Fouls of Church of Intercession to Bishop Potter, Standing Committee." n. d., Box #44, File 9. Archives of the Episcopal Diocese of New York.

Gallaudet, Thomas. "Correspondence: Gallaudet to Hodgson, March 4, 1896." Box #44, File 11. Archives of the Episcopal Diocese of New York.

——. "History." *Sacramental Register 1*. St. Ann's Church, 1852–1865. Box #44, File 12. Archives of the Episcopal Diocese of New York. 6–15.

——. "History." *Sacramental Register 2*. St. Ann's Church, 1865–1873. Box #44, File 13. Archives of the Episcopal Diocese of New York. 6–9.

——. "History." *Sacramental Register 3*. St. Ann's Church, 1873–1887. Box #45, File #1. Archives of the Episcopal Diocese of New York. 6–9.

——. "St. Ann's Church for Deaf-Mutes, New York." *American Annals of the Deaf* 7, no. 3 (April 1855): 158–66.

——. "A Sketch of My Life." Unpublished autobiographical manuscript. n.d., Thomas Gallaudet Papers, Gallaudet University Archives.

Hodgson, Edwin A. "Editor's Column." *Deaf-Mutes' Journal* 22, no. 44 (November 1, 1894): 2.

——. "Editor's Column." *Deaf-Mutes' Journal* 23, no. 44 (November 1, 1894): 2.

——. "Editor's Column." *Deaf-Mutes' Journal* 23, no. 48 (November 29, 1894): 2.

——. "Editor's Column." *Deaf-Mutes' Journal* 24, no. 9 (February 28, 1895): 2.

——. "Editor's Column." *Deaf-Mutes' Journal* 24, no. 10 (March 7, 1895): 2.

——. "Editor's Column." *Deaf-Mutes' Journal* 24, no. 14 (April 4, 1895): 2.

——. "Editor's Column." *Deaf-Mutes' Journal* 24, no. 17 (April 25, 1895): 3.

——. "Editor's Column." *Deaf-Mutes' Journal* 24, no. 21 (May 23, 1895): 2.

——. "Editor's Column." *Deaf-Mutes' Journal* 24, no. 39 (September 26, 1895): 2.

——. "Editor's Column." *Deaf-Mutes' Journal* 25 no. 35 (August 27, 1896): 2.

——. "Editor's Column." *Deaf-Mutes' Journal* 25 no. 52 (December 24, 1896): 2.

——. "Editor's Column." *Deaf-Mutes' Journal* 26 no. 6 (April 22, 1897): 2.

——. "Editor's Column." *Deaf-Mutes' Journal* 26 no. 19 (May 13, 1897): 2.

——. "Editor's Column." *Deaf-Mutes' Journal* 26, no. 25 (June 24, 1897): 2.

——. "Editor's Column: St. Ann's Church for Deaf-Mutes." *Deaf-Mutes' Journal* 26, no. 14 (April 8, 1897): 2.

King, Moses. *King's Handbook of New York City: An Outline History and Description of the American Metropolis*. 2nd ed. Boston, MA: Moses King, 1893.

Krans, Edward H. "Correspondence: Krans to Bishop Potter, December 1, 1894." Box #44, File 8. Archives of the Episcopal Diocese of New York.

——. "Correspondence: Krans to Secretary Rev. Seabury, Standing Committee, February 6, 1895." Box #44, File 8. Archives of the Episcopal Diocese of New York.

"Last Services in St. Ann's." *New York Times*. April 22, 1895. *New York Times* Archive 1851–1980. http://query.nytimes.com/search/query?srchst=p.

Legg, Jannelle. "'Not Consolidation but Absorption': A Historical Examination of the Controversy at St. Ann's Church for the Deaf." Master's thesis, Gallaudet University, 2011.

Manson, Alexander M. "The Work of the Protestant Churches for the Deaf in North America 1815–1949, 1." *American Annals of the Deaf* 95, no. 3 (May 1950): 265–79.

———. "The Work of the Protestant Churches for the Deaf in North America 1815–1949, 2." *American Annals of the Deaf* 95, no. 4 (September 1950): 387–433.

———. "The Work of the Protestant Churches for the Deaf in North America 1815–1949, 3." *American Annals of the Deaf* 95, no. 5 (November 1950): 461–85.

———. "The Work of the Protestant Churches for the Deaf in North America 1815–1949, 4." *American Annals of the Deaf* 96, no. 3 (May 1951): 363–81.

Many, P. H. "Correspondence: Clerk Many of St. Mary's to Seabury, Standing Committee, January 2, 1895." Box #44, File 9. Archives of the Episcopal Diocese of New York.

Maynard, Robert E. "The Deaf of New York." *The Silent Worker* 8, no. 6 (February 1896): 12.

———. "Greater New York." *The Silent Worker* 9, no. 10 (June 1897): 160.

———. "Greater New York." *The Silent Worker* 10, no. 6 (February 1898): 92.

———. "New York Letter." *The Silent Worker* 8, no. 7 (March 1896): 13.

Murray, Ambrose Spencer. "Copy of Minutes of Meeting of Committees of Conference Representing the Churches of St. Ann's and of the Annunciation," June 2, 1893. Box #44, File 8. Archives of the Episcopal Diocese of New York.

New York Times. "Church Consolidation." *New York Times*. April 12, 1897.

———. "Church Merging Blocked." *New York Times*. May 7, 1897.

———. "Churchwardens and Vestrymen." *New York Times*. April 17, 1895. http://query.nytimes.com/search/query?srchst=p.

———. "The Deaf and Dumb." October 12, 1852. New York Times Archive 1851–1980.

———. "'The Deaf and Dumb; Second Anniversary of the Organization of St. Ann's Church.'" *New York Times*. October 6, 1854. New York Times Archive 1851–1980.

———. "Deaf Mutes at Church; Interesting Services at St. Ann's Episcopal Church." *New York Times*. September 16, 1878. http://query.nytimes.com/search/query?srchst=p.

———. "Dr. Gallaudet's Farewell; His Last Sermon as Active Rector of St. Ann's." *New York Times*. October 3, 1892. http://query.nytimes.com/search/query?srchst=p.

———. "In the Real Estate Field." *New York Times*. October 31, 1894. *New York Times* Archive 1851–1980.

———. "Nearly a Riot in Church." *New York Times*. June 19, 1897. *New York Times* Archive 1851–1980.

———. "The New St. Ann's Church." *The Silent Worker* 11, no. 3 (November 1898): 37.

Olney, Kent Robert. "Religion and the American Deaf Community: A Sociological Analysis of the Chicago Mission for the Deaf, 1890–1941." PhD diss., University of Oregon, 1999.

Pach, Alexander L. "Greater New York." *The Silent Worker* 11, no. 4 (December 1898): 54–56.

———. "St. Ann's Bulletin." *St. Ann's Bulletin*, January 1938. St. Ann's Box #2, File 10. Gallaudet University Archives.

Patey. "Correspondence: Rector Patey of St. Luke's to Bishop Potter, December 21, 1894." Box #44, File 9. Archives of the Episcopal Diocese of New York.

Rider, Henry C. "Religious Service In Mexico." *Deaf-Mutes' Journal* 4, no. 22 (June 3, 1875): 2.

Satterlee, Henry. "Correspondence: Rector H. Y. Satterlee of Calvary Rectory to Bishop, February 18, 1895." Box #44, File 10. Archives of the Episcopal Diocese of New York.

Seabury, William J. "Memorandum (on the Consolidation of St. Ann's Church with the Church of the Annunciation)," April 29, 1893. Box #44, File 8. Archives of the Episcopal Diocese of New York.

"St. Ann's." *Deaf-Mutes' Journal* 26, no. 14 (April 8, 1897): 3.

"St. Ann's Church for Deaf-Mutes." *Deaf-Mutes' Journal* 24, no. 17 (April 25, 1895): 1.

"St. Ann's Church for the Deaf | The Parish of Calvary-St. George's." *The Parish of Calvary-St. George's in the City of New York*, 2010. http://www .calvarystgeorges.org/pages/st-anns-church-deaf.

Ted. "New York." *Deaf-Mutes' Journal* 23, no. 43 (October 25, 1894): 3.

———. "New York." *Deaf-Mutes' Journal* 26, no. 16 (April 22, 1897): 3.

———. "New York: St. Ann's–St. Matthew's Consolidation Matter." *Deaf-Mutes' Journal* 26, no. 25 (June 24, 1897): 2.

Tigg, Montague. "New York." *Deaf-Mutes' Journal* 27, no. 19 (May 11, 1893): 3.

———. "New York." *Deaf-Mutes' Journal* 27, no. 20 (May 18, 1893): 3.

Truax, Charles H. "Supreme Court Order for Union and Consolidation, October 27 1897." Box #45, File 9. Archives of the Episcopal Diocese of New York.

Van Cleve, John V. and Barry A. Crouch. *A Place of Their Own: Creating the Deaf Community in America*. Washington, DC: Gallaudet University Press, 1989.

Walters, Ronald G. *American Reformers, 1815–1860*, 2nd ed. New York: Hill and Wang, 1997.

Whiting, Eric. "A Brief History of St. Ann's Church for the Deaf And Its Founder, the Rev. Dr. Thomas Gallaudet," c.a. 1960. Henry L. Buzzard Papers, MSS 59. Gallaudet University Archives.

7

In Pursuit of Citizenship: Campaigns Against Peddling in Deaf America, 1880s–1950s

Octavian Robinson

THE LATE NINETEENTH CENTURY was an era of intense Americanization as the nation dealt with the aftermath of the Civil War and an influx of immigrants. During this era, a new way of thinking about membership in the nation emerged.[1] By the late nineteenth century as deaf people began formulating an identity as a distinct cultural minority, they found themselves subjugated to the category of partial membership in the nation. According to historian Douglas Baynton, during the late nineteenth century, deaf people were viewed with suspicion as outsiders because of their clannish behavior and the foreign nature of their language.[2] Sensitive to their status as second-class citizens in this new framework, the deaf community sought to secure their place as equal citizens, which to them, meant *legal and social rights* to employment and economic self-sufficiency.[3]

During much of the period under discussion, job discrimination, rapid industrialization, immigration, and recurring economic crises threatened the material security deaf people had accumulated earlier in the nineteenth century.[4] As the economy expanded, deaf people experienced social pressures related to employment discrimination, such as lack of opportunities to learn trades due to insufficient training venues, inferior education in schools for the deaf, and the encroachment of oralism, acutely aware of the connection between citizenship, power, and economic production.[5] They blamed the poor public image of deaf people due to the presence of peddlers and imposters in the public realm. The deaf community saw peddlers as the antithesis of the idea that deaf people could make valuable contributions to society in late nineteenth-century America.

The deaf community blamed deaf peddlers for conveying the impression that mainstream society should see deaf people as objects of charity due to their physical deficiency rather than as hardworking and self-sufficient contributors to the community. Many deaf people, like most non-disabled people, explicitly equated economic self-sufficiency with bodily and mental wholeness.

Leaders in deaf associations also accused peddlers as responsible for both the increasing popularity of oralism and employment discrimination deaf people faced.[6] Some deaf leaders feared that if the public believed that schools for the deaf teaching via sign language were not successful in their goal of producing self-supporting deaf citizens, states would either endorse the oral method or reduce appropriations for these schools.

Two national organizations, the National Association of the Deaf (NAD) and the National Fraternal Society of the Deaf (NFSD) took the lead in addressing these concerns, beginning with the NAD during the 1880s with the NFSD joining the fray after its inception in 1901. What began as rhetoric evolved into organized publicity, legislative, enforcement, and policing efforts during the early twentieth century, which then led to aggressive efforts toward the goal of eliminating peddling rings following World War II.

At the turn of the century, campaigns narrowed its focus on imposters rather than pursuing both them and peddlers. In the minds of deaf leaders, the marginalization of deaf peddlers was justified so as to advance the deaf community as whole. For example, Thomas F. Fox, a prominent figure in the deaf community suggested in his paper, "Social Status of the Deaf," presented at the 1883 NAD convention, that the American deaf community undertake a campaign to cast out deaf beggars and peddlers who exploited public sympathy.[7] As seen here, deaf community leaders did not undertake anti-peddling and -begging campaigns solely as a way of lifting these deaf people out of poverty, but also to promote an image of deaf people as able-bodied citizens.[8]

Anti-peddling crusades also associated peddling with criminality, exploitation, and poor public image. As convenient scapegoats, peddlers were used as part of the platform for educational and economic reform. The deaf community's anti-peddling campaign supported the belief that reforms of all kinds would benefit American society at large. Many American social reform efforts occurred during the Progressive era between 1900 and 1918, but also continued later in the form of New Deal legislation during the 1930s.[9]

Deaf people, in addition to seeking help combating peddling and employment discrimination during the early twentieth century, also shifted their priorities from hunting down peddlers to going after impostors. Impostors were a growing problem that had emerged in the consciousness of the white middle-class male elite, starting out small in the 1880s and growing in scope as the century turned. Impostors were hearing people posing as deaf people so as to exploit sympathy for deaf people, and therefore, use that sympathy as a way of extracting money from an unsuspecting public. Impostors had contact with many more people than did deaf peddlers. They used this to their advantage and increasingly shaped public perception of deaf people once again more as objects of charity, thus threatening, and partly undoing, the deaf community's efforts to show themselves as self-sufficient citizens.

Moving Beyond Rhetoric: Legislative and Local Community Action

Early action against impostors took place on the local and state level from 1880 to 1910 when deaf people took advantage of existing tramp and vagrancy statutes in investigating, helping police fine and/or imprison impostors. The earliest anti-vagrancy laws relevant to deaf people were on the books in New York in 1885 and Pennsylvania in 1897.[10] These laws were used as a weapon in the deaf elite's efforts to keep peddlers and impostors off the streets, and later were the basis for legislation aimed specifically at impostors.

Initially, individuals and state associations assumed responsibility for campaigns against impostors as early as 1893.[11] By 1905, numerous deaf newspapers in various states were reporting weekly arrests and punishments of impostors.[12] As of 1908, a number of state associations of the deaf had passed resolutions denouncing impostors with calls for legislative and community action in response to the problem.[13] For instance, the Minnesota Association of the Deaf began lobbying for anti-impostor legislation during this period.

The NAD discussed national action as early as 1901. The NAD president at the time, Thomas F. Fox, suggested that the NAD establish a publicity bureau as a way of undertaking a propaganda campaign against impostors by collecting and disseminating information about them to the public.[14] NAD President James Smith, in 1904, suggested a more expansive campaign by forming a committee to stamp out what the deaf community termed "the vagabond evil." He alluded to internal community policing by promoting the idea of vigilance committees. In larger cities, these committees were to network with each other and warn local deaf communities of vagrants and impostors.[15] At its 1904 national convention, the NAD recommended and passed a resolution saying that deaf people themselves should guard the public against impostors and promote enforcement and punishment for impostors.[16] The resolution's wording implied that each deaf *individual* was responsible for taking action against impostors. Because this official act at the convention only targeted impostors, and did not include deaf peddlers, this was when it became clear that the national deaf community's leadership had shifted its attention on impostors and, thus, had put the deaf peddler problem on the back burner.

At the NAD's 1910 convention in Colorado Springs, members passed a resolution mandating that the organization undertake a campaign to suppress activities of impostors and deaf beggars. The resolution also included more demands for more stringent legislation against impostor activity. After this, the NAD expanded its role by reshaping national strategies to include cooperative efforts between various state and local organizations. If anti-peddling and/or anti-impostor legislation was not present on the state or local levels, the NAD urged local and state associations to proactively pursue legislation, present model legislation, petitions, and secure the support from lawmakers by persuading them to present and pass such legislation.

They did this in various ways. The NAD produced a circular, *The Deaf Do Not Beg*, in the hopes of persuading lawmakers of the necessity and benefits of anti-impostor legislation. This circular contained information about impostors, promotion of stereotypes related to impostors, such as linking them to criminal behavior, and stressing the damage impostors did to deaf people's reputation. By portraying peddlers and impostors as criminals who committed other real and violent crimes, the circular suggested anti-impostor legislation would also target potential criminals. They wanted legislation that also protected deaf people from employment discrimination, in part, as a way of separating attitudes toward deaf people from the stigma associated with impostors.[17] By advocating for such legislation and portraying impostors as future criminals, Hanson and Howard portrayed deaf people as citizen-police who protected the community by pursuing impostors.

In 1911, Minnesota secured legislation against impostors.[18] In 1913, bills aimed at suppressing impostors were introduced before the legislatures in Illinois, Kansas, and Washington.[19] Understanding that the needs and requirements for legislation varied from state to state, Howard was lukewarm about introducing universal legislation during his tenure at the Impostor Bureau.[20]

When Olof Hanson became NAD president in 1911, he adopted and supported the anti-impostor agenda with vigor.[21]

This campaign, thus, became one of Hanson's priorities for the NAD, propelled by, in part, increasing interest in the issue. He established the Impostor Bureau in 1911 and appointed Jay Cooke Howard as bureau chief.The bureau's purpose was to investigate why hearing people faked being deaf (i.e., became imposters) and recommend anti-impostor campaign strategies to the organization.[22]

Howard structured the Impostor Bureau as "a cooperative committee with a national chairman, with a state chairman in each state and with a committee man in every town and city."[23] He believed that publicity and education were the best strategies, boasting they had been effective in Minnesota where he had been a state organizer.[24] Howard also supported internal community policing as well as rank and file enlistment for assisting law enforcement in the enforcement of existing anti-impostor statutes.

Howard agreed with Fox's strategy for dealing with impostors. He also believed that publicity against impostors would prevent hearing people from giving money to impostors and deaf beggars, and thus make the enterprise unprofitable.[25]

After Howard succeeded Hanson as president of the NAD, he appointed Jimmy Frederick Meagher, a publisher at the Washington School for the Deaf, to succeed him in 1915 as head of the Impostor Bureau. A flurry of legislation began when Meagher took the reins of leadership of the Impostor Bureau in 1915. Six states passed legislation in 1915. By 1917, eleven more states passed anti-impostor legislation. The new laws specifically prohibited the use of deafness or other disabilities for the purpose of soliciting alms from the public.[26] By 1920, fourteen states had legislation specifically targeting those who used deafness for peddling or begging. Eleven additional states had existing legislation that served the Impostor Bureau's anti-impostor purpose, but did not specifically prohibit peddling under false pretenses of being deaf.[27] Deaf leaders interpreted the passage of anti-impostor legislation as the government's affirmation of deaf people's legal right to "be secure in their reputation as law-abiding, self-supporting citizens."[28]

Adopting the role of "citizen-police," deaf individuals' goals were casting out from deaf social and political gatherings deaf people who peddled. Some went as far as to refer to themselves as agents of the law, even labeling themselves "police." Members of the bureau attempted to claim legitimacy by establishing relationships with local law enforcement, and some even requested actual police powers and badges. Using Meagher as an example of this attitude, he viewed himself and members of the Impostor Bureau as agents of law and order, in helping law enforcement officials uphold the anti-peddling and -impostor legislation as a way of preserving deaf people's reputation as law-abiding citizens.[29]

In 1915, after lobbying the chief of the Vancouver police and the mayor, Meagher was given a regular police badge by the Vancouver police department along with municipal-wide authority to make arrests.[30] As of 1916, Meagher claimed that the bureau was so successful in its work that arrests and convictions of impostors were no longer out of the ordinary.[31] By 1920, the Impostor Bureau had disseminated 10,000 circulars and 25,000 stickers. It had sent newsletters to 400 daily newspapers and secured the passage of legislation in a number of states. Meagher believed that the campaign had been successful even though the economic climate was difficult since impostors were caught more routinely. Although Meagher celebrated the decline of impostors in communities, the anti-peddling crusade of earlier years in the twentieth century was far from finished. He and his cohorts now confronted a new task, combating alphabet card peddlers and bona fide deaf peddlers, who seemed to proliferate within communities after World War I.

Broadening the Campaign: Pursuing Deaf Peddlers

By 1920, forty years of campaigns to improve trade instruction, eradicate impostors, and educate employers about the capabilities of deaf workers, and deaf people's job performance during the war had proven insufficient in cementing deaf people's status as equal economic citizens.[32] Keen awareness of such vulnerability drove the leadership's crusade against employment discrimination and economic inequality through anti-impostor activism, publicity campaigns, and continued efforts to improve trade instruction in schools for the deaf. Impostors remained a political priority for the NAD during the 1920s, although the association's main goal now was to deal more aggressively with deaf peddlers and labor bureaus.[33]

Prior to 1920, Meagher and the Impostor Bureau had maintained "a non-committal attitude on the question" of deaf peddlers because deaf peddlers relied upon "the fact that the NAD has never gone on record as condemning the practice."[34] The preceding four decades of anti-impostor activism had operated on the premise that the majority of deaf-mute peddlers were impostors. Deaf leaders' assertions that deaf people did not seek charity and were a class of hard-working, self-sufficient citizens were upturned by the proliferation of bona fide deaf peddlers. Deaf peddlers, like impostors, also threatened the deaf elite's efforts at portraying deaf people as self-sufficient citizens. They did this by peddling sign language alphabet cards, which implied a linkage of peddling with sign language. Following the emergence of alphabet card peddling, deaf peddlers became more visible and they could no longer be ignored.

Meagher brought the NAD's attention to the rising popularity of alphabet card peddling in the Chicago area in his 1920 report at the NAD convention.[35] He believed the Impostor Bureau could not address the question of deaf peddlers without a directive from the NAD.[36] In 1920, the NAD formally expanded the mission of the Impostor Bureau by redefining impostors to include deaf peddlers who sold items that were overvalued.[37] This directive especially targeted sign language alphabet card peddling.[38] Bona fide deaf peddlers could not be prosecuted for obtaining money under false premises as impostors. Instead, legislation was used to target deaf card peddlers by charging them with peddling without a license.[39]

Deaf people were especially bothered by card peddlers because of public stigma against them and many of them felt that the peddling of sign language alphabet cards only served to emphasize the relationship between deafness and beggary. Meagher described card peddling's stigma in a 1923 article in the *Deaf-Mute's Journal*, claiming that nearly every deaf person in Chicago had confronted a benevolent neighborhood shopkeeper who would flash the cards at them and remark that they had gotten it from a "poor dummy."[40] Alphabet cards left a lasting impression, explicitly tying peddling and beggary to deaf peddlers who used sign language.

As in the previous four decades, the deaf community leadership of the 1920s continued to encourage community self-policing as a primary strategy for discouraging impostors and peddlers. Deaf people, as community police, drove deaf beggars and peddlers out of their localities and assisted law enforcement authorities in detecting impostors, as redefined above.[41] Using the language of citizenship, deaf leadership exhorted deaf people to contribute to community self-policing by reporting any suspicions of fakery. "If you see a fake being enacted, it is your privilege and duty as a citizen to call the attention of the authorities to it."[42] In addition to turning impostors and peddlers in to law enforcement authorities, deaf elites pressured deaf people into socially ostracizing deaf peddlers, barring them from social and political membership.[43] The NFSD also established a policy in 1920 that denied membership to applicants who were known to peddle.

State Intervention

Beyond legislation such as anti-impostor laws, deaf elites believed it was time for states to more actively involve themselves in the crusade against peddlers. State bureaus were expected to gather statistics and information about deaf employment, assist in employment placement, publicize the deaf as capable workers, educate the public about impostors, and fight against discriminatory applications of liability laws.

The deaf elites' hope was that, in working with state labor bureaus would further legitimize deaf people's persuasion of employers to hire deaf workers. They also hoped that these bureaus would help the deaf community in its ferreting out of impostors since they viewed them as a significant threat against the legitimate employment of deaf people.

There was limited success in creating labor bureaus for the deaf on the state level during the 1920s and early 1930s. Minnesota established the first labor bureau for the deaf in 1913 after local activism by the Minnesota deaf community.[44] By the mid-1930s, North Carolina and Michigan also had labor bureaus for the deaf, and Pennsylvania had expanded its vocational rehabilitation services to include deaf adults.[45]

Efforts to secure a federal bureau of labor for the deaf with similar goals failed.[46] Although these efforts and those in many states failed, deaf leaders claimed that the successful establishment of such bureaus in some states secured deaf people's *legal right* to earn a living in the eyes of the state.[47]

During the Great Depression, deaf people confronted tremendous challenges as they encountered an economic downturn affecting all Americans. Deaf people complained of discrimination in the very programs that were designed to help the unemployed.[48] Logically, it would seem that the hard times would lead to a resurgence of deaf peddlers, impostors, and beggars. However, the silent press of the era recounts very little of this phenomenon. Throughout the Depression, the NAD focused on gaining access to employment for deaf people in addition to monitoring discrimination in government-funded work projects rather than on obtaining relief for able-bodied deaf people or in pursuing active campaigns against impostors.

Without assistance and access to government work projects and also coping with persistent employment discrimination, deaf people were driven to peddling out of desperation. During the early 1930s, the NAD reported an uptick in reports of peddler/impostors being discovered in communities around the country. "During the present depression . . . it is not astonishing that a few fakirs should ply their nefarious line of outwitting the sympathetic public.[49] The old story of the deaf and dumb man collecting funds . . . is again being worked."[50]

During the first two years of the Great Depression, deaf community newspapers continued their barrage against beggars, peddlers, and impostors by publishing anecdotes about how deaf people did—or should not—beg and reported on impostors being arrested. After 1931, the silent press focused less attention on the issue of deaf peddlers and impostors for the remainder of the Depression. The silent press's increasing silence on this topic throughout the 1930s occurred for a number of reasons. Editors wanted to avoid attracting attention to the increase in deaf beggary and vagrancy. They, along with deaf community leaders, were sensitive to the economic situation confronting deaf people during the Depression. One editorial lamented that the regular daily presses were already casting deaf people in a negative light. This editorial argued that any publicity from the deaf press during this time would only encourage more discrimination against deaf people's employability. They also worried about navigating the boundaries between condemning desperate deaf people and condemning predatory impostors.[51]

The deaf community tolerated peddling during the 1930s, tacitly acknowledging that the economic situation precluded many otherwise capable deaf people from participating in the workforce. In 1931, an editorial in the *Deaf-Mute's Journal* carefully delineated the difference between peddlers, fakirs, and legitimate salesmen. "It is quite honorable to peddle articles of value," the journal insisted, and such employment was acceptable as long as the items were legitimate and the peddler was licensed.[52] Those articles of value did not include alphabet cards.

The Depression also limited the activities of the Impostor Bureau. The Impostor Bureau, continuing from the 1920s, continued to concern itself with impostors and deaf peddlers. However, in 1934, the bureau, along with other deaf leaders, decided to redirect its efforts on the more pressing concern of improving employment opportunities for deaf people, given the dire economic condition.[53] Careful not to condemn desperate deaf people who were engaging in door-to-door sales, the bureau sponsored a resolution at the 1934 NAD convention that vigorously condemned peddlers who did not sell items at an honest value for the money received rather than deliver a wholesale condemnation of peddling.[54] Ayers claimed that many "otherwise honest and able deaf" were left with no choice but to resort to peddling.[55] He felt that it was not just to pursue deaf peddlers in those economic conditions, describing such persecution as robbing the deaf of their living by "taking the bread and butter out of their mouth."[56] Although peddling hurt the image of deaf people, he believed that most honest deaf people would cease peddling once the economy improved.

During the 1930s, deaf elites and leaders came to have contradictory views about peddling. They thought that it was the cause of deaf people's high unemployment rates *and* that it was a temporary solution to their unemployment in this period.

During World War II, this perception changed because deaf people experienced an uptick in employment and believed that they were now on equal economic terms as their able-bodied counterparts. An example of the changing perception of peddlers is found in an article that the Reverend Arthur G. Leisman penned in the *New York Journal of the Deaf* in April 1940, in which he attacked peddling.[57] He declared "money obtained by panhandlers, deaf or posing as deaf, is blood money. It saps public confidence in us, preys on the virtues of those of us who ever strive to abide by all that is decent and honorable. . . . In any case there is no excuse for panhandling. A man in need has recourse to county relief. No deaf person willingly risks his self respect and that of his comrades by stooping to vagrancy."[58] In the 1940s, when looking back at the Depression era, the deaf press acknowledged "there have been times during the depression when peddling was a dire necessity for some."[59] There were now no longer acceptable reasons to continue to engage in peddling. Leaders characterized those who chose to continue peddling as shiftless and unemployable.

A new concern regarding peddling emerged in the World War II era as the leaders of deaf organizations changed the direction of their anti-peddling campaign toward protecting vulnerable deaf people from organized peddling rings run by beggar kings. During the late 1930s, deaf community leaders had become increasingly aware that the widespread unemployment during the Great Depression coupled with defective educational systems for deaf children across the country contributed

Ladies and Gentlemen:
Pardon my intrusion. My deaf-
ness forces me to make my living
by selling the Best First Aid
Bandages for 25c.
Would you like to Buy One?
Thank You!
I AM AN AMERICAN

KINDLY RETURN THIS CARD

Peddler's card, circa 1940s. Courtesy of Gallaudet University Archives.

to some deaf people's practice of exploiting scores of undereducated, underemployed deaf people.[60] The silent press dubbed the deaf operators of peddling rings as "beggar kings." Those beggar kings were the targets of this revived activism against deaf peddling.

Tom Anderson, who became president of the NAD in 1940, assigned the deaf peddler exploitation issue to the Impostor Bureau.[61] Anderson declared at the 1941 Convention of American Instructors of the Deaf (CAID) that it was "our joint responsibility to prevent such heartless exploitation."[62] Anderson wanted to prevent "individuals of low intelligence to be led into and encouraged in activities symptomatic of begging."[63]

Young deaf peddlers working in peddling rings were often given cards such as the one pictured above.

Peddlers working for peddling gangs were given cheap trinkets and alphabet cards to sell, usually for either ten or twenty-five cents. The peddlers who worked within these operations were also encouraged to solicit alms, often called "tips," in addition to their sales of these wares. Some peddlers went from door to door, posing as families. Other peddlers staked out high traffic areas in large cities such as San Francisco and Chicago, selling their wares to passersby.[64]

As of 1942, there were three large organizations made up of deaf men and women working out of several eastern states under the supervision of a main leader.[65] The peddlers often carried cards with a doleful tale, canvassed towns marked by gangs, and kept a small percentage of their earnings while turning over most of their earnings to their bosses, the beggar kings.[66] In addition to keeping the skimpy remainder of their earnings, peddlers were compensated with rundown housing, promises of returns on their savings, and promises of exclusive peddling turf which never materialized. Peddlers in these rings who did not cooperate with their bosses and/or did not turn over enough earnings for the day were subject to physical assault by the gang's enforcers.[67] This exploitation of undereducated deaf people led the leadership of the deaf community to compare peddling rings to white slavery.[68]

An NAD pamphlet accused gang bosses of starving peddlers, beating them up for not giving over enough of their take, and forcing them to live in shabby rooms.[69] Some deaf leaders, such as Tom L. Anderson, theorized that peddling rings became rampant after World War II because so many youths had left school early to take advantage of wartime employment but were mentally, intellectually, and emotionally immature and, therefore, unprepared for the changing postwar workforce.[70] People involved with peddling rings also exploited young deaf people for sexual purposes. People were also concerned that peddling ringleaders themselves were sexually exploiting their female peddlers.[71] Arthur Roberts, president of the NFSD, not only tagged peddlers as criminals, but also labeled them as sexual deviants who molested women or used women in their peddling rings for immoral purposes.[72]

The deaf community was conservative in how they perceived women and had concerns about public perceptions of deaf women.[73] Deaf people dedicated to eradicating peddling rings, especially those that employed women, may have been driven by wanting to protect the public's perception of deaf women's virtues. Arthur Roberts did not distinguish between female peddling and prostitution; he thought that if a woman was peddling anything at all, she must also be selling the use of her body. A columnist in the *Frat* suggested this in a 1948 editorial, saying that "one comely young deaf girl, in this racket on her own, . . . she was peddling alphabet cards, and perhaps herself on the side."[74]

In addition to peddling rings' exploitation of some deaf people, deaf leaders remained concerned about public perceptions of them, as they had been since the 1880s. One example of a public perception that they wanted to dispel was that if there were too many deaf peddlers, the deaf would "come to be regarded as a dependent class."[75] In 1950, Fred Murphy, the NAD's anti-peddling chief, argued that peddlers held tremendous sway over shaping public perceptions of deaf people because they, by virtue of their profession, met hundreds of people daily and gave credence to the impression that all deaf people were like them.[76] Deaf people also continued to believe that widespread peddling directly contributed to the difficulties of the deaf in obtaining employment. An editorial in the *Frat* reported on this concern when it recounted an incident where a prospective employer told a deaf job applicant, "We do not employ deaf people. Why don't you go out and peddle like the rest of you do?"[77] Murphy argued in 1950 that the deaf community needed to take action against peddling because "in recent years the social and economic stability of the deaf has been subject to strong pressure by exploitation as practiced by itinerant bands of deaf peddlers."[78]

Deaf leaders were afraid that the public's negative perceptions of deaf peddling and, by extension, of deaf people in general would limit deaf people's employment and educational opportunities, key ways that deaf people used to show the larger community that they were good American citizens. Meagher, former chief of the Impostor Bureau, suggested in 1947 that peddling "is a racket which can cause us deaf to lose our full citizenship rights, and be treated as imbeciles—like the deaf are treated in Europe."[79]

While hearing peddlers had been characterized as con men and impostors since the late nineteenth century, deaf peddlers were not explicitly linked to criminality until the 1940s. Throughout the 1940s and early 1950s, deaf peddlers were described as criminals and troublemakers. Fred Murphy, a leader at the forefront of the anti-peddling campaigns during the post war period, connected peddling to criminality, "Other crimes stem from peddling-tax evasion, fraud, delinquency of minors, bribery, mayhem, thievery, immoral acts."[80] Peddling gangs were linked to criminality mainly because of their panhandling, but also because they did not pay their bills; committed forgery; drove recklessly, at times resulting in death, thus infringing on deaf people's battle to retain driving rights; selling obscene pictures; violating the Mann Act for engaging in prostitution and human trafficking; and even because of an instance in which a peddler molested a young child.[81] Peddling rings were thus viewed as epicenters of immoral activity and also because unmarried women and men traveled and worked together in these rings.[82]

In the 1940s, the leadership also looked for ways of linking deaf peddling activity to organized crime. They did this because they increasingly viewed organized peddling rings as a form of racketeering during the 1940s. Peddling rings were described more as rackets led by beggar kings, described as racketeers.[83] The *Frat*, the official newspaper of the NFSD, described this form of racketeering as organized gangs operating over wide territories in fleets of cars, using theft, playing confidence games, and incorporating immorality in their gangs.[84] A large part of the con was that peddlers were arranged into fake families and taught the use of pressure tactics as ways of successfully working in the way that gangs wanted.[85]

Another way of connecting peddling rings to organized crime was to point out examples of peddling gangs using physical violence, also a favored tactic of organized crime syndicates. In 1946, the *Frat* mentioned, for example, that peddlers who threatened anti-peddling activists with bodily harm were using "gangland's weapon to silence criticism."[86] The deaf press also compared the beggar kings to Al Capone, the most infamous Mafia leader of the time. The *Frat*, for instance, said of the beggar kings, "They turn into Al Capones—on a very small scale."[87] Newspaper editorials and community leaders also used terms such as "mob leaders" and "gangsters" to describe beggar kings as another way of connecting peddling rings with organized crime.[88]

The NFSD's decade-long national campaign in shutting down Leon Krakover's gang, the largest deaf peddling ring in the nation, continued during the 1940s. Deaf community leaders, however, put more emphasis on the need for local, state, and national deaf organizations to act against racketeering operations during this same period. These organizations' focused on eliminating peddling gangs rather than individual peddlers. Correspondence between Arthur Roberts of the NFSD and other deaf community leaders cover such strategies, as internal community policing, encouraging the use of local statues against peddling and vagrancy, and character attacks on beggar kings.[89]

The NAD Committee for the Suppression of Peddling recommended in 1949 that the NAD was not the proper channel for the deaf community's fight against peddling.[90] The committee suggested that they would work more effectively by using other strategies, such as pursuing an aggressive publicity and education campaign as ways of informing the public about the evils of organized peddling on the national level and that states and local communities should take action against specific peddling rings in their areas.[91]

Even though the NFSD continued as the primary force on the national level in anti-peddling campaigns from 1941 onward, the NAD's Committee for the Suppression of Peddling efforts on the national level was limited to seeking federal legislation against peddling rings and the enforcement of existing legislation. Leaders stressed the importance of localities taking advantage of existing legislation and urge law enforcement to follow through in using existing legislation to crack down on the peddling rings.[82] Deaf community leaders emphasized that local and state organizations use the legislation already in place because some deaf people complained about lax enforcement of laws against vagrancy and peddling.

In Defense of Peddlers

However, not all deaf people were against peddling or considered it a barrier to citizenship. Prior to the 1930s, deaf people did not defend deaf peddlers because those campaigns primarily targeted impostors. The campaigns against deaf alphabet card peddling in the 1920s were promoted as efforts toward limiting or eliminating peddling avenues for hearing impostors. By the 1940s, as campaigns narrowed their focus on deaf peddlers and peddling gangs, deaf people expressed either discomfort or indifference toward such campaigns. Roberts conceded to Joseph Grant, the NFSD's lawyer, that not all members of the organization were on board with their efforts to stamp out peddling. Roberts characterized this segment of the NFSD membership as indifferent or tolerant of peddlers. He believed that those members simply did not realize the "harm done to the honest deaf until they are confronted with the fact in their quest for honest employment."[93]

Many deaf people identified with deaf peddlers as part of the larger deaf community and advocated that solidarity among deaf people should be the most important objective of the community. The leadership was frustrated with deaf people who advocated deaf solidarity and refused to acknowledge the damage peddling did to deaf people.[94]

In fact, some deaf people accused the leadership of inducing "fear-hysteria" by invoking negative barbs aimed at deaf peddlers as part of their campaigns. In 1948, in a letter Altor Sedlow wrote to the editor of *The Cavalier*, a leading deaf newspaper of the day in response to the paper's anti-peddling editorials, Sedlow argued that the deaf community duty was not to demonize peddlers, but rather to advocate for alternative means of livelihood for them and support to peddlers who sought other ways to earn a living.[95] Anderson, one of the NAD's presidents, echoed Sedlow's sentiments and argued that the leadership should promote educational reforms that would provide deaf people with the necessary skills needed for succeeding in the postwar economy.[96]

Peddlers attempted to defend themselves in the silent press. They argued that selling goods was decent work and perfectly legitimate. They used patriotic language, in referring to "this great free country of ours—a land of free enterprises for all," appealing to the American sentiment of self-sufficiency and enterprise. They argued that by undertaking peddling, they were relieving the deaf community of the burden of supporting them.[97]

Some peddlers, in self-defense, went as far as to threaten legal action if the attacks on their reputations did not cease. Leon Krakover wrote a letter to the Pennsylvania Society for the Advancement of the Deaf and objected to their description of his business as a "nefarious racket." Krakover generously claimed that he didn't want to damage the deaf community's overall reputation with bad publicity so would not take action this time, but threatened legal action if publicity campaigns against him continued.[98]

Deaf community members who did not peddle also defended peddlers. Eric Malzkuhn, a well-known figure and actor in the deaf community, wrote to Tom L. Anderson in 1952, arguing that deaf people did not ask to be deaf or to be discriminated against. Why, he asked, censure deaf people for making the best they can by peddling as a "partial recompense" for their disability?[99] In 1950, a woman from Arkansas wrote to Emerson Romero, columnist and complier of "The Open Forum" section of the *Silent Worker,* inviting anti-peddling advocates to visit her state and see how many people were unemployed. She didn't have it in her "heart to condemn these men when, after months of struggling with their conscience, they take to peddling."[100] Romero responded that peddling was not the cause of employment difficulties for deaf people, but rather a consequence of a lack of employment available to deaf people. He argued that the focus of the post-war anti-peddling campaigns was beggar kings and not individuals, and that this could be seen in the attention they gave to peddling gangs rather than on individuals.

Some people even went beyond defending peddlers and lauded those who peddled. An anonymous author in the *Frat* said that the peddlers claimed that they should be respected for their sharp wit and ability to make a good living and should be viewed as benefactors of mankind by teaching hearing people the alphabet [fingerspelled].[101] Anderson recommended that the NAD not respond to defenders of peddling. Anderson believed that in responding to peddlers who defended themselves, the NAD would only affirm that peddling was a legitimate livelihood for deaf people.[102]

The end of anti-peddling campaigns in the 1950s cannot be attributed to a single event, but rather was a culmination of a number of factors. Individual personalities came to direct the campaigns rather than conducting them in consultation with and alongside their membership. Most other deaf leaders shifted their focus toward lessening employment discrimination toward deaf people and lowering the rate of deaf people's underemployment, including their acceptance of government assistance in the form of vocational rehabilitation, employment quotas, and programs designed to help deaf people obtain jobs. The leaders realized by this time that challenging public perception of deaf people would accomplish little and that anti-peddling campaigns no longer held the promise of breaking down employment barriers for deaf people.

Deaf leaders acknowledged that peddlers no longer represented a direct threat to the deaf community and culture, sign language, or to schools for the deaf that used sign-language-based pedagogical methods. Therefore, deaf leaders knew there was simply no longer a need to blame peddlers as for the employment issues that deaf people faced. Deaf leaders knew that the government would have to become involved for the successful integration of deaf people in the workforce and so they could achieve economic self-sufficiency. The meaning of citizenship also changed in the post–World War II period. "The prominent emergence of civil rights activism in particular has expanded the very meaning of American citizenship. The civil rights revolution has changed what it means to be an American. It has also challenged what it means to be a Deaf person."[103] Due to the commonly accepted premise that all people, by virtue of living in the United States, were entitled to all rights of citizenship such as obtaining an education and work thereafter, deaf people no longer felt pressured to prove themselves as citizens in order to obtain the rights of citizenship. This also meant that deaf people could now direct all their attention to combating unemployment and discrimination in hiring practices without having also to use their energy toward convincing others that they were good citizens and, therefore, worthy of employment.

Peddlers and other deaf people who were unable to or did not wish to work could secure economic help through the newly implemented Social Security Disability Insurance program (SSDI) as of 1956. The deaf community's response to SSDI was double pronged. With federal assistance available to combat the underemployment and unemployment of deaf people, the deaf community was able to lower public opinions of them as vagrants and preserve the public perception of deaf people as able workers as they had demonstrated in the factories during World War II. Although SSDI cushioned deaf people's economic status and hid deaf vagrancy from public view, deaf community leaders continued to feel the stigma of disability and poverty associated with many deaf people's continued need for SSDI benefits and vocational rehabilitation assistance for much of the twentieth century.

Recognizing that employment discriminatory practices were deeply entrenched in American society, deaf activists could no longer rely on education or voluntary approaches by the employment sector to proactively employ deaf people as they had for so long.[104] After the war, deaf leaders began lobbying for expanded higher education opportunities for deaf people and worked toward the establishment of a technical college for the deaf. Deaf leaders also invested their efforts in establishing access to federal and state vocational rehabilitation agencies. Leaders were careful to frame the purposes of rehabilitation agencies, as they had done earlier in the century with respect to the labor bureaus. Leaders, such as Tom L. Anderson, stressed that rehabilitation agencies, like the earlier labor bureaus, were in place to enable deaf people to become self-sufficient and were not government agencies that gave handouts or provided charity for deaf people.[105] Deaf community leaders combined their efforts towards the goals of increased access to rehabilitation agencies, expanding higher education for deaf people, and continued improvement in the education of deaf children, areas they believed would better help deaf people advance economically, thus cementing their place as citizens.

Notes

1. Frederick E. Hoxie, *A Final Promise: The Campaign to Assimilate the Indians, 1880–1920* (Lincoln, NE: University of Nebraska Press, 1984), xii.

2. Douglas C. Baynton, "A Silent Exile on This Earth: The Metaphorical Construction of Deafness in the Nineteenth Century." *American Quarterly* 44, no. 2 (1992): 127–128. Also see Robert Buchanan, *Illusions of Equality: Deaf Americans in School and Factory, 1850–1950* (Washington, DC: Gallaudet University Press, 1999), 21.

3. When deaf leaders spoke of economic self-sufficiency and equal citizenship for deaf people, they primarily meant that for deaf white men and, on occasion, for white deaf women as well.

4. Thomas F. Fox, "President's Address," *NAD Proceedings* (1893), 4–5 [hereafter NAD Proceedings].

5. Robert H. Wiebe, *The Search for Modern Order, 1877–1920* (New York: Hill and Wang, 1967), 40–41.

6. Ibid., 44. See source for more information on this topic.

7. Ibid., 40–41.

8. For more information on ableist rhetoric and efforts undertaken by the American deaf community see Octavian Robinson, "We Are of a Different Class: Ableist Rhetoric in Deaf America, 1880–1920," in *Deaf and Disability Studies: Interdisciplinary Perspectives,* ed. Susan Burch and Alison Kafer (Washington, DC: Gallaudet University Press, 2010), 5–21.

9. Richard Hofstadter, *The Age of Reform: From Bryan to FDR: Populism, Progressivism, and the New Deal- a stimulating new analysis from the perspective of our own time* (New York: Alfred A. Knopf Press, 1981), 3.

10. Jimmy Frederick Meagher, "Report of the Impostor Bureau," *Deaf-Mute's Journal* 49, no. 34 (August 19, 1920): 2.

11. Fox, "Associations of the Deaf in America," *World's Congress of Deaf Mutes' Proceedings* (1893): 30.

12. Theophilius d'Estrella, "The Itemizer," *California News* 20, no. 28 (March 18, 1905): 5.

13. "Colorado," *Deaf-Mute's Journal* 37, no. 35 (August 27, 1908): 1.

14. Hofstadter, *The Age of Reform*, 185.

15. James L. Smith, "President's Address," *NAD Proceedings* (1904): 50–51.

16. National Association for the Deaf "Resolutions," *NAD Proceedings* (1904): 178.

17. "Legislative Protection for 'Real' deaf Mutes Sought By State Chief," *The Silent Observer* 38, no. 14 (1915): 1.

18. "Resolutions," *Proceedings of the Twenty-Fifth Meeting of the Pennsylvania Society for the Advancement of the Deaf* (1911): 46–47. [hereafter PSAD Proceedings].

19. Jay Cooke Howard, "National Association of the Deaf. Report of the Impostor Bureau," *Deaf-Mute's Journal* 42, no. 9 (1913): 4.

20. Jay Cooke Howard to Olof Hanson, 25 January 1911. Olof Hanson Collection, Gallaudet University Library Archives.

21. Oscar Regensburg, "Impostor Bureau: A Report from Mr. Regensburg," *Deaf-Mute's Journal* 42, no. 13 (March 27, 1913): 2.

22. Susan Burch, *Signs of Resistance: American Deaf Cultural History, 1900–1942* (New York: New York University Press, 2002), 150.

23. Jay Cooke Howard to Olof Hanson, 25 January 1911. Olof Hanson Collection, Gallaudet University Library Archives.

24. Olof Hanson to Jay Cooke Howard, 6 February 1911, Olof Hanson Collection, Gallaudet University Library Archives.

25. "NAD Official Bulletin: Mr. Howard's Good Work," *Deaf-Mute's Journal* 41, no. 2 (January 11, 1912): 1.

26. Meagher, "Report of the Impostor Bureau," *Deaf-Mute's Journal* 49, no. 34 (August 19, 1920): 2; Ibid., *Deaf-Mute's Journal* 46, no. 21 (May 24, 1917): 1.

27. Ibid., *Deaf-Mute's Journal* 49, no. 34 (August 19, 1920): 2.

28. Michael Lapides, "National Association of the Deaf," *Deaf-Mute's Journal* 55, no. 13 (1926): 1.

29. Meagher, "Report of the Impostor Bureau," *Deaf-Mute's Journal* 49, no. 34 (August 19, 1920): 4. Ibid., *Deaf-Mute's Journal*: 2.

30. Ibid., *Deaf-Mute's Journal* 44, no. 46 (November 18, 1915): 4.

31. Ibid., *Deaf-Mute's Journal* 45, no. 6 (February 10, 1916): 2.

32. Octavian Robinson, "The Deaf Do Not Beg: Making the Case for Citizenship, 1880–1956." PhD diss., The Ohio State University, 2012, 80–81.

33. James H. Cloud, "President's Address," *NAD Proceedings* (1920), 9–10.

34. Meagher, "Report of the Impostor Bureau," *NAD Proceedings* (1920), 46.

35. Ibid.

36. Ibid.

37. "Resolutions," *NAD Proceedings* (1920), 97.

38. Meaghers, "Chicago," *Deaf-Mute's Journal* 52, no. 32 (August 9, 1923): 2.

39. Ibid.

40. Meagher, "Chicago," *Deaf-Mute's Journal* 52, no. 8 (February 22, 1923): 2.

41. Helen Hanson, "The Deaf," *Deaf-Mute's Journal* 53, no. 20 (May 15, 1924): 1.

42. "Editorial," *Deaf-Mute's Journal* 52, no. 28 (July 12, 1923): 2.

43. Arthur Roberts, "National Association of the Deaf: Official," *Deaf-Mute's Journal* 54, no. 6 (February 5, 1925): 2.

44. Burch, *Signs of Resistance*, 116–17.

45. Ibid., 117–20.

46. House Committee on Education. *House Resolution*, H.R.1109. 66th Cong., (1919).

47. Lapides, "National Association of the Deaf," *Deaf-Mute's Journal* 55, no. 13 (April 1, 1926): 1.

48. "The Deaf and National Legislation," *N.A.D. Bulletin* 2, no. 1 (October 1935): 1.

49. During the early twentieth century, the term *faker* was also spelled *fakir*.

50. "Impostors," *Deaf-Mute's Journal* 61, no. 5 (February 4, 1932): 2.

51. "Editorial," *Deaf-Mute's Journal* 63, no. 27 (July 5, 1934): 4.

52. "Editorial," *Deaf-Mute's Journal* 59, no. 47 (November 20, 1930): 2; and "Editorial," *Deaf-Mute's Journal* 60, no. 18 (April 30, 1931): 2.

53. Kreigh B. Ayers, "Report of the Impostor Bureau," *NAD Proceedings* (1930): 40.

54. "Resolutions Adopted at the Seventeenth Triennial Convention of the National Association of the Deaf at the Hotel Pennsylvania, New York City, July 27, 1934," *Deaf-Mute's Journal* 63, no. 33 (August 16, 1934): 2.

55. Ayers, "Report of the Impostor Bureau," *NAD Proceedings*, 40.

56. Ibid.

57. "Wisconsin," *New York Journal of the Deaf* 69, no. 14 (April 4, 1940): 5.

58. Ibid.

59. Ibid.

60. "A Racket That Must Be Stopped," *Western Pennsylvanian* 50, no. 9 (January 29, 1942): 67.

61. "National Association of the Deaf: Official Announcement," *New York Journal of the Deaf* 70, no. 24 (June 12, 1941): 5.

62. Anderson, "The Challenge to Leadership: An Address Delivered before the Convention of American Instructors of the Deaf" *NADIC* [hereafter NADIC] 1, no. 4 (August 1941): 5–7.

63. Ibid., "N.A.D. on the Trail of Impostors," *NADIC* 1, no. 3 (May 1941): 1.

64. "Beggar King Jailed in San Francisco," *The Cavalier* v. 7–8 (September 1946–August 1948), (no page number given).

65. H. Rodgers, "Let's Abolish The Deaf Racketeers," *Western Pennsylvanian* 50, no. 9 (January 29, 1942): 65–66.

66. Ibid.

67. Catherine Castera to Arthur Roberts, 9 December 1949, National Fraternal Society of the Deaf Collection, Gallaudet University Library Archives.

68. Arthur Roberts to Joe (no last name given), 12 July 1949, National Fraternal Society of the Deaf Collection, Gallaudet University Library Archives.

69. NAD Pamphlet, "The National Association of the Deaf: A Non-Profit Organization Representing All The Deaf Presents STOP THIS RACKET! An Educational Pamphlet of Interest to Everyone Concerned with Deafness," Tom L. Anderson Collection.

70. "Peddlers," *Frat* [hereafter *Frat*] 43, no. 11 (June 1946): 5.

71. Anderson to E. Ivan Curtis, 28 October 1941, Tom L. Anderson Collection, Gallaudet University Library Archives.

72. Arthur Roberts to Brother Cohen, 21 April 1946, National Fraternal Society of the Deaf Collection, Gallaudet University Library Archives.

73. Sara Robinson, "The Extended Family: Deaf Organizations from 1880–1950," in *Double Visions: Women and Deafness*, ed. Susan Burch and Brenda Brueggemann (Washington, DC: Gallaudet University Press, 2004), 40–56.

74. "We Can Do It," *Frat* 45, no. 8 (March 1948): 4.

75. "Jacksonville," *Frat* 46, no. 12 (July 1949): 4–5.

76. Ibid.

77. "Mendicants," *Frat* 49, no. 7 (February 1952): 8.

78. Fred Murphy, "The Curse of Deafdom: A Guidebook containing hints and suggestions for use by those who would like to see the PEDDLING RACKET suppressed."

79. Meagher, "Spotlight," *Frat* 45, no. 2 (September 1947): 2.

80. "Beggars' Progress: The Record and a Remedy," *Frat* 47, no. 3 (October 1949): 5–6.

81. Ibid.

82. Ibid.

83. Rodgers, "Let's Abolish The Deaf Racketeers," *Western Pennsylvanian* 50, no. 9 (January 29, 1942): 65–66.

84. "Racketeers," *Frat* 43, no. 10 (May 1946): 4–5.

85. Ben M. Schowe, "Fagins," *Frat* 46, no. 5 (December 1948): 4–5.

86. "Card Peddlers," *Frat* 44, no. 5 (December 1946): 4.

87. "On the Run," *Frat* 45, no. 5 (December 1947): 5.

88. "Educate Public," *Frat* 46, no. 9 (April 1949): 5; "Beggars Symposium: What They Are Doing Over the Country Highlights on the Racket," *Frat*, 5.

89. For examples on correspondence between local leaders on potential peddlers and troublemakers, see correspondence collections in NFSD and NAD manuscript collections, particularly amongst Fred Murphy, Arthur Leisman, Arthur Roberts, Byron Burnes, and local division presidents of the NFSD.

90. "Report of the Committee on Resolutions," in *NAD Proceedings* (1949), 51.

91. Byron B. Burnes, "President's Address," *NAD Proceedings* (1949), 13–14.

92. "Report of the Committee on Resolutions," *NAD Proceedings* (1949), 51.

93. Arthur Roberts to Joseph Grant, 15 March 1953, National Fraternal Society of the Deaf Collection, Gallaudet University Library Archives.

94. Nathaniel C. Garrison to Arthur Roberts, 4 April 1949, National Fraternal Society of the Deaf Collection, Gallaudet University Library Archives.

95. Altor L. Sedlow, "Rehabilitate the Peddlers," *The Cavalier,* 7 no. 8 (May 1948): 2.

96. Tom L. Anderson to Arthur Roberts, 25 July 1949, National Fraternal Society of the Deaf Collection, Gallaudet University Library Archives.

97. "Peddlers Selling Pencils Now," *The Cavalier* 11, no. 11 (September 1951): 1.

98. Clipping from Tom L. Anderson Collection, box 2, MSS 57, Gallaudet University Archives, Washington, DC: "We Are Threatened," dated 26 December 1941 —addressed to PSAD and published in *Pennsylvania Society News*, 5.

99. Eric Malzkuhn to Tom L. Anderson, undated, Tom L. Anderson Collection, Gallaudet University Library Archives (undated, TLA responds to this letter on 8 May 1952 and the response was attached to Malzkuhn's original letter).

100. Emerson Romero, "The Open Forum," *Silent Worker* 2, no. 9 (May 1950): 31.

101. "Panhandlers," *Frat* 43, no. 11 (June 1946): 4.

102. Thomas Northern to Tom L. Anderson, 17 February 1942, Tom L. Anderson Collection.

103. Burch, 171–74.

104. Buchanan, 125.

105. Ibid.

8

Revisiting the *Memoir*: Contesting Deaf Autonomy and the Real Tragedy of Alexander Graham Bell

Brian H. Greenwald

IN 1883, ALEXANDER GRAHAM BELL gave a presentation to the National Academy of Sciences in which he discussed deaf peoples' tendency to intermarry and stated that those marriages grew at an alarming rate during the nineteenth century. This pattern, Bell argued, would continue unabated if no action was taken to cease the spread of hereditary deafness. He also noted the cornerstones of the cultural deaf community such as social events including dancing, hosting state and national conventions, churches, newspapers, use of sign language, and usually marrying other deaf people. Following this, Bell discussed preventive and repressive measures as possible mechanisms to curtail the number of deaf people. The speech was published in 1884 as *Memoir Upon the Formation of the Deaf Variety of the Human Race* (hereafter *Memoir*), and it has sparked intense discussion among deaf people since its circulation and continues to be cited as damning evidence for its deleterious impact on deaf people. Historians have studied the *Memoir* largely through the lens of eugenics, identifying and elaborating on Bell's intentions and rationale to halt what he perceived as a troubling increase in the number of deaf people born. If left unabated, he argued, this pattern would lead to a "deaf variety of the human race."[1]

Historians have long used the labels "positive" and "negative" when describing specific aspects of eugenics as practiced in the United States during the Progressive Era. *Positive* eugenics typically referred to non-policy efforts, applying social pressure to encourage humans to make more informed decisions about procreation. In particular, supporters of positive eugenics encouraged genetically "healthy" individuals to increase their procreation. Practitioners of *negative* eugenics generally embraced public policy efforts including legislation, placing prohibitions on the activities of certain groups, or segregating them from society by physically distancing them to buildings such as specialized hospitals.[2] Despite the problematic labeling of eugenics—eugenics was eugenics—and eugenicists reflected a broad ideological swath. Bell was a eugenicist who favored positions generally supported by positive eugenicists; that is, Bell did not support sterilization, institutionalization, or marriage prohibition. Bell strongly pushed for deaf-hearing marriages and for deaf people to leave their cultural corner and embrace mainstream values, including oralism, attending day schools, and refraining from using sign language.

Alexander Graham Bell stood as a polarizing figure in the signing deaf community and his name remains synonymous with oralism even over ninety years after his death. Bell's legacy is complex—he is an American icon (even if he emigrated from Edinburgh, Scotland, to Canada, and then to the United States) with multiple patents including one for his invention of the telephone. Deaf people who grew up speaking and lipreading may claim Bell as their staunchest advocate, while signing deaf people demonize Bell for his work on eugenics and his multifaceted influence on oralism. One of Bell's earliest and most often studied polemics is the *Memoir*, a publication usually explored within the context of eugenics which was a growing movement in England before its transatlantic influence at the turn of the twentieth century. Rather than exploring Bell's influence on eugenics, this discussion concentrates on Bell's challenges to deaf autonomy (including marriage selection), ideologies surrounding deaf education, and cultural aspects important to deaf bodies and politics.

Bell's presentation to the National Academy of Sciences audience came at a time when he was very well informed about the history of deaf people, the value of sign language, residential schools, organizations, and other community ties that were important to the nascent signing deaf community. Bell learned and understood this from his own personal and professional experiences. He was born in 1847 in Edinburgh, Scotland, to a hearing father, Melville Bell, and deaf mother, Eliza Grace Bell.[3] Bell's father, Melville, and namesake grandfather, Alexander Bell, were both elocutionists who focused on speech delivery and voice presentation, two important areas associated with the teaching of speech. Melville Bell created "Visible Speech" which was a system of symbols that indicated tongue placement to generate sounds. Symbols were

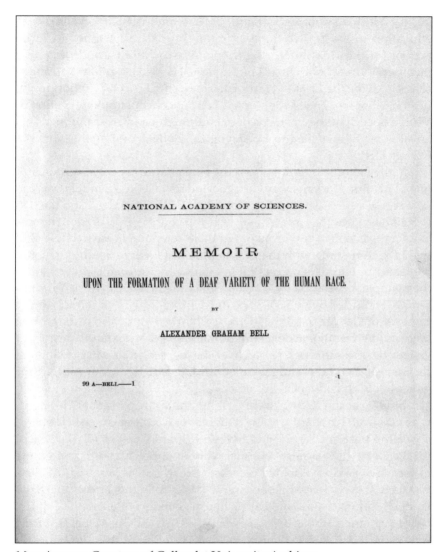

NATIONAL ACADEMY OF SCIENCES.

MEMOIR

UPON THE FORMATION OF A DEAF VARIETY OF THE HUMAN RACE.

BY

ALEXANDER GRAHAM BELL

99 A—BELL——1

Memoir cover. Courtesy of Gallaudet University Archives.

arranged in order from left to right and students would mimic these sounds, and thus, produce speech.[4] Visible Speech was used in private enterprise by Melville Bell and was a source of income that supported the family. Alexander Graham Bell learned the trade from his father, and used it himself in the United States.

As had his father in Scotland, Bell became very involved in deaf education in the United States. He taught for a brief time at Clarke School for the Deaf in Northampton, Massachusetts, and became a member of the school's Board of Trustees. He also taught at the American School for the Deaf in Hartford, Connecticut. An 1873 report to the Boston School for Deaf Mutes noted Bell's successful implementation of Visible Speech at the Boston school,[5] although he later abandoned this effort when he switched to a pedagogical model based on the works of George Delgarno.

In the fall of 1872, Bell opened his own private school in Boston and one of his first students was George Sanders.[6] George Sanders was the deaf son of a successful leather merchant, Thomas Sanders, and the two forged close ties that intersected over the course of Bell's life. Thomas Sanders was one of the investors in Bell's telephony research and Bell lived for some time with the grandmother of George Sanders. George Sanders came to depend on Bell in later years for financial assistance, for example, he secured a job at the Volta Bureau in northwest Washington, DC, founded by Bell. Perhaps most importantly, Bell came to know the love of George Sanders' life, Lucy Maria Swett, who came from a large multigenerational deaf familly. Bell learned of her family history of genetic deafness through research for the *Memoir*. In the years following the *Memoir*, Bell frequently testified in state legislatures in support for day schools and advancing oralism.[7]

In 1875, at the age of twenty-eight, Bell married Mabel Hubbard, who was deaf. Hubbard was the daughter of Gardiner Greene Hubbard, a wealthy Boston attorney and longtime Board Chair of Clarke School for the Deaf. She was also a former student of Bell's, and the two came to form a very close, lifelong marriage. Nearly all accounts show their marriage was a successful one, and it was exactly the kind of marriage that Bell endorsed—a deaf-hearing marriage independent of the cultural deaf community. Ironically, however, it was Bell and not Mabel Hubbard who kept close ties with the cultural deaf community.[8] Besides knowing sign language, Bell attended deaf gatherings, such as the unveiling of the Thomas Hopkins Gallaudet and Alice Cogswell statue on the Gallaudet College campus on June 26, 1889.[9] He maintained correspondence with numerous individuals in the deaf community and administrators of Gallaudet College and a large number of residential schools. Bell researched annual reports for the residential schools and gleaned data for his *Memoir* presentation, and he kept up with some of the deaf newspapers along with the *American Annals for the Deaf*. Bell, then, read very widely and was intimately familiar with the pressing issues, needs, and concerns of the deaf world at that time, more than most hearing people at the time. Because he was extremely well informed, Bell was in a position to cast tremendous influence over the contours of deaf education and deaf people, at least in the United States.

One year after Bell presented the *Memoir*, he pressed the National Education Association to move forward with the establishment of day schools to ward off the "great calamity" of deaf intermarriage that he feared. He claimed that oralism was the best pedagogical option for deaf children, and many educators of deaf students, encouraged by Bell, pushed for greater educational and social acceptance of this model. On October 1, 1883, before he delivered his *Memoir* address, Bell established a private school in Washington, DC, to further demonstrate his educational beliefs in oralism.[10] It was closely modeled after a school he had established in Greenock, Scotland, in 1878. The distinctive characteristic of this school was the integration of very young hearing and deaf students in a nonsigning environment. The DC school lasted some two years before Bell was forced to abandon plans after he became ensnared in litigation surrounding the telephone patent and the main teacher, Gertrude Hitz, married and left the school. Hitz's replacement lasted one year and Bell discovered he could not give the school the attention it needed to thrive, forcing its closure in November 1885.[11] Despite the closure, the DC school was another example of Bell's deep commitment to the expansion of day schools and rejection of deaf students' communication through sign language in favor of their use of speech and lipreading.

Bell's chief biographer, Robert V. Bruce, wrote "As late as 1884, Bell felt that the public at large still needed to be disabused of the notion that the deaf were physically or mentally unable to speak."[12] Bell was familiar with working in residential school settings, one-on-one with deaf children, but he advocated for the expansion of day schools that would not separate deaf children either from their (usually) hearing parents or from other hearing children. To help achieve this goal, Bell formed the American Association for the Promotion of Speech to the Deaf (AAPSTD) in 1890, becoming its first president.

Bell envisioned the AAPSTD as a counterweight to two other important organizations in the field of deaf education that favored sign language. The oldest of these was the Convention of American Instructors of the Deaf (CAID), established in 1850 and holding its first meeting at New York School for the Deaf. CAID served as space for educators to meet and exchange pedagogical techniques, discuss methodology, and new approaches important to deaf education.[13]

The second organization was begun by Gallaudet College President Edward Miner Gallaudet (EMG), who became concerned with the growing oralism movement after the Civil War that was beginning to establish roots in the United States. In 1869, nineteen years after CAID's establishment, the Conference of Educational Administrators Serving the Deaf (CEASD) was founded. First called the Conference of Superintendents and Principals of American Schools for the Deaf, it was an organization of administrators that focused on best practices in the field of deaf education. Meetings of both CAID and CEASD generally took place every two or three years depending on circumstances, and the organizations had some commonalities including shared publications and members. Although there was a strong overlap, CEASD grew to have larger political clout.[14]

After the *Memoir* speech, Bell bore the brunt of the deaf community's wrath since he was internationally famous and a committed oralist. The deaf community viewed the conclusions in Bell's *Memoir* as damning and irrefutable evidence that Bell sought to prevent deaf people from marrying one another. While he never explicitly discussed eugenics or sterilization in the *Memoir*, Bell's intention to strip deaf people from their cultural elements was evident from his statement that the "grand central principle . . . should be *the retention of the normal environment during the period of education.*"[15] By suggesting the removal of the foundation of a shared, visual signed language in place of oralism, Bell sketched a roadmap that not only fueled the ideological debates of manualism and oralism that were already in place in the United States, but also positioned oralism as the best option for deaf people. Bell was well educated about deaf people, their tendency to intermarry, and the deaf community's network of residential schools, publications, and organizations. Bell discussed the prominence of these focal points of the cultural deaf community.

Bell established the Volta Bureau in 1887 with funds from the Volta Prize that he had received from the French government, and he positioned it as a clearinghouse and ambassador for oralism in the United States. In 1890, the Volta Bureau moved to its present location in northwest Washington, DC, to house its collections and there it published a journal called *The Volta Review*, designed to counter the much older publication of the CAID, the *American Annals of the Deaf*, which typically supported the use of sign language as the primary form of com-

munication for deaf children. Through the Volta Bureau, Bell collected
and maintained annual reports of nearly every residential school in the
United States and corresponded with a number of superintendents.

Scholars have analyzed Bell's writings on eugenics and his relationship with key eugenicists in the United States during a critical period
in American history. A close textual analysis demonstrates that Bell
also had questions about deaf people, including those of language and
marriage, exactly the set of concerns that policymakers raised during
Progressive Era America.[16] Bell's concern with the genetics of deafness
and deaf marriage spilled over into debates on deaf education and deaf
lives in general.

Coincidentally, Bell's presentation to the National Academy of
Sciences occurred the same year that Francis Galton, an Englishman,
coined the term *eugenics*. Galton's view of eugenics was that it was a process by which to improve elements of English society through corrective
means, primarily focused on increasing knowledge and better breeding
practices, to reduce the incidence of poverty, alcholism, and other social
problems that England faced during the latter third of the nineteenth
century.[17] While Bell did not discuss the social problems that England
or other nations faced at the time, the *Memoir* can be considered a tool
of Progressivist thinking. A distinctive variety of the human race was a
social problem, Bell believed, which required intervention and reform.
Successful reform would halt the spread of genetic deafness and restore
the human race to that of speaking people.

Bell's findings in the *Memoir* had precedence in the speculations
of others before him.[18] Bell, in 1883, supported William W. Turner's, a
teacher and later principal at American School for the Deaf, claims with
layers of empirical data. Turner, first in 1847, wondered whether deafness could be passed down, and later, in 1868, he, like Bell, noted the
"distinct variety" of the human race could come about particularly if
deaf people married one another.[19] Attention to genetic deafness in the
United States was documented in the three decades before the *Memoir*
captured the attention—and wrath—of the deaf community. Scientists,
including Francis Galton, reviewed the *Memoir* and were impressed.[20]

Since humans had long controlled animal breeding, Bell deduced
that the same methods could be applied to humans. From the very beginning of his presentation to the Academy, Bell was explicit on his
opposition to interfering with marriage among humans since marriage
was assumed to carry childbearing responsibilities. "We cannot dictate
to men and women whom they shall marry," Bell said, "and natural

selection no longer influences mankind to any great extent."[21] However, the fact that deaf people married one another bothered Bell because, in part, it disrupted natural selection. Through research on residential schools and deaf people in general Bell deduced the "intermarriage of congenital deaf-mutes (born deaf) through a number of successive generations should result in the formation of a deaf variety of the human race."[22]

The data in the *Memoir* was collected from a number of residential schools, even as Bell noted these "institutions" actually had "very little information" on the topic of genetic deafness and deaf marriages in America, for the schools typically did not collect this information.[23] The *Memoir* was a platform that Bell used to demonstrate his familiarity with statistics and empiricism. Following the *Memoir*, Bell started collecting such data from his multi-nippled sheep breeding experiments on his Beinn Bhreagh Nova Scotia estate.[24] Bell gained experience in data collecting, organizing, and developing charts from his research for the *Memoir* and traveling to Martha's Vineyard for post-*Memoir* research. Bell's sheep breeding experiments led to direct correspondence with prominent eugenicist Charles Benedict Davenport, Director of the Station for Experimental Evolution at Cold Spring Harbor on Long Island, New York, a facility funded by the Carnegie Institution in 1904.[25] Davenport and Mary Harriman, the daughter of railroad magnate Edward Henry Harriman, established the Eugenics Record Office (ERO) in 1910.[26] The ERO came to be considered as America's clearinghouse on matters related to eugenics. Davenport and Bell corresponded, sharing research activities and results. Bell shared with Davenport that he had completed a special report on the census of the Blind and Deaf of the United States.[27]

Given the limited information provided through school records and the United States' Tenth Census report, Bell created some seventeen tables to flesh out information on the family histories of deaf students enrolled in residential schools. Beginning with, for example, a list recording the recurrence of surnames from 2,106 students at the American School School for the Deaf between 1817 and 1877, and 1,620 students from the Illinois School for the Deaf between 1846 and 1882, Bell tracked and calculated the frequency of these surnames. Deaf relatives of deaf students were also tracked at state residential schools in Ohio, Indiana, Illinois, and Texas. Overall, Bell calculated 29.5 percent of these deaf students had deaf relatives.[28] Bell also pointed to the Tenth Census which recorded some 33,878 deaf people and that more than 50 percent were "congenitally deaf."[29]

After presenting statistics establishing family relationships among pupils, Bell applied the laws of animal breeding to humans, and deduced that the "congenitally deaf would be more likely than those who became deaf from accidental causes to transmit their defect to their offspring" and those who had deaf relatives had a significantly higher likelihood of doing this than those born to non-congenital deaf relatives.[30] Aware of past studies on hereditary deafness, including that of Harvey L. Peet, teacher and superindendent at the New York School for the Deaf at Fanwood, Bell emphasized that future studies should include hearing relatives to ascertain a more precise calculation on the number of people carrying a "predisposition towards deafness." Bell again affirmed that "we have abundant materials in the United States for the formation of a deaf variety of the human race by selection in marriage."[31]

The first five chapters of the *Memoir* essentially follow classic scientific methodology. Starting with the question of "How can we ascertain the susceptibility of the human race to variation produced by selection?" and also again rephrased, "To what extent is the human race suspectible of variation by selection?" Bell collected data and organized tables to demonstrate his conclusion to the body of scientists: "I desire to direct attention to the fact that in this country *deaf-mutes marry deaf-mutes*."[32] Although his observation of genetic deafness had been previously noted by others, including W. W. Turner and Dr. Harvey L. Peet, none delved into social commentary.

In what may be considered a form of scientific methodology, Bell's question simply asked, "Do many of the deaf and dumb marry?"[33] Bell worked to ascertain the frequency of marriages by studying data he had obtained from residential school records. Bell noted, one year before his presentation to the National Academy of Sciences, that a "considerable proportion" of these deaf children marry. For example, 47.4 percent of deaf students who attended ASD between 1817 and 1877 married and 30.8 percent of deaf students from the Illinois school between 1846 and 1882 married.[34]

Bell cautioned that his study was incomplete for records were not as thorough as he preferred. Some schools recorded maritial status of their graduates, but did not indicate whether the marriage was to a deaf or hearing person. Bell offered strategies to improve record keeping—emphasizing empiricism—to enable these schools to engage

16   MEMOIRS OF THE NATIONAL ACADEMY OF SCIENCES.

then, we eliminate from the totals given in the above table, all the pupils of these institutions who
were born since the year 1839, we obtain the following results:

TABLE XIX.—*Proportion of the pupils of our institutions for the deaf and dumb who marry.*

Name of institution.	Date of opening.	Date of report.	Total number of pupils born before 1840.	Total number of these recorded to have married.	Percentage.
American Asylum	1817	1877	1,100	522	47. 4
Illinois Institution....... ...	1846	1882	159	49	30. 8
Total			1,259	571	45, 4

Whatever may be the exact percentage for the whole country, the indications are that *a
considerable proportion of the adult deaf-mutes of the United States are married.*

INTERMARRIAGES OF THE DEAF AND DUMB.

When we attempt to form an idea of the extent to which intermarriage takes place among
deaf-mutes, we are met by the difficulty of the imperfection of the institution records. In very
few cases is it specifically stated that a deaf-mute has married a hearing person.* The record
usually stands that the pupil has "married a deaf-mute," or that he is simply "married," leaving
it uncertain whether the marriage was contracted with another deaf-mute or with a hearing person.
When we eliminate all the uncertain cases we obtain from the institution reports the following
results:

TABLE XX.—*Proportion of the deaf and dumb who marry deaf-mutes.*

Name of institution.	Date of opening.	Date of report.	Total number of pupils recorded to have married.	Total number recorded to have married deaf-mutes.	Percentage.
American Asylum	1817	1877	642	502	78. 2
New York Institution.	1818	1854	191	142	74. 3
Ohio Institution..	1829	1854	56	39	69. 6
Indiana Institution.........	1844	1854	26	21	80. 8
Illinois Institution..... ..	1846	1882	174	152	87. 3
Total			1,089	856	78. 6

The large percentage of marriages with deaf-mutes reported from Indiana and Illinois suggests
the explanation that *intermarriages among the deaf and dumb may perhaps have become more common
of late years.* Both institutions are of comparatively recent origin (the one founded in 1844, the
other in 1846); and the report of the Illinois Institution, which exhibits the largest proportion of
deaf-mute intermarriages, contains the record of much later marriages than those mentioned in the
Indiana report, for the Indiana record stops at 1854, whereas the Illinois report gives the statistics
of the institution to October, 1882.

Unfortunately we are unable to ascertain from the reports the dates of the marriages. If we
assume, however, that as a general rule the older deaf-mutes were married before the younger, we

   * Only one case in the American Asylum and ten in the Illinois Institution. It is probable, however, that in
most cases where the pupil is simply recorded as "married" the record means marriage with a hearing person.

Table XIX. Proportion of the pupils of our institutions for the deaf and dumb
who marry. From *Memoir*, p. 16. Courtesy of Gallaudet University Archives.

in a more comprehensive approach to tracking its graduates.[35] These
schools provided a channel for Bell to collect, analyze, and interpret data
to answer his research questions. Bell concluded that deaf people married other deaf people; this pattern had continued for at least forty years,

and would continue. It was not an "ephemeral phenomenon, but a case of continuous selection . . . in the case of the deaf and dumb the work of selection will go on from generation to generation."[36] Bell declared that the *proportion of deaf-mute offspring born to deaf-mutes is many times greater than the proportion both to the people at large."*[37]

Bell assembled a number of genealogical trees to detail multi-generational families. The Hoagland family of Kentucky had over twenty members who were deaf and impressed Bell enough, calling them "one of the most remarkable families of America."[38] The Fullerton family of Hebron, New York, had at least fourteen deaf members. Other families had deaf descendents spanning at least two generations.

The first genealogical chart printed in the *Memoir* was a foreshadowing of events that took place in 1891 with the marriage of Lucy Maria Swett and George Sanders. Nahum Brown, of Henniker, New Hampshire, sired two deaf children. His daughter married Bela Swett, of Henniker, and had three sons. One son, William B. Swett married Margaret Harrington, who was deaf, and they had five children. Two of them were deaf—Persis H. and Lucy Maria Swett.[39] Bell was familiar with the Swett-Brown relationship, and his personal views on deaf marriages were tested when his first student, George Sanders, married Lucy Swett.[40] As mentioned earlier, Bell maintained a lifelong relationship with George Sanders, but when Sanders was a child, Bell did not know of the Brown-Swett family and its extensive multigenerational deaf relatives.[41]

Even though Bell compiled copius data, and later (1885–1889) spent time on Martha's Vineyard to test his hypothesis, he remained flummoxed by patterns of genetic deafness. Unaware of Mendelian genetics, Bell's understanding of biological inheritance reflected Victorian era science. Bell was aware that to some extent heredity had a role in deafness in offspring. A wide range of variables came into play that further exacerbated the complexities of genetic deafness. Two hearing parents could give birth to deaf offspring, or some hearing and deaf offspring. Other cases may show that two deaf parents, without clear hereditary deafness, may have hearing or deaf children. Possibilities on the etiology of deafness ran a wide spectrum, and Bell faced a puzzling quandry— why did some deaf parents have hearing offspring? Why did others have deaf offspring? Despite his years of research, Bell never came to have clear answers to these questions.

The *Memoir* was historically significant for several reasons. It generated widespread discussion and reaction among the Deaf community through the deaf newspapers printed by state residential schools and other periodicals, such as the *American Annals of the Deaf*. A common reaction was that the *Memoir* represented irrefutable and damning evidence that Bell sought to prohibit deaf people from marrying, thus stripping them of autonomy and free will in their choice of who to marry. Arguments about protecting the right of deaf people to marry one another persisted for decades. Some deaf people including architect Olof Hanson and advocate Alice Terry argued against deaf marriage. Terry, despite marrying a deaf man and having a family of her own, argued that people with hereditary deafness should refrain from childbearing.[42] The National Association of the Deaf went on record in 1920 as disapproving of marriages between congenitally deaf people.[43] Bell's polemics captured the attention and support of Francis Galton, who published a positive review of the *Memoir*. Finally, through the *Memoir*, it was beginning to be understood throughout science that deaf people held a propensity for marrying other deaf people.

The final chapter of the *Memoir* was a radical departure from the scientific method. Unlike others who observed a predisposition to genetic deafness among certain deaf people, Bell ventured into social commentary on the personal lives of deaf people. Through the options he raised and discussed to halt the "great calamity" of the "deaf variety of the human race," we gain an understanding of boundaries intersecting genetics, culture, and the autonomy of deaf people. Had Bell ended his observations of genetic deafness without proposing social change, following in the footsteps of Turner and Peet, the virulent sentiments against Bell would not have been as pronounced.

Bell's declaration that a deaf race would be a "great calamity to the world" and his search for a "remedy" interjected himself into the politics of the deaf world. Bell noted that before the spread of residential schools deaf people did not receive much in the way of formal schooling and thus deaf intermarriage "was so rare . . . as to be practically unknown." Once these schools appeared, an increase in deaf marriages followed, and Bell surmised that deaf to deaf marriages had "in some way been promoted by our methods of education."[44]

Bell was keenly aware of the strong community ties that formed as a result of deaf marriages through several generations, and if such a deaf variety of the human race was "desired. . . . we could not invent a more complete or more efficient method than those that actually exist and which have arisen from entirely different and far higher motives."[45] If the goal was to preserve and protect autonomy, and allowing such a variety of the human race to unfold, deaf and hearing children would be separated early, interacting with their own peers by living together, "carefully guarding them [deaf children] from the possibility of making acquaintances among hearing persons of their own age."[46] Deaf children, Bell argued, were already attending residential schools at this time. Following graduation and as adults, deaf people came together at reunions, organized religious services, state organizations, and the national organization. Large gatherings offered social opportunities and had the potential to lead to relationship building.

Newspapers printed in the residential schools, collectively known as the Little Paper Family, served several purposes. They contained information and announcements related to employment opportunities, reunions, marriages, deaths, births, and other personal information to keep alumni connected to their residential schools.[47] These papers also had more practical benefits—for example, students working for the school newspapers learned valuable vocational skills. Many male students became printers, and if they were fluent in English, editors of newspapers. The newspapers also served as physical, tangible proof that the schools responsibly used state funds, training students to become productive citizens during the late nineteenth and early twentieth centuries. In addition to the school papers, several deaf men independently established newspapers for the Deaf community, among them the *Deaf-Mutes' Journal* edited by Edwin A. Hodgson, *The Gallaudet Guide and Deaf-Mutes' Companion* edited by William Martin Chamberlain, and the *The National Exponent* edited by O. H. Regensburg.[48] In essence, Bell understood that the network of these newspapers served as a medium to bring together students, alumni, and other deaf adults into a cohesive community.

Bell, thus, understood that the cornerstones of the deaf community— namely, its schools, organizations, reunions, and newspapers, bound together by a shared visual language—generated opportunities for deaf adults to gather socially, creating pathways toward marriage and childbearing. These patterns would continue if there was no interference in marriage. Yet, Bell took another tack—what about interacting with hearing people, specifically those hearing from deaf families? He also attacked the use of sign language by comparing deaf people to foreigners—"What more powerful or efficient means could be found than to teach the deaf-mutes to think in a different language from that of the people at large?"[49] Bell charged that deaf people "*think* [Bell's emphasis] in the gesture language" leaving spoken English as a "foreign tongue," even if these deaf people were American citizens by birthright. Essentially, in labeling deaf people as foreigners in their own land, Bell's condescending attitude revealed how great his concerns were about the translation of sign language into written English.[50] Deaf people could exchange written notes to facilitate dialogue through "broken English," not dissimilar to what a foreigner might do in similar circumstances. Deaf people's use of sign language, Bell believed, further compounded problems they had with developing English fluency and, thus, rendering them unable to comprehend significant current events beyond what they could understand from school newspapers widely circulated among deaf people.

If sexual selection continued without interference, Bell warned, two other factors could lead to a distinct group of deaf people. One was the possible creation of "sign writing"—what Bell called "ideography," a system similar to Egyptian hieroglyphics.[51] The second factor was that hearing people had limited knowledge of the intellectual competencies of deaf people. Because most Americans had never met a deaf person Bell reasoned, they had "the idea they [deaf people] are dangerous, morose, ill-tempered . . . he is sometimes looked upon as a sort of monstrosity, to be stared at and *avoided*."[52] If this idea was perpetuated, it would lead to exclusive gatherings of deaf people at residential schools, "away from public observation." Bell dismissed these concerns, especially those about the intelligence of deaf people, in his paper *Fallacies Concerning the Deaf and the Influence of these Fallacies in Preventing the Amelioration of their Condition*. However, in the same paper, Bell was unfailingly critical of sign language as an "artificial and conventional language derived from pantomine," and he labeled sign language an impediment to acquiring the English language. In other words, the visual language was directly responsible for cementing the cultural ties of deaf people and their shunning of hearing people, preference for deaf marriage, and the "propogation of their physical defect."[53]

While Bell was critical of sign language as a language, he noted most deaf children were born to hearing parents and did not learn sign language before enrolling in school. Bell also recognized the complexities and nuances of learning sign language and that it would take at least a year or even longer for teachers to become "thoroughly qualified" in using the language so that they could successfully instruct their students. Speech, lipreading, and written English, discussed in the *Memoir* was the desired goal and they would be constantly emphasized as Bell became one of the most identified individuals associated with the movement known as oralism. Oralism spread across the nation and severely undercut the vitality of sign language during the late nineteenth and early twentieth centuries.

At the 1883 National Academy of Sciences lecture, Bell presented his case through statistics, evidence of community building, and a negative analysis of sign language. He then arrived at his conclusion—an "object of remedy" was necessary to halt the genetic expression of deafness, and he outlined "repressive" and "preventive" measures in order to remove the "physical defect" of genetic deafness and prevent the perpetuation of a class of deaf Americans who used a distinct shared, visual sign language. Bell presented this material during such a critical period in American history, a time when immigrants, mainly from southern and eastern Europe, had begun to enter the United States in significant numbers.[54]

Bell's "repressive measures" included a number of possible scenarios for halting the transmission of genetic deafness, but he noted objections to each of them. A law prohibiting deaf intermarriage "might only promote immorality." Legislation directly prohibiting deaf unions would not be feasible because it was a state matter, and deaf people would simply move to a location that permitted their marriage. Additonally, it was nearly impossible to determine with certainty if someone was "congenitally deaf," which Bell mistakenly believed indicated genetic deafness. The presence of deaf relatives in the family might allow scientists to make these inferences; however, legislation targeting multi-generational deaf families including hearing relatives and consanguineous marriages "would be more practical."[55] Bell called for additional research on this question via a more thorough and detailed reporting on marriages of residential school graduates, but his summary stated his position clearly: "a due consideration of all the objections renders it doubtful whether legislative interference with the marriage of the deaf would be advisable."[56]

Turning away from legislative options, Bell considered social pressure to "prevent undesirable marriages." Family and friends could be recruited to apply pressure in "individual cases," but here, too, he discovered a problem. Widespread influence on restricting marriage was thought to be next to impossible as it was a "subject on which a man will so little brook interference as one of this kind where his affections are involved."[57] Bell would later discover this to his own chagrin with George Sanders.

Rejecting repressive measures, Bell turned to preventive measures as the "most promising method of lessening the evil." To achieve this,

Bell determined to identify the "causes" of deaf marriages, and to "remove them."[58] Bell was was very specific about what he deemed as the causes for this—the residential schools and the use of sign language. He advocated for changing a deaf child's "social environment" through the "retention of the normal environment during the period of education."[59]

Bell's favored "preventive measures" became the basis for much of his work with deaf education later in life. "Segregation really lies at the root of the whole matter," said Bell.[60] As long as residential schools were left intact, deaf people would continue to gravitate together, sign language would continue to flourish, and articulation would be neglected. Thus, Bell advocated for the expansion of day schools or educating deaf children in small classes, framing these alternatives as less expensive than residential schools.

The primary objective of Bell and other committed oralists, however, was to minimize contact between deaf people. This meant removing each part of the community's institutions. Removing sign language from the curriculum, and introducing articulation and speechreading, would come to have negative repercussions for deaf teachers, as they would be replaced by hearing teachers at the turn of the twentieth century due to the changing teaching methods. Thus, as deaf children progressed through school, they would no longer be exposed to deaf adults, sign language, and the deaf community. They would then turn to hearing matrimonial partners, as did Bell's mother and wife. If his strategies had prevailed, the method by which most deaf people became socialized as a self-identified group with particular shared interests would come to an end. Bell sought to implement measures which would strip deaf people of the autonomy to meet with one another in a cultural community.

The very last sentence in the final chapter of the *Memoir* is worth considering—"Having shown the tendency to the formation of a deaf variety of the human race in America, and some of the means that should be taken to counteract it, I commend the whole subject to the attention of scientific men."[61] In Bell's address to the National Academy of Sciences, he was explicit that scientists, including Bell himself, could not enforce marriage restrictions on humans. Others before Bell had made the social observation that deaf people tended to marry other deaf people. Bell developed a hypothesis, collected data from at least five residential schools, and arrived at the same conclusion. In his final chapter, Bell outlined the causes that led to the "segregation" of deaf children from mainstream society—specifically, the network of residential schools, unarrested use of sign language, and access to deaf teachers.

His preventive measures became the model that Bell himself adopted in deaf pedagogy, for example, testifying at state hearings on the value of day schools.

It is unknown precisely how these scientific men who attended the 1883 lecture responded. At the very least, as Francis Galton noted, the topic was "startling." Bell's presentation came at an important juncture in American Deaf history. There were at least forty residential schools for the deaf in the country plus the National Deaf-Mute College in Washington, DC. White deaf Americans had established the groundwork for a thriving deaf community. There were national and state organizations, at least three dozen school newspapers, and deaf churches. The black deaf schools in the South were segregated from the white schools— sometimes in close proximity to the white schools and sometimes in other locations many miles away.[62] Yet, even as deaf white and African American deaf students remained segregated for decades, the network of residential schools and communities that formed near the schools helped spread sign language throughout the country. Deaf people had a shared visual langauge, and most deaf adults secured employment. Deaf leaders, many of them college graduates, consistently argued for a fair chance at self-reliance and self-sufficiency. Only when it was evident to the community that rampant discrimination existed did they turn to organized protest to protect their autonomy.[63]

Paradoxically, Bell was keenly aware that deaf people organized around a common language even as oralism was gaining steam in the United States. Buried deep in the report of the 1900 United States Census Special reports on the Blind and Deaf that Bell himself organized, he noted that deaf people from residential schools "are mainly responsible for the fact that the deaf from childhood no longer constitute a dependent class," and those deaf people who used sign language they had learned at residential schools were "more self-supporting than the deaf from adult life. This is especially surprising when we consider the fact that the deaf from childhood include practically all of those who are deaf and dumb."[64]

Despite Bell's admission that residential schools allowed deaf children to become responsible citizens, Bell continued to push for educational and social acceptance of oralism throughout the United States. By the turn of the twentieth century, hearing school administrators had accepted Bell's model and had banned sign language in schools throughout the United States. The tragedy was that hearing adults and administrators largely disregarded the advice and experiences of deaf adults and proceeded with what they thought was best for deaf children. Deaf teachers were dismissed from residential schools and deaf children lost convenient access to adult role models. Despite these changes, deaf people fought to maintain their autonomy while oralism deepened the crisis in deaf education.[65]

The firestorm that followed the *Memoir* is well established. Deaf people engaged in debates about protecting the right to marriage and discussed questions surrounding citizenship. They kept sign language alive and contested the right to deaf spaces in schools and community settings. Even though oralism gained currency and day schools and classes began to spread throughout the country, deaf marriages continued. However, they did not create the new and distinct variety of the human race that Bell had feared in the *Memoir*. The "great calamity" that he had predicted in the *Memoir* never came to pass. And after his personal experience with the relationship between George Sanders and Lucy Swett that culminated in their marriage in December 1891, Bell relinquished attempts to constrain deaf autonomy in marriage.[66] To be sure, deaf people continued to discuss marriage in their newspapers and organization meetings (see Malzkuhn's paper in this volume). Community instututions such as the National Fraternal Society of the Deaf (NFSD), the NAD, and other state organizations supported deaf people's campaign for civil rights.

Paternalism was tragic indeed; however, the real tragedy was the educational and social acceptance of oralism that undermined community building efforts of the late nineteenth and early twentieth centuries. The American eugenics movement may have threatened the deaf community, but deaf people were not legally sterilized in the United States. Alexander Graham Bell was much more than an eugenicist—his educational and social ideologies earned the respect and praise of many hearing administrators across the nation at the expense of deaf autonomy that had been built over eight decades. That is the real tragedy and the painful legacy of Alexander Graham Bell; it serves as a constant reminder that deaf people always need to reaffirm their autonomy.

Notes

Thanks to John V. Van Cleve and Joseph J. Murray for their insightful comments and critique.

1. Jack R. Gannon, *Deaf Heritage: A Narrative History of Deaf America* (Silver Spring, MD: National Association of the Deaf, 1981), 75; Harlan Lane, *When the*

Mind Hears: A History of the Deaf (New York: Vintage Books, 1984), 353; Richard Winefield, *Never the Twain Shall Meet: The Communications Debate* (Washington, DC: Gallaudet University Press, 1987), 85–96; John Vickrey Van Cleve and Barry A. Crouch, *A Place of Their Own: Creating the Deaf Community in America* (Washington, DC: Gallaudet University Press, 1989); Douglas C. Baynton, *Forbidden Signs: American Culture and the Campaign Against Sign Language* (Chicago: University of Chicago Press, 1996); Douglas C. Baynton, "'Savages and Deaf-Mutes': Evolutionary Theory and the Campaign Against Sign Language in the Nineteenth Century," in *Deaf History Unveiled: Interpretations from the New Scholarship*, ed. John V. Van Cleve (Washington, DC: Gallaudet University Press, 1993), 92–112; Susan Burch, *Signs of Resistance: American Deaf Cultural History, 1900 to World War II* (New York: New York University Press, 2002); Brian H. Greenwald, "The Real 'Toll' of A. G. Bell: Lessons about Eugenics," in *Genetics, Disability, and Deafness*, ed. John V. Van Cleve (Washington, DC: Gallaudet University Press, 2004); Brian H. Greenwald, "Taking Stock: Alexander Graham Bell and Eugenics," in *The Deaf History Reader*, ed. John V. Van Cleve (Washington, DC: Gallaudet University Press, 2007); Brian H. Greenwald and John V. Van Cleve, "'A Deaf Variety of the Human Race': Historical Memory, Alexander Graham Bell, and Eugenics," *Journal of the Gilded Age and Progressive Era* 14 (2015): 28–48.

2. Daniel J. Kevles, *In the Name of Eugenics: Genetics and the Uses of Human Heredity* (Cambridge: Harvard University Press, 1985), 85.

3. Robert V. Bruce, *Bell: Alexander Graham Bell and the Conquest of Solitude* (Ithaca, NY: Cornell University Press, 1973), 9, 13–16.

4. Ibid., 42–44.

5. City of Boston School Committee, *Report of the Committee on the School for Deaf Mutes* (Boston: Rockwell & Churchill, 1873), 8–9.

6. Bruce, *Bell*, 90–91.

7. John V. Van Cleve, "The Academic Integration of Deaf Children: A Historical Perspective" in *The Deaf History Reader*, ed. John V. Van Cleve (Washington, DC: Gallaudet University Press, 2007), 116–35.

8. Bruce, *Bell*, 380.

9. Michael J. Olson, "The Thomas Hopkins Gallaudet and Alice Cogsell Statue: Controversies and Celebrations" in *A Fair Chance in the Race of Life: The Role of Gallaudet University in Deaf History*, ed. Brian H. Greenwald and John V. Van Cleve (Washington, DC: Gallaudet University Press, 2008), 46. Robert V. Bruce also notes Bell's familiarity and use of sign language and interpreting at banquets and meetings (383).

10. Bruce, *Bell*, 389–90.

11. Ibid., 390.

12. Ibid., 382.

13. Jerome D. Schein, "Convention of American Instructors of the Deaf," in *The Gallaudet Encyclopedia of Deaf People and Deafness*, vol. 1: A-G, ed. John V. Van Cleve (New York: McGraw-Hill Book Company, Inc, 1987), 202–3.

14. Jerome D. Schein, "Conference of Educational Administrators Serving the Deaf" in *The Gallaudet Encyclopedia of Deaf People and Deafness,* vol. 1 A-G, ed. John V. Van Cleve (New York: McGraw-Hill Book Company, Inc, 1987), 200–202.

15. Alexander Graham Bell, *Memoir Upon the Formation of a Deaf Variety of the Human Race* (National Academy of Sciences: Washington, DC, 1884), 46.

16. Nathaniel Comfort, *The Science of Human Perfection: How Genes Became the Heart of American Medicine* (New Haven: Yale University Press, 2012), 45–66.

17. Kevles, 3–19.

18. In terms of studying hereditary deafness or, at the least, speculating on genetic deafness, Bell's arguments were not entirely new and had been noted for at least three decades. W. W. Turner, "The Causes of Deafness," *American Annals of the Deaf* 1, no. 1 (1847): 32; W. W. Turner, "Conference of the Principals of the American Institutions for the Education of the Deaf and Dumb," *American Annals of the Deaf* 13, no. 4 (1868): 245; Dudley Peet, "The Remote and Proximate Causes of Deafness," *American Annals of the Deaf* 8, no. 3 (April 1856): 132; "Editorial Note," *American Annals of the Deaf* 13, no. 1 (March 1861): 33.

19. W. W. Turner, "Causes of Deafness" *American Annals of the Deaf* 1 (October 1847), 32; Ibid., "Conference of Principals of the American Institutions for the Education of the Deaf and Dumb" *American Annals of the Deaf* 13 (November 1868), 245.

20. Francis Galton, "Hereditary Deafness,"*Nature* 31, no. 795 (January 22, 1885): 269–70.

21. Bell, *Memoir*, 3.

22. Ibid.

23. Ibid., 5.

24. Bruce, *Bell*, 415.

25. Alexander Graham Bell to Charles Benedict Davenport, 20 September 1904, Mss. B.D27, Box 4, Folder 1, Charles B. Davenport papers, American Philosophical Society; Bell to Davenport, 18 May 1906, Charles B. Davenport papers, Box 4, Folder 2; Garland E. Allen, "The Eugenics Record Office at Cold Spring Harbor, 1910–1940: An Essay in Institutional History," *Osiris* 2nd series, vol. 2 (1986): 227–28.

26. Allen, 227–28; Kevles, 54–55.

27. Bell to Davenport, 11 July 1906, Mss. B.D27, Box 4, Folder 2, Charles B. Davenport papers, American Philosophical Society.

28. Bell, *Memoir*, 11.

29. Ibid., 12.

30. Ibid., 12.

31. Ibid., 14.

32. Ibid., 4, 19.

33. Ibid., 15.

34. Ibid,. 16.

35. Ibid., 16; 21.

36. Ibid., 19.

37. Ibid., 27. Italics are original as published.

38. Ibid., 30.

39. Ibid., 28–29.

40. The relationship between these deaf people has been documented. Joseph J. Murray, "'True Love and Sympathy': The Deaf-Deaf Marriages Debate in Transatlantic Perspective," in *Genetics, Disability, and Deafness,* 56–60; Lane, 361.

41. Harlan Lane, Richard C. Pillard, and Ulf Hedberg, *The People of the Eye: Deaf Ethnicity and Ancestry* (New York: Oxford University Press, 2011), 91–92. For background on the organization, see Van Cleve and Crouch, 89–91. Thomas Brown, a deaf son of Nahum Brown, attended American School for the Deaf and established the New England Gallaudet Alumni Association. A number of Brown's descendants lived on Martha's Vineyard, and left the island to receive an education at the Connecticut school.

42. Olof Hanson, "The Tendency Among the Deaf to Exclusive Association with one Another," *American Annals of the Deaf* 33, no.1 (January 1888): 31–32; Alice Terry, "Eugenics," *The Silent Worker* 30 (March 1918): 96.

43. National Association of the Deaf, *Proceedings of the Thirteenth Convention of the NAD,* vol. 5 Detroit, Michigan August 9–14 (1920), 96.

44. Bell, *Memoir,* 41.

45. Ibid.

46. Ibid.

47. Robert M. Buchanan, *Illusions of Equality: Deaf Americans in School and Factory, 1850–1950* (Washington, DC: Gallaudet University Press, 1999); Van Cleve and Crouch, 164–68.

48. Van Cleve and Crouch, 98–105.

49. Bell, *Memoir,* 42.

50. For a good discussion on deaf people as foreigners in their own land, see Baynton, *Forbidden Signs,* 27–35.

51. Bell had learned about sign writing by reading the works of George Hutton, principal of the Institution of the Deaf and Dumb in Halifax, Nova Scotia. George Hutton, "Upon the Practicability and Advantages of Mimography," *American Annals of the Deaf* 14, no. 1 (January 1869): 157–82.

52. Bell, *Memoir,* 43.

53. Alexander Graham Bell, "Fallacies Concerning the Deaf," *American Annals of the Deaf and Dumb* 29, no. 1 (January 1884): 58.

54. Roger Daniels, *Coming to America: A History of Immigration and Ethnicity in American Life* (New York: Harper Perennial, 2002).

55. Bell, *Memoir,* 45.

56. Ibid., 46.

57. Ibid.

58. Ibid.

59. Ibid.

60. Ibid.

61. Ibid., 48.

62. Carolyn McCaskill, Ceil Lucas, Robert Bayley, and Joseph Hill, *The Hidden Treasure of Black ASL: Its History and Structure* (Washington, DC: Gallaudet University Press, 2011), 14–48.

63. Robert M. Buchanan, *Illusions of Equality: Deaf Americans in School and Factory, 1850–1950* (Washington, DC: Gallaudet University Press, 1999), 36.

64. Alexander Graham Bell, "The Deaf" in the Department of Commerce and Labor, Bureau of the Census, *Special Reports: The Blind and the Deaf, 1900* (Washington, DC: Government Printing Office, 1906), 147.

65. Baynton, 149–52. Baynton argues oralism "failed . . . and sign language survived because deaf people themselves chose not to relinquish the autonomous cultural space that their community and language made possible."

66. Joseph J. Murray, "'True Love and Sympathy': The Deaf-Deaf Marriages Debates in Transatlantic Perspective" in *Genetics, Disability, and Deafness*, 56–59.

9

Compromising for Agency:
The Role of the NAD during the American
Eugenics Movement, 1880–1940

Melissa Malzkuhn

> As deaf-mutes among the other inhabitants of this country,
> we have interests peculiar to ourselves, and which can be
> taken care of by ourselves.
>   —Theodore A. Froehlich, 1880[1]

CONCERNED BY THE LACK of organized representation to protect and
assert the rights of deaf people, Edmund Booth, Edwin Hodgson, and
Robert P. McGregor, organized a national meeting, which led to the
establishment of the National Association of the Deaf (NAD) in August
1880. The three deaf men knew each other through the National Deaf
Mute College, today known as Gallaudet University. Initially, the NAD
focused on obtaining employment opportunities within the federal government and strived to project a positive image of deaf people as hard-
working and capable self-sufficient citizens.

From 1880 to 1940, the NAD was led by a succession of fourteen
different deaf presidents who shaped the organizations' priorities. Although priorities over that period shifted, the NAD largely focused
on employment opportunities, driving rights, sign language use, and
sought to "normalize" deaf people by presenting them as American citizens. During this critical period in American history, there was a huge
influx of immigrants of nearly twenty five million people, mostly from
southern and eastern Europe, which, in part, led to a rise in the eugenic
ideology. Coined in 1883 by English scientist Francis Galton, "eugenics"
is a systemic idea of improving the human race by selective breeding.[2]
The concept gained traction and recognition among Americans as they

began defining an able-bodied, intelligent, and fit citizen as being of Anglo-Saxon descent, deeming all other races, ethnic backgrounds, cultures, and non-English languages as inferior.[3]

Eugenicists encouraged careful selection of marriage partners, and others pushed for governmental involvement in improving citizens' lives. The result of the theory then is that "if natural selection yielded the Darwinian fit, only artificial selection—by governmental means, where appropriate—could multiply the eugenically fit."[4] Some state governments soon adopted what is now referred to as "negative eugenics": employing sterilization or legislative means to halt procreation among "undesirables." In 1907, the first sterilization law was passed in Indiana. These laws allowed the sterilization of those labeled "unfit," among those classified as such were criminals, alcoholics, the impoverished, the physically and mentally defective, and the disabled. By 1920, twenty-four states had passed sterilization laws and "by [the] mid-thirties, some twenty thousand sterilizations had been legally performed in the United States."[5] The classification of being included in these groups was a considerable threat to the deaf community; while the majority viewed them as disabled, deaf people viewed themselves as able-bodied and functioning citizens.

As the eugenics movement expanded during the early twentieth century, eugenicists delivered lectures at colleges and universities, advertising on the importance of selecting appropriate marital partners. The goal was to encourage young men and women to think about procreating to produce healthy offspring, in hopes that "some knowledge of eugenics would in many cases prevent falling in love with the wrong people."[6] To counter these efforts, deaf people were placed in situations where they "sought to normalize the view of Deafness by showing Deaf people's abilities as citizens."[7] The deaf community found themselves differing on principles when the details of their personal lives grew into a public concern, the right to marriage and procreation among deaf community members was starting to be scrutinized. Deaf people would find themselves disagreeing with other community members on the topic of deaf marriage; this disagreement would shift with the definition of who should or could marry whom and procreate with whom, focusing primarily on the rights of the congenitally deaf.

The NAD's leaders treaded a delicate balance of preserving deaf people's agency, in their right to choose in a spouse, and the individual freedom in making decisions, without societal pressure to acquiesce to the sentiments of mainstream opinion. While the NAD sought to defend and project deaf people as productive and participating citizens, the concept of what a "good citizen" entailed was encroaching into their communal mentality. "Good citizenship" in mainstream America included marrying well, choosing a right partner to have healthy and fit children, and that deafness was not desired. The Deaf community agreed with that, but they wanted to preserve their agency, their right to choose a partner without any legal interference. On this issue, the NAD showed resistance and presented a unified voice for the community in their stance to prevent any form of legislation that affected deaf people's rights as autonomous citizens; their efforts specifically focused on preventing deaf people from the classification as "unfit" and halting possible legislative action related to marriage and sterilization laws. Marking the words of Theodore Froehlich of New York, in his paper titled: "Importance of Association Among Mutes for Mutual Improvement" presented at the first NAD convention in 1880, "as deaf-mutes, we have interests peculiar to ourselves, which can be taken care of by ourselves," this mind-set is a summation of the stance the NAD and the deaf community maintained throughout the eugenic movement in the United States.[8]

The Early Years: Talking Deaf Marriages, 1880–1904

> [The] statistics on the intermarriage of the deaf, and their results, are so mixed that the subject has become one of controversy.
>
> —Thomas Fox, 1889

One of the founding members of the NAD was Robert P. McGregor, a talented storyteller with a commanding presence, who became the first NAD president.[9] The goals of his administration focused primarily on improving employment opportunities for deaf people. Yet, less than a month after the inception of the NAD in 1880, an international congress on the education of the deaf took place in Milan, Italy, and is commonly referred as the Milan Conference. A majority of the attendees voted in favor of the oral method, a method of communication and education that focuses on speaking, lipreading, and speech training.[10] Although oralism existed in the United States prior to the Milan Congress, most schools for deaf children up until that time used sign language as the

primary method of instruction. The Milan Congress represented a mile-
stone in the shift of method in deaf education as schools for deaf students gradually adopted oralism, banned sign language, and replaced
deaf teachers with hearing teachers.[11]

Soon after, defending sign language quickly became a leading priority on the NAD's agenda. Alexander Graham Bell was an outspoken
advocate of the oral method. His support of the oral method was based
on the perception that spoken English would help deaf people assimilate into mainstream society; he encouraged them to meet and marry
hearing partners. Although Bell was better known for his invention of
the telephone, he also had many ties to deaf people, including the fact
he had a deaf mother and a deaf wife, and knowledge of conversational
sign language. Bell dabbled in a variety of scientific pursuits, including
technology, genetics, and breeding, which ultimately led to an interest
in eugenics.[12] Bell believed that deaf marriages increased the likelihood
of having deaf children, and he did not shy away from educating the
public of his concerns. Bell argued that having a deaf child was a burden
and it would be wiser for a deaf person to marry a hearing partner. For
this reason, Bell was opposed to the use of sign language asserting that
it would encourage the "clannish nature" in deaf people, increasing
their chances of marrying one another. In 1883, he presented a paper to
the National Academy of Sciences in Connecticut titled *Memoir Upon
the Formation of a Deaf Variety of the Human Race.* In it he outlined his
thoughts on deaf marriages and revisited Galton's original ideas of selective breeding.[13] He was adamant that if deaf people continued marrying one another, it would lead to a "deaf variety" of the human race and
thus impose an inevitable burden on society. Bell's rationale included
ideas for formulating "practical plans that might lead to the breeding
of better men and better women," although he admitted, "the problem
is one of great difficulty and perplexity, for its solution depends upon
the possibility of controlling the production of offspring from human
beings." Advocating what is now referred to as "positive eugenics,"
Bell viewed this as an educated choice, advocating that any good citizen
should consider if they had the "desire that their offspring may be fully
up to the average of the race in every particular, if not superior" and
did "not desire for a weak, sickly, defective or physically and mentally
inferior child."[14] Bell visited the Gallaudet College campus in 1891 to
deliver a paper titled *Marriage: An Address to the Deaf.* In his paper he
outlined his concern that "there would be an unidentifiable deaf variety
of the human race, separate from the hearing community and, presum-

ably, a drain on that community's resources."[15] He also stressed that deaf people could also be happy with hearing companions.[16]

In an attempt to investigate hereditary deafness, Bell commissioned Edward Allen Fay, then editor of the *American Annals of the Deaf*, to compile an extensive database on deaf marriages.[17] Fay sent and collected surveys questioning deaf Americans, about deaf parents, deaf children, and deaf spouses. Completed in 1898, the result was a 528-page report titled *Marriages of the Deaf in America: An Inquiry Concerning the Results of Marriages of the Deaf in America*, and was published by Bell's Volta Bureau Association in Washington, DC.[18] Fay's "careful research suggested that deaf-deaf marriages did not produce a higher proportion of deaf offspring than deaf-hearing marriages."[19] His research, a result of surveying 4,471 deaf individuals, concluded that "marriages of the deaf are far more likely to result in hearing offspring than in deaf offspring."[20] With this finding, the report discredited Bell's theory on the possibility of a "deaf variety" of humanity occurring from deaf marriages.[21]

The NAD initially did not concentrate on opposing Bell's work with eugenics, but rather focused on his efforts to promote the oral method in deaf education. Edward Miner Gallaudet, son of a deaf mother and the first president of Gallaudet University, was often at odds with Bell. But, he spoke at the third NAD convention in 1889, at which he stated: "Bell is the friend of the deaf. Meet his theories by facts and prove them wrong. He is sincere and generous, full of enthusiasm in all that he does."[22] Like Bell, Gallaudet disapproved of deaf marriages, more specifically marriages between congenitally deaf persons. Gallaudet believed that "it is generally better for a deaf person to marry one who hears, rather than to take a deaf partner."[23] *The Silent Worker*, a significant deaf newspaper, was "viewed as a tool for education, advocacy, and cultural expression,"[24] mentions that the congenitally deaf "fourth class" (out of different classifications of deafness) was the ones that Gallaudet would not advise to marry based on "general principles."[25]

At the third NAD convention, the controversy of deaf marriages erupted. Thomas Fox, who became president of the NAD in 1893, presented his paper on establishing a federation of the deaf, also touching on the topic of deaf marriage:

> It's evident that on such subjects, as "statistics," intermarriage," "clannishness," and "system" or "method" the deaf are fully aware of their importance as controlling elements in their lives

and happiness, and they feel that it is about time they put a curb to the practice of a few interested parties, who promulgate false views of those subjects under the cloak of scientific theories.[26]

Fox's statement is the first documented response to deaf marriage in NAD proceedings; it indicated that NAD leaders and members were aware of Bell's work and Fay's research.

At the next NAD convention in 1893, participants specifically criticized Bell. Two papers were presented, both bearing the same title: "Should the Deaf Marry the Deaf?" One paper was by Jean Olivier, from France and the second was by Dudley W. George, who was the outgoing NAD president at the time. George, deaf himself, had a deaf father and had married a deaf woman, emphasized in his paper the importance of happiness and liberty of choice and supported deaf marriages.[27] He stated that "the deaf have no more desire to see their children deaf than hearing parents, but should any of them happen to have a deaf child, they would know what to do with him."[28] In sum, both Olivier and George emphasized the right to pursue happiness and that it is relatively rare for deaf marriages to produce deaf offspring.

There was no mention of deaf marriage at the subsequent NAD conventions, held in 1896 and 1899. However, at the 1904 convention, held in St. Louis (just one year after the American Breeders' Association was first organized in the same city), the NAD released a formal statement advocating deaf marriages. "The deaf often marry the deaf. Such marriages are generally more happy than when the deaf marry hearing partners. Divorces are relatively fewer among the former than the latter."[29] Although there was nothing to indicate discussions on marriage in that year's convention proceedings, deaf people perceived this statement as a proclamation of their right of agency and the right to choose; echoing the sentiments of Dudley W. George. In the early days of the American eugenics movement, the NAD thus emphasized the significance of happiness and communication over assimilation.

Veditz's Terms as NAD President: 1904–1910

> Bell is the most feared enemy of the Deaf that came in the guise of a friend.
>
> —George W. Veditz, 1910

The seventh president of the NAD, George W. Veditz, was the first to serve two consecutive terms (1904–1907; 1907–1910). In his presidential address, marking the start of his second term, Veditz warned of

Dudley W. George, third president, National
Association of the Deaf (1889–1893). Courtesy
of Gallaudet University Archives.

the potential negative implications that eugenics and potentially related
legislation posed to the community; stating that "there is another matter
in which we are vitally interested and that should engage our attention. I refer to the old spectre of the greatest menace yet offered to the
happiness of the adult deaf—the proposition to forbid or restrict their
intermarriage." Veditz shared that the American Breeders' Association
(ABA) decided to propose a "restriction of matrimony" and planned to
introduce the concept to all American states. Veditz went on to explain
that in the previous year, 1906, the ABA had established a division on
eugenics and a "Committee on Eugenics," even more revealing was that
"our old friend" Bell was on that committee. Veditz regarded this action as a threat and asked for the end of this "humiliating and unjust
classification," although "so far, on paper and is merely a threat still I
would call upon this convention to express itself in indignant protest."[31]
The NAD quickly formed a committee to "confer with [the ABA] Committee on Eugenics, looking toward the removal of the deaf and dumb
from its list."

James L. Smith, NAD president (1990–1904) and
chair of the NAD's Committee on Eugenics.
Courtesy of Gallaudet University Archives.

James Lewis Smith of Minnesota, who served as president preceding Veditz (1900–1904) was named as chair of the NAD Committee on
Eugenics. Among those appointed to the committee were Albert Berg,
John B. Hotchkiss, Amos G. Draper, Edwin Hodgson, Alexander Pach,
George Dougherty, C. C. Goodman, and Francis P. Gibson. Each of those
deaf men held prominent positions within the deaf community, ranging
from NAD presidents to editors of residential school news publications,
known as "The Little Paper Family."[30] They were familiar with one another through their tight-knit social network and were active members
of the deaf community.

The NAD Committee on Eugenics delivered their report at the
NAD Convention in 1910. It was reported that Smith wrote to David
Starr Jordan, the chairman of the ABA Committee on Eugenics, inquir-
ing whether deaf people were among those being classified on the bill

Jordan, then president of Stanford University, replied "The Committee of Eugenics has not recommended and has never thought of recommending the prohibition of the intermarriage of the deaf."[32] Prior to this correspondence, Smith also wrote to Bell, mistakenly thinking Bell was the chair of the ABA's Eugenics Committee. Bell wrote back, correcting him and directed Smith to Jordan, he also was sure to state that he had never supported any legislation that restricted deaf marriages.[33] Shortly after, Bell published an article that appeared in the February 1908 issue of the Volta Bureau's *Association Review*, titled "A Few Thoughts Concerning Eugenics," which also appeared in the *National Geographic* in February 1908.[34] In this article, Bell repeated that he was not in favor of legislation restricting deaf marriages, but that marriage was a matter of choice between the two concerned individuals. Bell believed that creating laws would not have made a difference, but that educating people about hereditary defects would help them choose the "right" partners.[35] In this sense, Bell shows himself to be a eugenicist in the positive mold, opposing coercive restrictions.

After determining that deaf people were not at risk of being classified for sterilization, according to the correspondence with Starr Jordan and Bell, the NAD Committee on Eugenics was disbanded. Smith was also the editor of *The Companion*, a deaf publication printed in Faribault, Minnesota. During that time, there were series of editorials and columns in *The Companion* that continued the discussion on deaf marriages. Smith wrote an editorial about marriage, and although he was in opposition of legislative action barring deaf marriages, he did not support deaf marriages personally. In his editorial, he wrote that deaf adults should "take a strong stand in opposition to mating of deaf persons who have the hereditary tendency on both sides."[36] *The Companion* also published a column titled "Hits and Misses" written using the penname of Ichabod Crane.[37] In that column, the mysterious author wrote in a sardonic tone, which ridiculed Smith for trying to be "the matrimonial adviser of the deaf" and wrote that no one would listen anyway. This showed conflicting views between popular societal views and what went on, which was found repeatedly what could be best put as "between the lines."

In the 1910 NAD conference proceedings, Veditz's and Smith's addresses, the NAD Committee on Eugenics actions, and *The Companion* showed apparent divisions in the deaf community.

Not all agreed on which position to take on deaf marriages, but remained decidedly against legislation; positing that deaf people were capable of handling differing opinions and debates without government involvement. One instance of this was Smith who asserted that deaf people should marry responsibly, especially if they had deaf parents.

Shifting Views: The 1920 and 1930 Resolutions

> Unless we take our own initiative in this matter, society will get after us.
>
> —Clayton McLaughlin, 1917

After Veditz's eight-year term as NAD president ended, his mantle was passed on to Olof Hanson, a trained architect. Under Hanson, NAD president from 1910–1913, the priorities of the NAD focused largely on the right to use sign language in schools, the oral method of instruction had since become widespread and established in the United States. The NAD also pushed for eliminating boundaries surrounding employment discrimination.[38] Following Hanson, Jay Cooke Howard stepped in as president for two terms from 1913 to 1917. Deaf marriages were mentioned briefly at the eleventh NAD convention in San Francisco and again at the twelfth convention in a paper titled "The Intermarriage of the Deaf" by Clayton McLaughlin. McLaughlin cautioned that, according to him, offspring with hereditary deafness was increasing, which presented a risk that deaf people would be classified with the feeble-minded. McLaughlin encouraged the prevention of marriages between two congenitally deaf adults in order to eliminate hereditary deafness. He warned that "unless we take our own initiative in this matter, society will get after us." He concluded his paper by recommending that the NAD "should declare itself against the intermarriage of the congenitally deaf, and begin a propaganda of education with the view of discouraging intermarriage between persons possessed of hereditary deafness."[39] McLaughlin proposed that the NAD should gain control (essentially, agency) and inform eugenicists, organizations, and politicians that it was the responsibility and right of the deaf community, not theirs, to "control" who they marry. "I would also keep this matter from being handled by legislative bodies, we may then, and only then feel that we are doing our duty to society."[40] This statement by McLaughlin's was the most revealing and in line with the true intentions of the NAD, particularly in how it would represent its constituents and how the deaf community fought to preserve their agency during the eugenics movement.

The twelfth NAD convention in 1917 passed a resolution to establish a committee to investigate and gather "reliable statistics" on marriages of the deaf, with McLaughlin as chairman. The 1917 *Proceedings* show that attendees regarded Fay's study, published nineteen years earlier, as outdated. At the 1920 NAD convention, in Detroit, McLaughlin and his Committee on Statistics reported that based on "statistics and observations," deaf marriages led to an increase in hereditary deafness.[41] There were no further details or information on how the statistical data was collected. At the 1920 convention, a resolution was passed:

> Whereas, Statistics and observation have shown that the liability to deaf offspring is increased to a marked extent by (1) the inter-marriage of the congenitally deaf, and (2) the marriage of the con-genitally deaf into families having deaf relatives. Resolved, that the National Association of the Deaf go on record as viewing such marriages with disapproval and earnestly urge the deaf to avoid such unions if possible.[42]

Taking this resolution into perspective, along with McLaughlin's "studies" and the general consensus that deaf people wanted to seize agency, this was the first time the NAD went on record to disapprove of marriages between congenitally deaf people. Their stated intention was to avoid any future legislation, which could potentially restrict the marriages in the larger deaf community. This, of course, did not mean that congenitally and non-congenitally deaf people refrained from mar-rying one other.[43] However, this also posed specific societal expectations among those born from deaf families. These marriages were now put under a stigma, one which could be avoided only by taking hearing partners.

At the next NAD Convention in 1926, the issue of eugenics was again raised and the NAD made an official statement titled "Eugenics."

> The Association has had, and probably always will have the obli-gation and responsibility of safeguarding the deaf from inclusion in laws tending to classify them with the unfit and inferior and putting restrictions on their marriage and the raising of families. The question of eugenics has a great vogue among so called re-formers, many of them densely ignorant of even the elemental facts of biology and of inheritable tendencies among human be-

ings. Some time ago, the Chicago papers carried a story with a Madison, Wisconsin, to the effect that the reformers and upbuilders of the human race in that State proposed to enact a measure putting restrictions on the intermarriage of the unfit. The Association took immediate steps to investigate the report and to ascertain whether the deaf were included. The proposal died in committee in the Wisconsin legislature.[44]

It was following this statement that a resolution was passed, condemning "any and all efforts to classify the deaf as defective." This resolution described the deaf as "respectable, loyal, self-supporting citizens" and not as "Insane Imbeciles, Chronic Alcoholic, or the like."[45] By then, over twenty-four states had sterilization laws in place, barring the feeble-minded from marriage, and sterilization was routine in some states for those classified "unfit."[46]

In effect, the NAD acted as a watchdog for the American deaf community against any possible classification in categories of people seen as eugenically unfit and from any legislative restrictions on marriage. However, at the 1930 convention there was a marked shift in how the NAD represented its constituents. At this convention, a resolution was passed recognizing "that deafness, is after all, something of a handicap to success—through having the manifold blessings in this noise-crazed civilization," that medical sciences have progressed much, "the National Association of the Deaf . . . commend and encourage efforts of the American Otological Society to discover and cure causes of deafness, and appoints a standing committee to co-operate with Science to the fullest extent."[47] This statement revealed another shift in the NAD's approach to eugenics, going on to support and commend scientific efforts on finding a cure. However, there was no indication of the NAD actually forming a committee, unlike previous resolutions, which sought immediate action.[48] The NAD and deaf leaders strongly opposed any form of legislation preventing marriages, or legislation that "wrongly" classified the deaf among undesired groups.

As educated citizens, deaf people agreed that hereditary deafness was a burden, and generally favored openly opposing such marriages instead of being forced by legislative action that might endanger all deaf marriages. In the eyes of the NAD, that was sufficient, and the deaf would continue to do what they had done, which was to take matters into their capable hands. In light of sterilization laws, which continued to gain momentum in many states, the NAD issued warnings for deaf members to keep watch for any new restrictions on their reproductive freedom.[49]

The Later Years: Sterilization Laws 1930–1940

> It is heartening to know that we have strong allies in the Catholic Church, which opposes sterilization.
>
> —NAD *Bulletin*, 1935

The NAD continued to monitor sterilization laws in place in several US states, which it addressed in its periodical, the *N.A.D. Bulletin* (*Bulletin*). In April 1935, the *Bulletin* issued a statement titled "The Deaf and Sterilization," in which it was explained that, by that time 27 states had adopted sterilization laws. However, in those laws, deaf people had not been included as a target for sterilization. The NAD urged every deaf citizen to "keep their eyes open on these sterilization laws and report to us IMMEDIATELY any effort being made to include the deaf in the category of 'mental defectives." It also warned that sterilization laws could later target those who depended on public funding (welfare) and those who were hereditarily deaf, but, if not carefully monitored, it may become a hazard for *all* deaf people. The statement closed with a sentiment, stating that "it is heartening to know that we have strong allies in the Catholic Church, which opposes sterilization."[50] The Catholic Church viewed every man, woman, and child as a creation by God and if they were indeed afflicted with "undesirable traits," then it was God's will, and it is only their duty to "help."[51]

The *Bulletin* ran several notifications on proposed bills on sterilization, keeping all NAD members up to date. Whenever informed of a possible bill making the rounds in state legislatures, a member of the NAD would be sent to investigate by requesting that copies of the bill be sent to the NAD board for careful scrutiny. Other than a few mentions in the *Bulletin* by 1940, the NAD had fewer concerns about eugenics. The eugenics movement, by the mid-1930s, had lost much of its public approval in the US. "Generally been recognized as a farrago of flawed science," much of the movement died out by the 1940s especially when it became closely associated with medical experiments of the Nazi regime. This led to a loss of public support in the US and abroad.[52] Yet, between 1909 and 1960, nearly sixty thousand people had been eugenically sterilized in the US. They were immigrants, and people labeled as "undesired" (mentally ill, alcoholics, and disabled). California led the trend with more than one third of these operations.[53] The NAD's main concern, however, was to safeguard deaf people from sterilization and marriage restrictions. Under the NAD's watch, proposed bills never became laws, and this was result of a vigilant and watchful body.

Agency Over Representation

> If we would keep abreast with times, we must acknowledge we owe a duty to society in so far as the control of hereditary deafness is concerned.
> —Clayton McLaughlin, 1918

The NAD's representation of deaf people during the eugenics movement can be best summed up in the words of Theodore Froehlich, a prominent deaf community member, who said at the inaugural conference, "matters peculiar to ourselves, to be taken care of ourselves." Those words had been a long mantra of the NAD, particularly as it strategically responded to eugenic ideals. However, how deaf people handled agency differed greatly over time, influenced by who presided over the Association.

For instance, Dudley W. George, the only NAD president during that time to have a deaf parent, focused his administration on the liberty of choice and happiness.[54] This is different from that of George Veditz, who paid close attention to eugenic practices and warned about possible threats.

Out of fourteen presidents in the first sixty years of the NAD during the eugenics movement none stood out as an advocate for deaf agency more than George W. Veditz.[55] It is likely that through his activities in chicken breeding and horticulture, which he won several awards for, Veditz came across the American Breeders Association and read about their activities.[56] The year he warned the NAD, through his presidential address at the 1907 convention, was also the same year as the first sterilization law was passed in Indiana, granting the state authority to sterilize criminals.[57] By 1914, some thirty states had such laws in place, barring the "feeble minded" from getting married, and by 1917 fifteen states enacted sterilization laws, allowing criminals to be sterilized, preventing any genetic disposition from passing on.

As president, Veditz had held a firm ground in face of eugenic values calling it "the greatest menace yet offered to the happiness of the adult deaf."[58] In those later years of the eugenic movement, there was a shift in how deaf people perceived their own agency, going from George's liberty and happiness to Veditz's more defeatist view. This shift was succinctly expressed by Clayton McLaughlin, in 1918:

> Now, there is no gainsaying that the whole [eugenics] movement which is aimed at social welfare has the endorsement of taxpayers and may yet become a regular function of the State government. If we would keep abreast with the times, we must acknowledge that we owe a duty to society in so far as the control of hereditary deafness is concerned. Unless we take our own initiative in this matter, society will get after us.

This coincides with the strong rise and influence of eugenics, with sterilization laws in place in some states. For deaf people to protect their agency, it seemed like a wise course of action to agree with society, although only in concept but not practice.

Deaf people continued to intermarry, and the majority of the four-teen NAD presidents married deaf women. Ironically, regardless of the 1920 resolution in which the NAD went on record to disapprove of deaf marriages, there was a wedding at the NAD convention. Having a wed-ding at the convention showed that the NAD made statements to ap-pease societal values while deaf people continued on with their lives. It was a constant negotiation of agency during a time when eugenic ideals took root in the United States.

Not all deaf people had unified disdain for eugenic ideologies, many stood in support, such as James L. Smith, who held views against deaf marriage, and throughout the 1917 conference proceedings, the gen-eral consensus was that the "congenitally deaf" should not marry one another. Most NAD presidents were postlingually deaf and came from hearing families; they were not carriers of any markers of hereditary deafness. What is also evident, is that the NAD compromised by nar-rowing the eugenic values to apply only to the congenitally deaf, as stated by Clayton McLaughlin in 1917:

> [Eugenicists] generally concede that hereditary deafness is a condi-tion that can be controlled through education, and that the solution is best left to the deaf themselves who are graded high in the strata of eugenic society.[59]

Also, at the time, the consensus appeared that no one wanted to intentionally have deaf children. Dudley W. George, who was of deaf parentage, even stated that "no one wishes to have deaf children."[60]

The 1930 resolution passed by the NAD convention, had the NAD agreeing to work with scientists to find a cure for deafness, was a shift from previous actions. Did this mean that the NAD was acquiescing to eugenic ideals and societal expectations or was it more of a strategic move to ideally "cooperate" with the larger society to safeguard deaf people's agency?

During his tenure as president from 1904 to 1910, Veditz also campaigned for employment rights, improved fundraising efforts, and, in 1913, his address concerning the importance of sign language preservation was filmed. Veditz recognized Bell's role and beliefs as a eugenicist, stating that Bell was "the most feared enemy of the Deaf" that came "in the guise of a friend" in his presidential address in 1910.[61] Veditz's term ended in 1910, and the eugenics movement continued to gain ground in other areas of American life, which both influenced and changed how deaf people represented themselves through the NAD.

In 1917, McLaughlin argued that the NAD should employ statements in agreement with general societal views, rather than being put in a position where deaf citizens could possibly face legislative restrictions. This continued to resonate with the early days of the NAD, when Froehlich specified that deaf people would take care of matters themselves. Historian Susan Burch states, that "deaf people viewed themselves as self-sustaining and not in need of significant legal intervention on their behalf."[62] While at the same time, deaf people believed themselves as capable citizens and could prove themselves agreeable to societal values and ideals. In doing so, it was necessary to reach compromise on such issues as congenitally deaf marriages in order to maintain agency to maneuver through other issues of concern to them.

The actions of the NAD were a reflection of a larger complicated picture of conflicting and constant negotiations pertaining to personal views versus societal expectations. It is impossible to overlook the sentiment that deaf people have long struggled to portray and prove themselves as capable, fit, and hardworking citizens. The debates over agency and personal rights shaped the course of action for the NAD, when confronted with threatening legislature, possible reclassification of deaf people as a group, and sterilization; the NAD banded together and presented a united force. The NAD, throughout the six decades, never showed mainstream society that its members held varying views on intermarriage. The NAD was stoic in its position, that deaf people were able to challenge the eugenic debates and resolve external debates internally. As historical artifacts, the convention proceedings, publications, and articles, demonstrate the struggles of the late nineteenth and early twentieth centuries. It also demonstrates how the National Association of the Deaf acted to protect and safeguard the rights of the American deaf community.

Notes

1. Theodore A. Froehlich, "Importance of Association," 39–40.
2. Kevles, *In the Name of Eugenics*, 91.
3. Roger Daniels, *Coming to America: A History of Immigration and Ethnicity in American Life* (Cambridge, MA: Harvard University Press, 1990); Alan M. Kraut, *The Huddled Masses: The Immigrant in American Society, 1880-1921* (Arlington Heights, IL: Harlan Davidson, Inc., 1982); John Higham, *Strangers in the Land: Patterns of American Nativism, 1860–1925* (New York: Atheneum, 1970).
4. Kevles, *In the Name of Eugenics*, 91.
5. Ibid., 111–112.
6. Ibid., 89.
7. Burch, *Signs of Resistance*, 91.
8. Froehlich, *Importance of Association*, 39.
9. The third issue of *Deaf Studies Digital Journal* (2012, http://dsdj.gallaudet .edu), features Robert McGregor in "The Irishman's Flea," part of the NAD's 1913 Preservation of ASL collection.
10. *Collection of International Congresses on the Deaf*, 1963. Retrieved from http://www.gallaudet.edu/library_deaf_collections_and_archives/collections /manuscript_collection/mss_079.html
11. Buchanan, "Oralism," 679–81.
12. Bell owned flocks of sheep at his Nova Scotia estate and systemically bred sheep with extra nipples, which he wrote about in *Science*, "The Multi-Nippled Sheep of Beinn Bhreagh," in 1904.
13. Greenwald, "Taking Stock," 138–39.
14. Bell, "A Few Thoughts Concerning Eugenics," 119.
15. Bell, "Marriage," 1891.
16. Greenwald, "Taking Stock," 140.
17. Van Cleve and Crouch, *A Place of Their Own*, 151.
18. Fay, *Marriages of the Deaf in America*, 1898.
19. Greenwald, "Taking Stock," 141.
20. S. W. A. Review of Marriages of the Deaf in America. *Publications of the American Statistical Association* 6 (47), 1899, 353–56.
21. Greenwald, "Taking Stock," 125.
22. Gallaudet, "Closing remarks," 66.

23. *The Silent Worker,* Dec 25, 1890, 1.

24. Soulier, "The Silent Worker," 828–29.

25. *The Silent Worker,* Dec 25, 1890, 1.

26. *Proceedings of the Third Convention,* 14.

27. Gannon, *Deaf Heritage,* 251.

28. George, "Should the Deaf Marry the Deaf?," 112–15.

29. *Proceedings of the Seventh Convention,* 68–69.

30. Little Paper Family (LPF) is a term used to classify publications by schools for the deaf that were widely distributed from 1870s to 1930s. LPFs served as the main mode of communication and news exchange for the deaf community during that time. During the rise of oralism and changing of school administrators who supported the oral method, it affected LPFs as community news. LPFs became less political and shifted focus on school activities, rather than reporting activities of the national and local deaf communities, which included recaps of NAD's convention proceedings. Many prominent deaf leaders (including NAD presidents) also served as editors of LPFs, and took pride in their work.

31. *Proceedings of the Eighth Convention,* 15–16.

32. Ibid., 69.

33. All this correspondence between the NAD committee and the ABA Committee on Eugenics occurred in 1908, following the seventh NAD convention in 1907.

34. Bell, "A Few Thoughts," 171–73.

35. Greenwald, "The Real 'Toll' of A. G. Bell," 37.

36. Smith, *The Companion,* March 25, 1908, 9.

37. A letter to the editor from Jay Cooke Howard appeared in a 1914 issue of *The Silent Worker* titled "Was One-Third Ichabod," 68. In the letter, Howard revealed he was one of three co-authors who wrote under that pen name. However, he did not reveal the true names of the other two men. Being deaf himself, Howard was also married to a deaf woman, and he later became NAD president after Hanson's term ended in 1913, 68.

38. Burch, *Signs of Resistance,* 112–14.

39. McLaughlin, "The Intermarriage of the Deaf," *Proceedings of the Twelfth Convention,* 111–12.

40. Ibid.

41. McLaughlin reported at the fourteenth convention, that the committee "had no findings to present before the Convention." *The Silent Worker* 37, no. 5 (February 1925). Records did not show if the committee continued.

42. *Proceedings of the Thirteenth Convention,* 96.

43. The *Deaf-Mutes Journal* ran a news blurb with the headline, "Mutes Wed While at the N.A.D. Convention" and described a lavish wedding with many "valuable presents received" (September 1920).

44. "Proceedings of the Fifteenth Convention." *Deaf-Mutes Journal.*

45. Ibid.

46. Kevles, *In the Name of Eugenics*, 111.

47. *Proceedings of the Sixteenth Convention*, 88.

48. A mention of the 1930 resolution appeared in the *American Annals of the Deaf*, with a completely different interpretation: "The convention adopted a series of resolutions . . . (3). Endorsing the efforts of science in the systematic study of the problems of deafness . . . " (328–29). "Systematic study" carries a very different meaning from "finding a cure."

49. *N.A.D. Bulletin*, April 1935.

50. Ibid.

51. Kevles, *In the Name of Eugenics*, 118–119.

52. Kevles, *In the Name of Eugenics*, 169.

53. Stern, *Eugenic Nation*, 85.

54. Nearly a hundred years would pass until the NAD again had a president who came from a deaf family. Gertrude Galloway was also the first female president in 1980.

55. A news brief appeared in the April 1910 edition of *The Companion* mentioning that Veditz had sent two delegates to the Laryngological, Rhinological, and Otological Association convention. "Mr. Veditz, by this action, has given another evidence of his policy of keeping abreast with the times" (Smith).

56. Veditz wrote for journals and magazines on poultry and horticulture, and garnered recognition and won awards for his work, along with his wife, Bessie.

57. Kevles, *In the Name of Eugenics*, 100.

58. Veditz, "President's Address."

59. McLaughlin, "The Intermarriage of the Deaf."

60. George, "Should the Deaf Marry the Deaf?" 113.

61. Veditz's comments on Bell as an enemy of the deaf are published in several places, including Newman's book *Sands of Time* (2006). However, those publications have taken Veditz's words out of context, leading people to believe that he was referring to Bell's advocacy work on oralism. When this quote is examined in its original context, from the proceedings of the eighth NAD convention in 1907, it was delivered immediately after Veditz warned the audience about Bell's work in eugenics and of a possible legislation prohibiting deaf marriages, not about oralism. It was in this setting that Veditz stated Bell was "the most feared enemy of the American deaf, past and present" from the "President's Address," 12–16.

62. Burch, *Signs of Resistance*, 115.

References

Bell, Alexander G. "A Few Thoughts Concerning Eugenics," *The National Geographic Magazine* (February 1908): 119. Also published in *The Association Review* (1908): 171–73.

———. "Marriage: An Address to the Deaf," presentation to Gallaudet College, 1891.

———. "Memoir Upon the Formation of a Deaf Variety of the Human Race." Paper presented to the National Academy of Sciences, 1883.

———. "The Multi-Nippled Sheep of Beinn Bhreagh." *Science* 19, no. 489 (1904): 767–68.

Buchanan, Robert. "The Silent Worker Newspaper and the Building of a Deaf Community, 1890–1929." In *Deaf History Unveiled: Interpretations from the New Scholarship*, edited by John V. Van Cleve, 172–97. Washington, DC: Gallaudet University Press, 1993.

———. "Oralism." In *Encyclopedia of American Disability History*, 679–81. New York: Facts on File, 2009.

Burch, Susan. *Signs of Resistance: American Deaf Cultural History, 1900 to World War II*. New York: New York University Press, 2002.

Collection of International Congresses on the Deaf, 1963. Gallaudet University Archives. Retrieved November 20, 2014: http://www.gallaudet.edu/library _deaf_collections_and_archives/collections/manuscript_collection/mss _079.html

Colorado Index. September 29, 1911. Colorado Springs: Colorado School for the Deaf and Blind. Retrieved from Gallaudet University, on microfilm.

Colorado Index. March 22, 1912. Colorado Springs: Colorado School for the Deaf and Blind. Retrieved from Gallaudet University, on microfilm.

Daniels, Roger. *Coming to America: A History of Immigration and Ethnicity in American Life*. Cambridge, MA: Harvard University Press, 1990.

Fay, Edward A. *Marriages of the Deaf in America: An Inquiry Concerning the Results of Marriages of the Deaf in America.* Washington, DC: Volta Bureau, 1898.

Fox, Thomas, F. "The Federation of the Deaf." In *Proceedings of the Third Convention of the National Association of the Deaf.* 1889. New York: Office of the *Deaf Mute Journal*, 1890. Gallaudet University Archives, on microfilm, 14–17.

Froehlich, Theodore A. "Importance of Association among Mutes for Mutual Improvement. *Proceedings of the First Convention of the National Association of the Deaf.* 1880. Gallaudet University Archives, on microfilm.

Gallaher, James. *Representative Deaf Persons of the United States of America: Portraits and Character Sketches of Prominent Deaf Persons (Commonly called "Deaf Mutes") Who Are Engaged in the Higher Pursuits of Life.* Chicago, 1898, Gallaudet University Archives.

Gallaudet, E.M. Closing remarks. In *Proceedings of the Third Convention of the National Association of the Deaf.* 1889, 66. Gallaudet University Archives, on microfilm.

Gannon, Jack. *Deaf Heritage: A Narrative History of Deaf America.* Silver Spring, MD: National Association of the Deaf, 1981.

George, Dudley W. "Should the Deaf Marry the Deaf?" In *Proceedings of the Fourth Convention of the National Association of the Deaf: Held in Chicago, Illinois, 1893*, 112–15. Gallaudet University Archives, on microfilm.

Greenwald, Brian. "The Real 'Toll' of A. G. Bell." In *Genetics, Disability, and Deafness,* edited by John Van Cleve, 35–41. Washington, DC: Gallaudet University Press, 2004.

———. "Taking Stock: Alexander Graham Bell and Eugenics 1883–1922." In *Deaf History Reader,* edited by John Van Cleve, 136–52. Washington, DC: Gallaudet University Press, 2006.

Higham, John. *Strangers in the Land: Patterns of American Nativism, 1860–1925.* New York: Atheneum, 1970.

Howard, Jay Cooke. "Was One-Third Ichabod." *The Silent Worker* 27, no. 4 (1914): 68.

Kevles, Daniel. *In the Name of Eugenics: Genetics and the Uses of Human Heredity.* Cambridge: Harvard University Press, 1985.

Kraut, Alan M. *The Huddled Masses: The Immigrant in American Society, 1880–1921.* Arlington Heights, IL: Harlan Davidson, Inc., 1982.

Malzkuhn, Brian. "The Irishman's Flea." *Deaf Studies Digital Journal* 3 (2012): accessed August 14, 2014, http://dsdj.gallaudet.edu.

McLaughlin, Clayton. "The Intermarriage of the Deaf." In *Proceedings of the Twelfth Convention of the National Association of the Deaf: Held in Hartford, Connecticut, 1917,* 109–12. Gallaudet University Archives, on microfilm.

———. *The Silent Worker* 37, no. 5 (February 1925).

"Mutes Wed While at the N.A.D. Convention," *Deaf Mutes Journal.* September 1920.

N.A.D. Bulletin, 1, no. 6 (April 1935). Gallaudet University Archives.

N.A.D. Bulletin, 1, no. 7 (May 1935). Gallaudet University Archives.

Newman, Lawrence. *Sands of Time: NAD Presidents 1880–2003.* Silver Spring, MD: National Association of the Deaf, 2006.

Proceedings of the First Convention of the National Association of the Deaf. 1880. Gallaudet University Archives, on microfilm.

Proceedings of the Third Convention of the National Association of the Deaf. 1889. New York: Office of the *Deaf Mute Journal,* 1890. Gallaudet University Archives, on microfilm.

Proceedings of the Seventh Convention of the National Association of the Deaf. 1904. Gallaudet University Archives, on microfilm.

Proceedings of the Eighth Convention of the National Association of the Deaf: Held in St. Louis, Missouri, 1907. Gallaudet University Archives, on microfilm.

Proceedings of the Thirteenth Convention of the National Association of the Deaf. 1920, 96. Gallaudet University Archives, on microfilm.

"Proceedings of the Fifteenth Triennial Convention of the National Association of the Deaf." *Deaf-Mutes Journal* no. 33 (August 19, 1926). Retrieved from Gallaudet University, on microfilm.

Proceedings of the Sixteenth Convention of the National Association of the Deaf. 1920, 88.

S. W. A. Review of *Marriages of the Deaf in America. Publications of the American Statistical Association* 6 (47). Taylor & Francis, Ltd., 1889.

The Silent Worker 4, no. 27. (December 25, 1890).

The Silent Worker. 27, no. 4 (1908): 68.

The Silent Worker 37, no. 5 (February 1925).

Smith, J. L., ed. *The Companion* 33, no. 12 (February 27, 1903), 9–10. Retrieved from Gallaudet University Library, on microfilm.

——. *The Companion* 33, no. 13 (March 11, 1908), 4. Retrieved from Gallaudet University Library, on microfilm.

——. *The Companion* 33, no. 14 (March 25, 1908), 8–9. Retrieved from Gallaudet University Library, on microfilm.

——. *The Companion* 33, no. 18 (May 20, 1908), 2–3. Retrieved from Gallaudet University Library, on microfilm.

——. *The Companion* 35, no. 16 (April 27, 1910). Retrieved from Gallaudet University Library, on microfilm.

Soulier, Sylvie. "The Silent Worker." In *Encyclopedia of American Disability History*, 828–29. New York: Facts on File, 2009.

Stern, Alexandra M. *Eugenic Nation: Faults and Frontiers of Better Breeding in Modern America*. Berkeley: University of California Press, 2005.

Van Cleve, John, and Barry Crouch. *A Place of Their Own: Creating the Deaf Community in America*. Washington, DC: Gallaudet University Press, 1989.

Veditz, George W. "President's Address." In *Proceedings from the Eighth Convention of the National Association of the Deaf: Held in St. Louis, Missouri, 1907*, 12–16, 68.

10

Normalization and Abnormal Genes: Hereditary Deafness Research at the Clarke School for the Deaf, 1930–1950

Marion Andrea Schmidt

SINCE THEIR ESTABLISHMENT in the early nineteenth century, schools for the deaf have been entangled in a network of beliefs and assumptions about who deaf people should be and what they could accomplish. Whether manualist or oralist in their orientation, educators believed that deaf children could achieve an independent and fulfilled life. More than just educational paradigms, these assumptions reflected contemporary notions about the characteristics of a good citizen. The Clarke School for the Deaf, founded in 1867 in Northampton, Massachusetts, as one of the nation's first oralist institutions, operated within these societal expectations of citizenship and humanness. Aiming to turn deaf children into independent citizens, oralism promised to be a transformative tool. In teaching deaf children speech and lipreading, a 1929 fundraising brochure explained, the school bestowed upon them "something they were born without, and the lack of which would forever shut them out from human intercourse." Thus demonstrating "past all doubting that the deaf need not be 'dumb'," oralist educators expected deaf people to overcome their otherness and isolation in order to become productive and integrated citizens.[1]

Five decades after the school's founding, science and medicine expanded this promise of normalization. In 1929, the Clarke School established a research department that included divisions for audiology, psychology, and heredity. Investigating these diverse aspects of hearing loss, the school's educators believed, would help students to better integrate into hearing society. Combining oralist education with an optimistic belief in medical and technological progress, the school aimed to minimize the effects of deafness on its students. In the future, they hoped, it could be treated, and eventually, with the help of heredity research, prevented altogether. Analyzing the first decades of the school's hereditary deafness research makes visible the continuity of eugenic motives in the emergent field of genetic counseling. Yet it also shows how perceptions of deaf people influenced eugenic policies. Rather than promoting coercive measures, the school pursued their goals through education and counseling about heredity, thus maintaining an image of the deaf as responsible citizens. Through these pedagogic measurements, teachers tried to instill in their students what historian Wendy Kline has called the "reproductive morality" of foregoing the individual desire for a family in order to prevent passing on unfavorable traits.[2]

The founding of the school's heredity research division came at a time in which the deaf population, like other groups perceived as physically or mentally defective, were potential targets of eugenic legislation. When assessing sterilization laws and other eugenic measures, historians have predominantly focused on the "feeble-minded." The moral, intellectual, and physical threat this ill-defined group allegedly posed to society was used to justify measures such as institutionalization and coercive sterilization. In order to successfully campaign for restricting the rights of "feeble-minded" people, sociologist Allison Carey argues, eugenicists relied on pre-existing institutional settings and perceptions. Hereditary deafness research likewise operated within an older framework of assumptions about the worth and abilities of deaf people. Both oralists and the culturally deaf community insisted that they were responsible, self-supporting, and productive citizens. Yet, as Susan Burch and Octavian Robinson have pointed out, deaf organizations had to constantly rally to establish and maintain this image, often at the cost of excluding deaf people who supposedly did not fit these criteria, such as multiply disabled or non-white deaf people.[3]

Other examples help to place research on hereditary deafness into a larger negotiation over the value of a social group in terms of their (perceived) self-reliance and contribution to society. The feeble-minded were placed firmly on one end of the spectrum and decried as social and moral degenerates, incapable of holding steady work, relying on charity and welfare, and thus wasting the tax money of respectable citizens. The other end was occupied by those whose conditions presumably had a hereditary component, but who were also thought to contribute valuable—and equally hereditary—traits to society that would outweigh any negative impact. Historian Arleen Tuchman has shown how the contemporary perception of diabetes shaped the debate over the benefits and disadvantages of sterilizing diabetics. The general perception of diabetic sufferers as predominantly white, educated, and middle class, she argues, made coercive eugenic measures seem unnecessary. In contrary, some physicians asserted that diabetics' intellectual standards and extraordinary self-control outweighed the negatives of diabetes when it came to procreation. On this range of possible eugenic preconceptions, the deaf stood somewhere in the middle, closer to the supposedly normal and rational end of the spectrum, yet were still considered defective. Such preconceived notions of selfhood and ability had a significant impact on eugenic policies. While coercive measures were usually deemed unnecessary to regulate deaf people's reproduction, their positive traits were not enough to outweigh the negative eugenic impact of passing on their condition.[4]

Deaf people thus did not necessarily fit the pattern of de-individualized genetic determinism that is often seen as a characteristic of the eugenics movement. Rather, the Clarke School's heredity research operated within a paternalistic framework that, in preparing students for citizenship and normalcy, perpetually medicalized deafness and negated deviating cultural and linguistic beliefs. The school's strong belief in individual educational redemption counteracted a generalizing biological determinism. It was not hereditary deafness, but rather a child's ability to learn speech and lipreading that revealed—and determined—his or her abilities and educational direction.

Hereditary research operated within this alliance of medicalization and normalization, defect and correction. To realize a deaf child's inherent normalcy, the school insisted that they should be educated about the medical, audiological, and potentially genetic nature of deafness. Expanding scientific knowledge on these fields transferred expertise and agency away from deaf people to the professional groups—psychologists, teachers and geneticists—involved in gaining and applying this knowledge in their respective fields. Researchers claimed interpretative authority over family history, pedigrees, and future reproductive choices. Teachers took on the role of paternalistic counselors for a group portrayed as unaware of the mechanisms and dangers of inherited deafness. These professionals were optimistic that deaf people shared their belief in the transformative power of progressive science. If educated about their genetic makeup, the school believed, those affected by genetic deafness would opt for a "normal" family.

The Coolidge Fund for the Deaf—The "Plight of the Deaf" and Promises of Normalization

To this day, hereditary deafness research is often associated with Alexander Graham Bell and his 1883 *Memoir Upon the Formation of a Deaf Variety of the Human Race.* A dedicated eugenicist and one of the most prominent and ardent proponents of oralism, Bell feared that deaf people's dangerous tendency to marry each other would increase the incidence of hearing loss and thus eventually produce a deaf human sub-race. Bell ignited a heated debate, as scientists, educators and deaf people themselves tried to confirm or disprove his theory and discussed the justification of marriage restrictions. Bell's solution, however, was more pedagogic than eugenic. He believed that integrating deaf people into day schools and society at large and discouraging them from associating with each other would automatically decrease the incidence of harmful deaf intermarriages.[5]

In Northampton, Bell's ideas found a receptive audience. Visiting the Clarke School in 1871, he had introduced the staff to Visible Speech, a phonetic method developed by Bell's father for teaching speech to the deaf. Bell himself would remain connected to the school for the rest of his life and from 1917 to 1922 served as president of the school board. In 1921, he envisioned a future research department that—like his own work—would integrate science and education to achieve the overcoming of deafness. Though Bell died in 1922, the school was determined to realize this ambitious plan. School officials shared with him an understanding of research as part of a larger program of alleviating deaf people's otherness by educational reform, identifying and preventing hearing loss, and improving diagnostic and assistive equipment.[6]

In 1929, after nearly a decade of fundraising, the school established the Clarence W. Barron Research Department. It was named after the influential financial journalist Clarence W. Barron, president of Dow Jones, who had used his contacts and influence to help gather the substantial sum of two million dollars for the endowment. The cause of saving the deaf from their isolation had also mobilized other well-known figures. Among them were President Calvin Coolidge and First Lady Grace Goodhue Coolidge. Before her marriage, the latter had been a teacher at the Clarke School, where for "three years she gave herself wholly to the work of guiding little children across the narrow, perilous bridge which leads the deaf to the Promised Land of normal fellowship with their kind." The fund was named in the Coolidges' honor, and their contribution was remembered in a commemorative booklet, *The Coolidge Fund for the Clarke School and the Deaf.*[7]

The booklet painted a dire picture of the situation of American deaf people. The existence of an estimated ten million deaf and hard of hearing people in the United States pointed to the "vital need for an organization which will meet and grapple with the problem of the deaf in America on a national scale." The implication that America lacked such an institution was true only from an oralist point of view—and even then the booklet only expressed the partial truth of fundraising rhetoric. By the early twentieth century, a host of organizations addressed deaf people's concerns, among them national organizations of educators, the highly active National Association of the Deaf (NAD), and Bell's own Volta Bureau.[8]

There was, however, no school-based research unit that approached deafness from the medical and scientific angles. It was because deafness had been long treated as "an incurable affliction," the booklet informed its readers that "we are today further behind in adequate practical dealing with the problem of deafness than with any other social problem." The booklet thus rendered deafness as a social ill, a potentially curable disease on the scale of polio, tuberculosis, and other afflictions deserving of large-scale public attention. Yet, the authors lamented, society still was ignorant about the fate of the deaf: "The plight of the deaf is not, like that of the blind or the crippled, obvious." Contrary to the attempts of the culturally Deaf to assert their normalcy, the Clarke School stressed the otherness of those who had not yet been reached by the normalizing effect of oralist education. "Because they *look* like us, we suppose they must *be* like us," the booklet described this harmfully naïve perception that left people unaware of the "depth of misery [. . .] hidden under their apparent normality." It was just this apparent normalcy that allowed for deaf people's salvation by the means of education, medicine, and science. After the school had proven that the deaf were indeed capable of speech, it now set out to establish itself as a pioneer in the treatment and prevention of deafness.[9]

The research department was organized into three subdivisions, each with an ambitious scope. The Division of Experimental Phonetics worked on developing instruments to amplify sound in order to help teachers improve students' speech and employ their residual hearing. The second division was dedicated to researching the psychology of deafness, investigating the emotional and intellectual differences between deaf and hearing children with a particular emphasis on their "conscious thinking." The third division, headed by anthropologist Morris Steggerda (1900–1950), was concerned with hereditary deafness.[10] This threefold focus combined short- and long-term goals that targeted both the individual and the population. For a child already deaf, oralist education promised a means to attain the normalcy of hearing society. More and more, this quasi-cure was supported by diagnostics tests and technological devices. Heredity research similarly relied on scientific means and knowledge, but promised preventive long-term relief to the "suffering" of the deaf.

Between Gratification and Confusion: The First Two Decades of Research

Like other institutions and researchers investigating the heredity of mental and physical traits in this period, the school modeled their research methodologies after the principal American institution for human genetic analysis in the 1930s—the Eugenics Record Office (ERO) at Cold Spring Harbor, New York. Founded in 1910 by zoologist Charles Davenport, the ERO cooperated with a wide range of researchers and institutions. One of the researchers associated with the ERO was Steggerda, who had worked closely with Davenport since 1926 and brought the ERO's methodology to the Clarke School. In 1928, he became assistant professor of zoology at Smith College and by 1929 directed the Clarke School heredity research division. In 1930, Steggerda gave up his positions in Northampton to become a full-time researcher at the ERO.[11]

During his short time at the Clarke School, Steggerda was responsible primarily for data analysis and setting up the program. Research and data collection were carried out by two women from Clarke's staff; Ruth Pierce Guilder and her assistant, the teacher and audiologist Louise A. Hopkins. With a BS from Simmons College and an MD from the University of Illinois, Guilder had been working as an editor for the American Medical Association before she came to the Clarke School in 1930. Hopkins had just graduated from Clarke's teacher-training program in 1929 when she became an associate member of the Research Department. She worked there for the rest of her life, administering audiological tests to incoming as well as current students and recorded their general and hereditary health. In 1936, when Guilder left the school due to an illness, Hopkins replaced her as head of the heredity research division.[12]

Anthropologist Morris Steggerda
served as director of the Clarke School
Hereditary Research Division, 1929–
1930. The photograph is from the Hope
College alumni magazine, January
1950. Used by permission of the Joint
Archives of Holland; courtesy of the
University of Massachusetts, Amherst.

The Clarke School investigators faced methodological and analytical problems typical of heredity research in the first decades of the twentieth century. Deafness was a particularly confusing and complex trait. Bell, Edward Allen Fay, and other early researchers had begun their research in the 1880s with a pre-Mendelian understanding of genetics. However, the introduction of the Mendelian principles of dominant and recessive traits by the turn of the century did not do much to clear the picture. In the first half of the century, researchers assumed that deafness came in an unknown number of dominant and mostly recessive forms, yet they could not distinguish them clearly or tie them to a particular gene. The problems of identifying recessive carriers and defining syndromes from a vast array of phenotypical expressions were vexing. This raised eugenic questions about marriage and family planning. Why did marriages of two deaf people sometimes result in hearing children and other times did not? What about their hearing siblings' marriages? Moreover, a large number of infectious diseases, such as measles, mumps or meningitis can cause hearing loss—did these have a hereditary component? In the early decades of the twentieth century it was far from clear where to draw the line between acquired and hereditary causes of deafness. Often, the term congenital was used without clearly distinguishing between hereditary factors and environmental influences on prenatal development.[13] "The many devious ways in which deafness appears and disappears in all these studies," Guilder wrote in a 1931 research report, "make it apparent that the problem is by no means simple." Her division attempted to tackle this complexity with a combination of methods. The "problem of inheritance of deafness," Guilder concluded, "must be approached from three angles: the genetic, the otological and the general medical." She thus anchored their work in two scientific fields that, at the time, were perceived as groundbreaking and highly promising of practical application.[14]

The school set out to gather genetic, medical and otological information from the students and their families. Just as the ERO field workers did, Guilder and Hopkins visited students' families, inquiring about the incidence of deafness and other possibly connected traits. Interviews, questionnaires or family histories could be used to create pedigrees that, in turn, were analyzed for Mendelian patterns. Information from the children's medical records, collected and updated by Guilder and Hopkins, added to the genealogical data. Outside physicians, geneticists, neurophysiologists, or anthropologists also examined some of the children and made the program a multi-disciplinary and multi-institutional affair.[15]

Audiological measurements offered another way to distinguish between different types of deafness. Audiometers, devices that measure the range of hearing by generating the respective range of sound, had been developed soon after the invention of the telephone. Bell himself had constructed one of the first types and by the 1880s, commercially produced models were available. As these early models were still rather unreliable, the school long had mainly depended on teachers' experience to evaluate a student's degree of hearing loss. This changed by the early 1920s, when the first electric audiometers were developed and replaced subjective judgement with a more objective and scientific assessment. The Clarke School had purchased its first audiometer in 1924, and by the 1930s used a smaller and more affordable electric model. Hopkins, who had expanded her qualifications in 1936 with an MS in audiology, administered hearing tests to incoming students and—if their pedigree revealed other cases of hearing loss—their families.[16]

Guilder's and Hopkins' tests helped them develop four different categories of hearing loss that "served as a working basis for both scientific and educational purposes." Heredity and audiological research combined to benefit the school in their quest to understand and ameliorate deafness. An individual's profile, Guilder explained, was the base for a successful oralist education. At the same time, she continued it was "in many ways . . . the foundation for our research in the heredity of deafness."[17]

As extensive hearing tests became the school's standard, it was no longer enough just to know that a child was deaf. Now, one needed to know the exact type and degree of an individual's hearing loss. This stricter classification went hand in hand with a relabeling of those affected. With the advent of oralist education, the use of old labels such as "deaf-mute"or "deaf and dumb" had been discouraged and consecutively replaced by a simple "deaf" in the names of schools and institutions. Associations like the NAD, too, engaged in public awareness campaigns to project a more able and positive image of deaf people. Distancing deaf people from associations with mental disability was an important part of this endeavor.[18] At the same time, however, deafness increasingly became a condition to be identified, monitored and treated not only by educational, but also by medical and audiological interventions. The increasing emphasis on the medical and technological aspects of deafness during this period thus went hand in with redefining who a deaf person could become. While oralism promised normalization via these means, it also pathologized identities beyond this strongly medicalized framework.

In 1931, Steggerda, Guilder, and Hopkins presented their first "Report of the Research Department." Mainly a collection of (hand-drawn) pedigrees, divided into hereditary, non-hereditary, and mixed cases, it correlated deafness with data on birth date and place, cause of death and general health, and noted characteristics such as "Alcoholism," "Tuberculosis," or "Feeble-minded." Rather cautiously, the report noted higher rates of hearing impairment in combination with tuberculosis, "circulatory diseases," and inflammatory ear conditions. Yet the researchers' limited analytic means allowed no judgement about whether these characteristics and diseases were a result of environmental or hereditary factors. Rather than defining clearly identifiable types, the study mainly confirmed the notion that some forms of deafness were indeed hereditary. General eugenic and oralist preconceptions influenced analysis of the findings. Pedigree 4, an example of three generations of deafness, "illustrates the idea of 'like marrying like.'" This, the authors warned, "is a dangerous practice when the heredity of an abnormality is involved." Six years and many pedigrees, audiograms, and examinations later, the division did not know much more about the genetic basis of deafness. "It is still too early," Guilder summarized in the 1936–37 report, "to undertake a detailed analysis or to determine the final significance of this material."[19]

After Guilder retired in 1936, Louise Hopkins continued to collect pedigree and health information from incoming students, tested their hearing, and filed the data. In 1939, the school invited geneticist Madge T. Macklin to analyze the material accumulated since Steggerda's time at Clarke. Macklin, a Johns Hopkins–trained clinician, had been an outspoken advocate for eugenics and genetics in medical education and practice since the 1920s. The Clarke School, with its clear preventive goals, ambitions for furthering education on the principles of heredity, and ties to earlier eugenic research, was naturally of interest to her. The school gave Macklin access to their vast collection of pedigrees and medical data, as well as the chance to educate an allegedly high-risk population. Delayed by wartime restrictions, the result of this cooperation, the *Clarke School Studies Concerning the Heredity of Deafness* (Studies) was at last published in 1949. Conceding that analysis had not progressed enough for "accurate predictions," the 162-page volume was more a call for "cooperative analysis" than a conclusive statement. The Clarke School remained, as Hopkins had written in 1946, "extremely concerned and puzzled by the problem of inheritance of deafness."[20]

Applied Research: Education, Counseling, and Normalization

Despite the monograph's inconclusive results—a characteristic it shared with other contemporary publications on hereditary deafness— the *Studies* had a keenly interested readership. The Clarke School material became part of an international set of pedigrees scientists employed to theorize about different hereditary types of hearing loss and their connections with other disorders. Over the next decade, scientists and laymen from all over the world wrote to the school for information or advice. Outside researchers requested copies of the pedigree information as data for use in their own research. Among these were Japanese geneticist Toshiyuki Mori, Egyptian Hearing Center researchers, and Dutch physician L. S. Wildervanck after whom a syndromic form of deafness is named. The Clarke School material thus became part of an international set of pedigrees that scientists used to theorize about different types of genetic hearing loss. The Dutch ophthalmologist and geneticist Petrus Johannes Waardenburg, for example, referred to the school's pedigrees to argue for the existence of several different recessive forms.[21]

The school also received more personal letters. Persons with a family history of hearing loss, or in which a family member intended to marry a deaf person, inquired about the probability of having deaf or hearing offspring. Even though the then-current knowledge did not allow for a reliable prognosis, the school self-confidently maintained their expertise for anything pertaining to deafness.[22]

With their mixture of genetic advice and research the school shared some important qualities with the heredity clinics that had emerged in the early 1940s. These clinics, including the ones located at the University of Michigan, Wake Forest University Medical School, or the Dight Institute for Human Genetics at the University of Minnesota, pursued the medical and eugenic goals of preventing and relieving suffering for both individuals and in the wider population. For this, they, like the Clarke School, relied on counseling as the only available form of treatment. Like the Dight Institute's Sheldon Reed, one of the founding figures of genetic counseling, school officials assumed that once adequately educated on genetic risk, the desire for a "normal" family would guide alumni's reproductive decisions.[23]

Unlike the heredity clinics which narrowly focused on genetics, medicine, and reproduction, counseling at the Clarke School was embedded in a larger network of pedagogy and research encompassing all aspects of deafness. With their work, Guilder explained, the division would eventually "be of greater assistance to the teachers through our studies of the individual child. It is our hope that the study of each child may begin at the time he enters school and continue through the years of his attendance."[24] In addition to their scientific work, Guilder and Hopkins served as the school's audiologists, health center staff, and heredity counselors. In their work, they accumulated new knowledge on deafness, interpreted it and, in turn, applied their expertise with the goal of preventing deafness in future generations. Serving as both the school's health workers and researchers offered Guilder and Hopkins the double reward of scientific exploration and the gratification offered by the role of the altruistic teacher and counselors. They identified at least as much with the school's mission of providing individualized education as with the more abstract eugenic applications of their research. In particular, the school's use of audiological profiles demonstrates how closely intertwined were the short-term goals of special education and the long-term goals of heredity research. A student's audiogram, medical file, and pedigree served as indicators of his or her educational needs and potential. The accumulation of these varied records provided school staff with information to reduce the impact of deafness on the level of student education, medicine, and heredity.

Like at the ERO and the hereditary clinics, the Clarke School's hereditary research pursued two goals—accumulating and analyzing data on hereditary factors and, at the same time, educating those affected as well as their family members, physicians, or teachers. Talks to "prospective teachers and graduate students" from Smith College and "a group of social workers and public health nurses who are members of the Hampshire County Social Welfare Workers' Club" targeted those who might come into contact with deaf persons. At least as important were the "demonstration and interpretation of family charts . . . given to the members of our own graduating class." "Upon request," Guilder reported, "those who wished it were given an opportunity for individual conferences." Whether these were mandatory was not noted, though presumably participation was at least recommended, if not expected. Through such activities, heredity research merged with education and applied eugenics. Clarke's graduating students had been prepared for secondary education, marriage, or professional life through years of rigorous oral education. With their normalcy and fitness for participating in hearing society thus established, this group now received additional advice on their genetic makeup in order to perpetuate their normalcy in future generations.[25]

Eugenicists' focus on biological limits and educators' emphasis of human malleability have often been considered incompatible paradigms. Historian Diane B. Paul concluded that hereditary determinism contradicted the American belief in education and experience. "Eugenicists," she wrote, "had to counter the powerful American faith in education and in the efficacy of moral effort."[26] The Clarke School, however, reconciled both strands. Unlike in contemporary debates about feeblemindedness, it was not the (hereditary) hearing status that implied a person's worth, but his or her ability to overcome his handicap through the laborious effort of learning oral communication and thus to pass as "normal." Hard work, the school never tired of repeating, was rewarded with acceptance by and success in hearing society. Assessing a child—and by extension his family—for hereditary deafness did not necessarily change this set of values. Within the larger scheme of eliminating the plight of the deaf, heredity research was yet another new and promising tool to prevent deafness or even eradicate it in the future.

Conclusion

Until its closure in 1983, the Clarke School heredity division operated under a consistent paradigm. The school had been founded to prove the inherent normalcy of deaf people, profiting from the rise of oralism that dismissed sign language as socially isolating and educationally outdated. The oralist ideal promised the inspirational success of overcoming disability and isolation in order to realize one's full human potential. This was not only an educational achievement, but increasingly also one of science and medicine. In both realms—the teaching of speech and the use of medicine and assistive or diagnostic technology—the Clarke School saw itself as a pioneer.

Whether applied at the individual or a general level, the Clarke School research points to the ongoing medicalization and professionalization of deafness throughout the twentieth century. Along with educators and psychologists, geneticists and audiologists increasingly appropriated deafness as their field of expertise. In this hierarchy of knowledge, agency was transferred from students and their families to the teachers and scientists who applied their expertise. Whether or not Clarke's alumni eventually followed their advice, research and counseling marked their encounters with the medical world during their school years and beyond.

Education, research and counseling intertwined, demonstrating the comprehensive character of oralist schooling. The school espoused the position that teachers, parents, and physicians were not the only parties who should be aware of the cause and extent of the students' hearing loss. The children, too, the school maintained, needed to learn about their condition's character and its implications. Only with this information could they navigate doctor visits, effectively use available adaptive technology, and make the "right" decision when it came to starting a "normal" family.

Clarke's oralist education prepared students for appearing as normal as possible for a life as self-supporting citizens in hearing society.

In the eyes of the school, access to citizenship relied on normalcy, and to some extent, this normalcy relied on the medicalization of deafness. In order to restore deaf students to hearing standards, it was necessary to first determine how they differed on the psychological, audiological, and medical levels. The school's research was to provide valuable insights for this enterprise. Medicalization thus was a double-sided enterprise. While the oralist paradigm praised the inherent normalcy of the deaf, its reliance on science and medicine marked them as different.

At the Clarke School, the perpetuation of normalcy was not achieved through crude force or coercion. Unlike other agencies of the period, the school avoided a simplistic biological determinism that denied the potential of full human development to those labelled as defective. Rather, theirs was a persuasive paternalism that assumed medical and cultural agency over its students. Just as teachers steered students away from the conspicuous use of sign language and other expressions of Deaf culture, the school aimed to instill in them a sense of responsibility for preventing deafness in future generations. The school's oralist paradigm portrayed citizenship and participation in hearing society as its ultimate goal. Yet maintaining these elusive ideals came with the price of forfeiting linguistic and reproductive choices to cultural norms.

Notes

1. Clarke School for the Deaf, *The Coolidge Fund for the Clarke School and the Deaf*, 6, 23. For the history of the Clarke School, see Numbers, *My Words Fell on Deaf Ears*.

2. Kline, *Building a Better Race*, 2.

3. Carey, "2003. Beyond the Medical Model," 413; Burch, *Signs*; Robinson, "We are a Different Class," 5–21.

4. Tuchman, "Diabetes and 'Defective' Genes," 1–33; Burch, *Signs*, 133.

5. Bell, *Memoir*. For an in-depth discussion, see Greenwald, "Alexander Graham Bell through the Lens of Eugenics, 1883—1922"; For recent references to Bell, see e.g., Arnos, "Genetics and Deafness: Impacts on the Deaf Community," 150–68; Nance, "The Genetics of Deafness," 109–19.

6. Numbers, *Words*, 33; Bell, "Report of the Corporation," 7–10.

7. Yale, *Years of Building*, 293; Clarke School, *Coolidge Fund*, 9–11.

8. For the history of deaf organizations see e.g., Van Cleve and Crouch, *A Place of Their Own*, 87–97. For the Volta Bureau, see Greenwald, "Alexander Graham Bell," 23, 66.

9. Clarke School, *Coolidge Fund*, 3, 17, 18, 42–8.

10. Eberhardt, "Report of the Research Department," (1929): 25; Clarke School, *Coolidge Fund*, 48.

11. For Davenport and the ERO see e.g., Witkowski, "Charles Benedict Davenport, 1866–1944," 36–58; Allen, "The Eugenics Record Office at Cold Spring Harbor, 1910–1940: An Essay in Institutional History," 225–64. For Steggerda see Sledzik, The Morris Steggerda Human Biology Collection, 281–86.

12. Biographical sketches of Ruth Guilder and Louise Alice Hopkins, Clarke School Archive.

13. See e.g., Tinkle, "Deafness as a Eugenical Problem," who assumed the involvement of two pairs of recessive genes; Hopkins, Louise A. and Richard H. Post, "Deafmutism in Two Pairs of Identical Twins," 87–90.

14. Guilder, "Report of the Research Department," (1931): 28; Ibid., "Report of the Research Department," (1932): 25.

15. Numbers, *Words*, 101; Guilder, "Report of the Research Department," (1931): 27–9; Ibid., "Report of the Research Department," (1932): 25–9. For the Eugenic Record Office field workers, see Bix, "Experiences and Voices," 625–68.

16. Hopkins, "Influence of the Type"; Numbers, *Words*, 81, 101; For the development of audiometers, see Stephens, "Audiometers from Hughes," 17–23.

17. Numbers, *Words*, 102; Guilder, "Report of the Research Department," (1935): 26; Ibid., "Report of the Research Department," (1933): 36.

18. Burch, *Signs*, 36.

19. Sledzik, The Morris Steggerda Human Biology Collection: 281–86.; Guilder, "Report of the Research Department," (1931): 14, 90; Hopkins, "Report of the Research Department," (1937): 27.

20. Reiter, "Report of the Principal," 17–22; Hopkins, "Report of the Research Department," (1930): 41; Hopkins and Guilder, *Clarke School Studies*, (1939): 3. Both Macklin and Hopkins had published their analyses of the material before 1949. See Macklin, "Studies on the Inheritance," 570–82; Ibid., 583–601. For information on Macklin's work, see Comfort, "'Polyhybrid Heterogeneous Bastards,'" 415–55.

21. Toshyuki Letter to Hopkins, 17 January 1957; Wildervanck Letter to Hopkins, 28 March 1953; Letter to Hopkins, 10 July 1951; Waardenburg, "Intermarriages of Hereditarily Deaf Mute and of Hereditarily Blind People, Marriage Counselling and the Question of Sterilization," 113–21.

22. Connor, Letter of 4 June 1956, Correspondence Hereditary Deafness.

23. For the history of hereditary clinics and counseling, see e.g., Stern, *Telling Genes*; Comfort, *The Science of Human Perfection*, ch. 4; Ladd-Taylor, "'A Kind of Genetic Social Work'," 67–83.

24. Guilder, "Report of the Research Department" (1932): 28.

25. Ibid., "Report of the Research Department" (1937): 28, 29. Hopkins, "Report of the Research Department" (1940): 41.

26. Paul, *Controlling Human Heredity*, 11.

References

Allen, Garland E. "The Eugenics Record Office at Cold Spring Harbor, 1910–1940: An Essay in Institutional History." *Osiris 2nd series* 2 (1986): 225–64.

Annual Reports of the Clarke School for the Deaf. Northampton, Massachusetts. Northampton, MA: Metcalf Printing Company, 1920–1983.

Arnos, Kathleen S. "Genetics and Deafness: Impacts on the Deaf Community." *Sign Language Studies* 2, no. 2 (2002): 150–68.

Bell, Alexander Graham. *Memoir Upon the Formation of a Deaf Variety of the Human Race.* Washington, DC: U.S. Government Printing Office, 1884.

Bell, Alexander Graham. "Report of the Corporation," *Fifty-Fourth Annual Report of the Clarke School for the Deaf. Northampton, Mass. For the Year Ending August 31, 1921.* Northampton, MA: Metcalf Printing Company, 1921, 7–10.

Bix, Amy Sue. "Experiences and Voices of Eugenics Field-Workers: 'Women's Work' in Biology." *Social Studies of Science* 27 (1997): 625–68.

Burch, Susan. *Signs of Resistance: American Deaf Cultural History, 1900 to World War II.* New York: New York University Press, 2002.

Carey, Allison. "Beyond the Medical Model: A Reconsideration of 'Feeblemindedness,' Citizenship, and Eugenic Restrictions." *Disability & Society* 18, no. 4 (2003): 413.

Clarke School Archive, Division for Hereditary Deafness, Northampton, MA. (Relocated to the University of Massachusetts, Amherst Archives).

Clarke School for the Deaf, Northampton, Mass. *The Coolidge Fund for the Clarke School and the Deaf.* New York, 1929.

Comfort, Nathaniel C. "'Polyhybrid Heterogeneous Bastards': Promoting Medical Genetics in America in the 1930s and 1940s." *Journal of the History of Medicine and Allied Sciences* 61 (2006): 415–55.

Comfort, Nathaniel C. *The Science of Human Perfection: How Genes Became the Heart of American Medicine.* New Haven: Yale University Press, 2012.

Connor, Clarence D. 4 June 1956, Correspondence Hereditary Deafness, File 3, Drawer 3, Clarke School Archive, Division for Hereditary Deafness. 4 June 1956.

Eberhardt, Margarete. "Report of the Research Department." *Clarke School Annual Report* (1929): 25.

Greenwald, Brian H. "Alexander Graham Bell through the Lens of Eugenics, 1883–1922." PhD diss., The George Washington University, 2006.

Guilder, Ruth. "Report of the Research Department." *Clarke School Annual Report* (1931): 28.

——. "Report of the Research Department." *Clarke School Annual Report* (1932): 25–29.

——. "Report of the Research Department." *Clarke School Annual Report* (1933): 36.

——. "Report of the Research Department." *Clarke School Annual Report* (1935): 26

Hopkins, Louise A. "Report of the Research Department." *Clarke School Annual Report* (1930): 41.

———. "Report of the Research Department." *Clarke School Annual Report* (1937): 27.

———. "The Influence of the Type of Audiogram upon the Child's Ability to Interpret Speech Sounds." MS thesis, Massachusetts State College, Amherst Massachusetts, 1939.

———. "Studies on the Inheritance of Deafness in the Pupils of the Clarke School for the Deaf; the Collection of Family Histories, Pedigrees and Audiometer Readings." *The Laryngoscope.* 56, no. 10 (1946): 570–82.

Hopkins, Louise A., and Richard H. Post. "Deafmutism in Two Pairs of Identical Twins." *Journal of Heredity* 47, no. 2 (1956): 87–90.

Hopkins, Louise A., and Ruth P. Guilder. *Clarke School Studies Concerning the Heredity of Deafness: Pedigree Data 1930–1940.* Northampton, MA: The Clarke School, 1949.

Kline, Wendy. *Building a Better Race: Gender, Sexuality, and Eugenics from the Turn of the Century to the Baby Boom.* Berkeley: University of California Press, 2001.

Ladd-Taylor, Molly. "'A Kind of Genetic Social Work': Sheldon Reed and the Origins of Genetic Counseling." In *Women, Health and Nation: Canada and the United States since 1945,* edited by Georgina D. Feldberg, 67–83. Montréal: McGill-Queen's University Press, 2003.

Macklin, Madge T. "Studies on the Inheritance of Deafness in the Pupils of the Clarke School for the Deaf; Genetic analysis of Data and Pedigrees." *The Laryngoscope* 56, no. 10 (1946): 583–601.

Nance, Walter E. "The Genetics of Deafness." *Mental Retardation and Developmental Disabilities Research Reviews* 9, no. 2 (2003): 109–19.

Numbers, Mary E. *My Words Fell on Deaf Ears: An Account of the First Hundred Years of the Clarke School for the Deaf.* Washington, DC: Alexander Graham Bell Association for the Deaf, 1974.

Paul, Diane B. *Controlling Human Heredity: 1865 to the Present.* Atlantic Highlands, NJ: Humanities Press, 1995.

Reiter, Frank H. "Report of the Principal." *Clarke School Annual Report* (1939): 17–22.

Robinson, Octavian. "'We are a Different Class.' Ableist Rhetoric in Deaf America 1880-1920." In *Deaf and Disability Studies: Interdisciplinary Perspectives,* edited by Susan Burch and Alison Kafer. Washington, DC: Gallaudet University Press, (2001): 5–21.

Sledzik, Paul S. The Morris Steggerda Human Biology Collection Ethnological Series at the National Museum of Health and Medicine, 281–86. Washington, DC, 2001.

Stephens, S. D. "Audiometers from Hughes to Modern Times." *British Journal of Audiology* Supplement 2 (1979): 17–23.

Stern, Alexandra. *Telling Genes: the Story of Genetic Counseling in America*. Baltimore: Johns Hopkins University Press, 2012.

Tinkle, William John. "Deafness as a Eugenical Problem." PhD diss., The Ohio State University, 1932.

Toshyuki, Mori. Letter to Louise Hopkins, January 17, 1957.

Tuchman, Arleen. M. "Diabetes and 'Defective' Genes in the Twentieth-Century United States." *Journal of the History of Medicine and Allied Sciences* 70, no. 1 (2013): 1–33. doi: 10.1093/jhmas/jrt037.

Van Cleve, John V., and Barry A. Crouch. *A Place of Their Own: Creating the Deaf Community in America*. Washington, DC: Gallaudet University Press, 1989.

Waardenburg, Petrus Johannes. "Intermarriages of Hereditarily Deaf Mute and of Hereditarily Blind People, Marriage Counselling and the Question of Sterilization." *Acta Genetica Et Statistica Medica* 6, no. 1 (1956): 113–21.

Wildervanck, L. S. Letter to Louise Hopkins, 28 March 1953.

Witkowski, Jan A. "Charles Benedict Davenport, 1866–1944." In *Davenport's Dream: 21st Century Reflections on Heredity and Eugenics* edited by Jan. A. Witkowski and J. R. Inglis. Cold Spring Harbor, NY: Cold Spring Harbor Laboratory Press, (2008): 36–58.

Yale, Caroline Ardelia. *Years of Building: Memories of a Pioneer in a Special Field of Education*. New York: L. MacVeagh, The Dial Press; Toronto: Longmans, Green, 1931.

11

The "Breakaways": Deaf Citizens' Groups in Australia in the 1920s and 1930s

Breda Carty

IN THE LATE 1920s AND EARLY 1930s, a spate of newspaper stories reported on "wild meetings" and "breakaways" among Deaf organizations in Australia. New national organizations were formed, and disappeared within a few years. Deep divisions emerged about the rights of deaf people to control their organizations and "manage their own affairs." In a large country with a small population, just thirty years after self-government, these developments seem unusually turbulent. Examination of the disputes and the people involved shows that ideas of citizenship, autonomy, and ownership were key issues, and that these movements within Deaf organizations paralleled those in some other marginalized groups in Australia, who were also agitating for autonomy and for the right to be treated as citizens.

Other groups were also seeking equality and a voice in public affairs during the 1920s and 1930s, and using the idea of "citizenship" as a way of articulating their aims. Australian women, who had gained the vote in 1902, continued to organize and educate each other. The Australian Federation of Women Voters, active during the 1920s, was originally called the Australian Federation of Societies for Equal Citizenship, and was committed to the goal of social equality.[1] Members educated each other in the skills needed for good citizenship, such as running meetings, debating, public speaking, and using the media; and sought involvement in national and international organizations which embodied their aims, such as the League of Nations.[2] Aboriginal Australians were also beginning to organize as "citizens," although this happened to a greater extent in the 1930s.[3]

Deaf people appear in Australian history from the beginnings of British colonization in 1788, with a number of deaf convicts transported from Britain and Ireland.[4] Deaf children occasionally appeared in the records of the early colonial period; some of them were sent back to Britain to be educated. The first schools for deaf children appeared in Sydney and Melbourne in 1860, and were established in other parts of the country over the next several decades. As adult Deaf communities began to grow in the capital cities during the second half of the nineteenth century, they and their supporters began to establish Deaf Societies (sometimes called "Missions") modeled on the organizations that were then widespread in Britain.[5] These institutions have been described by Ladd, and their organization and activities are recorded in the British Deaf newspapers of the time, such as *The British Deaf-Mute* and *The British Deaf Times*.[6] Deaf Societies were usually established as Christian missions, with church services and welfare services for Deaf people providing their rationale and the basis of their charitable fundraising. However, they also served as social and sporting centers for Deaf communities, and were the primary centers of adult Deaf socialization and support.[7]

In Australia, Deaf Societies began to emerge in the 1880s, and by the early decades of the twentieth century, each state had its own Deaf Society. Deaf people were usually very active in the beginnings of these organizations, working with hearing allies to establish them, raise funds for them, participate on their boards of management, and occasionally to work for them (Deaf leaders in these organizations included, for example, Eugene Salas in South Australia, Samuel Showell in Queensland, and James Johnston in Victoria).[8]

As in Britain, Australian Deaf Societies were charitable institutions which employed a system of "collectors" to travel throughout the state and solicit regular donations (which were known as subscriptions) from the public. This was the funding model used by most charitable organizations in Australia at that time, including early Deaf schools. The charitable collection system was regulated by state governments, which issued licenses to approved organizations. During the late nineteenth and early twentieth centuries, Australian Deaf Societies in all states were able to raise enough capital to buy buildings and employ "welfare" staff to support Deaf people.

Once Deaf Societies had been established—which usually involved close collaboration between Deaf communities and hearing allies or sometimes family members—the new organizations began recruiting prominent citizens onto their boards of management. The politicians, lawyers, religious leaders, and businessmen who took these roles not only contributed their expertise and reputations, they also fulfilled the public's ideas of how charities should be administered, and ways in which successful men (they were always men) should contribute to society. Charity was the responsibility of the affluent and altruistic.[9] By the 1920s these hearing men were becoming entrenched and powerful, and funds and publicity for the Deaf societies depended on the particular image of benevolent hearing people "looking after" Deaf people. Deaf people, even those who had been active in setting up the Deaf societies, often seemed to accept this portrayal of them, with one prominent Deaf leader, Fletcher Booth, saying in 1922:

> . . . we can trust the hearing Board to look after the interests of the Deaf and Dumb. . . . The best way is to leave our troubles and disputes and grievances to the hearing Board of Management, they will look after us very well.[10]

Despite such comments, their increasing marginalization by boards of management concerned many Deaf people, and these dissatisfactions became more prevalent when arrivals from other countries told stories of more active and autonomous Deaf organizations elsewhere. By the end of the 1920s conflict was brewing within the Deaf societies of New South Wales (hereafter NSW), Queensland, and Victoria. As Deaf people sought to define themselves in opposition to the charity model of the Deaf societies, they used the idea of citizenship and the insistence on their right to manage their own affairs to describe their aspirations.

The Breakaway in New South Wales

The Adult Deaf and Dumb Society of New South Wales (NSW) was established in 1913. Deaf people had been active for several years in the struggle for its existence and felt a sense of pride and ownership of the organization, especially when it purchased its first permanent building in the city center in 1927. By that time its board had recruited many high-profile professional hearing men, and had amassed enough funds to not only purchase its first social and administration center, but also to recruit a missioner from Britain to replace the largely volunteer workers who had been managing the Society by providing welfare and interpreting assistance to Deaf people and leading their church services.

The missioner they recruited, Herbert Hersee, was not who the conservative board members expected. He was a young man with Deaf parents active in British Deaf organizations, and he had grown up seeing his father work as a missioner in North London—one of a number of Deaf missioners working throughout Britain in the mid- to late nineteenth century. Hersee had been a pilot in the First World War and had forged connections with the service organization Toc H (Talbot House), established on the Western Front.[11] He himself had worked as a missioner with Deaf people in Portsmouth, where he had a reputation as an energetic, forward-thinking leader, who believed in providing access for Deaf people to the activities, philosophies, and practices of other organizations. He was reported to have written in his first annual letter to Portsmouth mission members saying, "I found it necessary to drop a bomb, for you were all asleep."[12]

Hersee appears to have galvanized the NSW Deaf community and supported them in challenging the controlling practices of the board. In the months after his arrival, Deaf leaders, such as Fletcher Booth, became more active in requesting access to information and demanding a greater role in the workings of the Society. Booth later wrote about an unsuccessful meeting with the Society's board to discuss these issues:

> The Executive's policy was apparently to keep information and knowledge away from the deaf: they did not want them to know what was being said at the meetings and this despite the fact that the society was reared up by the deaf and dumb themselves after many years of hard work.[13]

Another Deaf leader, Ernest Quinnell, challenged the board to employ more Deaf workers in the Society, and pointed out that board members did not employ any Deaf workers in their own companies.[14] Their complaints were dismissed and the board chair emphasized that an organization such as the Deaf Society must be firmly controlled by its executive, "with all the weight of our names."[15] This reflects the view of many similar charity boards that well-known and influential men were essential for raising funds from the public and instilling confidence that the organization would be well-managed. This was destined to clash with Deaf people's feelings of ownership of such organizations and their aspirations for more autonomy. As elsewhere in the world, these events were taking place against the backdrop of economic, political, and social upheaval. During the first months of 1929, Australian government efforts

Fletcher Booth, deaf leader of the New South Wales breakaway. Courtesy of The Deaf Society.

to contain financial crises and lower wages led to strikes by waterside workers, timber workers, and miners. Unions, Communists, and the unemployed frequently led demonstrations, which sometimes became violent. The conservative government was crumbling amid increasing anti-Empire sentiment, more people were becoming disillusioned with those in power, and dole queues were growing longer.[16] Although there is no direct evidence of Hersee's or the Deaf community's response to these developments, it was a time when a dissatisfied minority group, such as theirs, could readily take inspiration from events happening around them.

After almost a year of increasing tensions with the board of the Deaf Society, Hersee was dismissed from his position on May 8, 1929.[17] A meeting of Deaf people was scheduled at the Society for that evening, and attended by over 100 people. As news of Hersee's dismissal spread,

the gathering transformed into what was later described as a "demonstration"[18] and a "riot."[19] Fletcher Booth and other Deaf people addressed their outrage at Hersee's dismissal. Newspaper reporters were
soon on the scene, and watched as deaf people smashed framed photographs of the board President and Executive Officer, throwing one
into a urinal and turning the other to face the wall. The next day a
Sydney Morning Herald reporter attempted to describe the unusual scene
of rebellion:

> Fists were flourished . . . Hats were thrown into the air. Those
> persons who were not entirely voiceless shrieked with excitement.
> Others stamped and clapped their hands. The noise could be heard
> out in the street.[20]

The Society's caretaker summoned the police, but the lone constable
who arrived found himself unexpectedly out of his depth when he loud-
ly told the crowd to leave the hall. "Although nobody could hear him,
everyone understood his mission," observed the same *Herald* reporter.
However, instead of a docile and obedient retreat, "someone wrote on
the blackboard, 'We are a hundred to one,' and those present showed
that they intended to stand their ground." The constable called for re-
inforcements, but the five additional police officers who arrived were no
more effective, "—and so the meeting continued until 10 o'clock, when
it disbanded. The police thankfully left."[21] In this altercation, the reporters were observing a classic Deaf strategy of defiance—even when the
shouted words and flailing gestures of the hearing are transparent, Deaf
people choose to retain their privilege of "not hearing."
     The article, appearing in the *Sydney Morning Herald* the next day,
was accompanied on the following page by a photograph of a score of
Deaf people emerging from the building, smiling broadly, waving ju-
bilantly at photographers, and throwing their hats in the air. It was an
image of people asserting independence and equality, not one of meek
and grateful recipients of charity.
     Hersee and his Deaf supporters acted swiftly. When they found
themselves locked out of the Society's building on the following night,
they "formed a silent procession to the Headquarters of Toc H in
Hamilton-street where they held a breakaway meeting under the Chair-
manship of Mr. Hersee . . ."[22] It was at this meeting that the decision to
form a new organization was made, with Hersee as Superintendent and

Secretary. Gordon Winn, a former councilor and life member of the Deaf Society, who immediately switched his allegiance to the new organization, guaranteed Hersee's salary for three months, but did not have to pay it, as Deaf people raised enough funds themselves.[23]

The breakaway group quickly established itself as a viable alternative and rival to the Deaf Society. It was initially called the New South Wales Society for the Adult Deaf and Dumb.[24] However, within a few weeks it was re-named the New South Wales Association of Deaf and Dumb Citizens.[25] It was usually referred to as the "Association" as distinct from the "Society." Its new name not only avoided any possible legal injunction from the Deaf Society against the use of a similar name, but also signaled a clear departure from other Australian Deaf organizations. All of the existing Deaf Societies had been established with the British mission model as their management method, which—even with extensive Deaf involvement—was predicated on the need for Deaf people to be supported and given succor by benevolent helpers. Identifying themselves as "citizens" was these Deaf people's rejection of this model. As citizens, Deaf people declared that they had the same rights as everyone else to a free, public education (not yet guaranteed for Deaf children in NSW), jobs at the basic wage, and independent access to government support if needed. They also declared that they were capable of fulfilling the obligations of citizens, such as providing assistance to others and participating in civic duties and in the life of the broader community. Later commentators often affirmed and praised the way the Association fulfilled these obligations. For example, at the Association's Third Annual General Meeting in 1932, the NSW attorney general declared that its members fulfilled the "obligations of citizenship"—self respect and social intercourse, and mutual assistance.[26]

The Padre of Toc H, Rev. E. J. Davidson (a hearing man who was elected a vice president of the new Association), wrote soon afterwards:

> The Deaf and Dumb of this city of Sydney have passed through a troublous time. Through the failure of that fine sensitiveness which is the characteristic mark of gentlemen, they have been subjected to treatment worthy only of naughty children . . . the writer has no hesitation in appealing to all friends of the deaf and dumb to support them in this courageous attempt to secure that measure of self-determination which is surely the prerogative of any and every citizen, whether he can hear or not![27]

Davidson said elsewhere in the article, "They do not need, nor do they want, our 'Charity'." He signaled the key themes which were to be articulated by the new Association. The Association held the position that Deaf people were not children, they were capable of self-determination and of managing their own affairs, and they rejected "charity" and claimed equality with hearing people and the rights of citizens.

The Deaf Society's annual general meeting was held on August 23 of that year, and members' perceived what seemed to them, a grim indication of the new state of affairs. Fletcher Booth described it as follows:

> The Annual Meeting of the Society was awaited with anxiety, in the hope that things would improve and reconciliation take place. About 200 deaf and dumb from the Association, accompanied by sympathizing supporters, attended the Annual Meeting in August, 1929, and were surprised to find that the Executive of the Society already had the police patrolling the hall, even before the meeting commenced.
>
> The meeting turned out to be an utter farce, as several speakers were rudely ordered by the President to sit down, with the assistance of the police; even a Press reporter was asked by the Organizing Secretary, Mrs. Gore Jones, not to report the speeches of any but Executive members. I myself was described to a reporter by an official of the Society as "mentally deficient." . . . Mr. Winn moved an amendment to the Report, and in his speech he was frequently applauded by the deaf for his remarks. The amendment of Mr. Winn was carried by a very large majority, but the Chairman refused to accept the voting result, saying the deaf were not financial members of the Society. This caused a scene of demonstration and protest, as the deaf and dumb always voted at their Annual Meetings for the last fifteen years, and as a demonstration they got up and left the hall. While they were doing this, and with only a very few people remaining, the President declared the Report carried, and the Council elected themselves for another year of office.[28]

Newspaper reports the following day were less restrained. Under the headline, "Wild Meeting. Policemen Present," the *News* described "Rowdy scenes, which terminated in the wildest uproar," reporting that "police officers watched the proceedings from the rear, and were frequently compelled to caution rowdy members."[29]

When the president insisted that only the small number of financial members could vote (a clause in the constitution which had never been invoked before), "Disorder broke loose . . . the audience gesticulating wildly, and the din drowned all efforts of the Committee to restore peace. Intervention of the police, however, somewhat relieved the situation."[30] A similar report was carried in the *Daily Telegraph Pictorial*, which quoted a hearing supporter of Winn's amendment calling out to the president, "You're fooling the deaf and dumb!" The man was "cautioned by a policeman."[31]

While it is astonishing to read of a charitable organization's annual general meeting being patrolled by the police, 1929 was a time of widespread unrest in Australia. Arranging a police presence to deter possible protests was probably a more routine precaution at that time. Newspaper reporters were used to describing scenes of "uproar," "disorder," and police intervention, and may have reverted to such stock phrases to describe these scenes. They were, however, unused to Deaf people being the source of such unrest, and their lack of experience with Deaf people's communication is reflected in their use of phrases such as "gesticulating wildly" to describe sign language being used. This would also indicate that the interpreter at the meeting might not have interpreted everything that Deaf people said. When a reporter wrote that "a man jumped to his feet waving his hands in an effort to be understood," and in the next sentence quoted a hearing person's comments verbatim, they provide a useful reminder that most of what survives is the commentary of the hearing, and that the contributions of Deaf participants have often been reduced to descriptions of people "gesticulating wildly."[32]

The executive committee of the Society continued to dismiss all suggestions that Deaf people should have any significant control of the Society, or even that this was what Deaf people wanted. In a letter to the NSW Minister for Education in July 1930, the Society's president repudiated further proposals for a conference with the Association, and defended the Society's stance on the relative powers of Deaf and hearing people:

> what is called the essential difference between the old Society and the new is on the question of complete self determination and control in what is described as their own affairs, by the Deaf. The policy of our Society from the commencement has been to allow the Deaf as much say and control in the internal and domestic affairs of the Society as is possible by Deaf Committees. It is however, a

definite procedure [*sic*], and has been ever since its formation, that the policy and finances of the Society must necessarily be under the control of an Executive and a Council. On the Executive no Deaf members are considered to be practicable. On the Council there are five deaf members. This arrangement has always worked admirably until the advent of Mr. Hersee, and is still so working.

Brooks did not mention that the council met only a few times a year, whereas the executive committee met monthly (sometimes more frequently), and made almost all administrative and policy decisions for the Society.

The New South Wales Association for Deaf and Dumb Citizens

The Association soon leased premises in central Sydney and acquired a license to employ its own Deaf collectors to travel through the state soliciting public subscriptions just as the Deaf Society continued to do. Hersee was immediately employed as its superintendent-secretary. The Association provided the same services as the Society: welfare work (assistance with employment, domestic, legal, and financial problems), interpreting, church services, and (later) limited accommodation facilities for deaf people from rural areas or those who were temporarily homeless. It also provided a meeting place and a rich variety of social activities, which were important in binding the community together. Deaf people comprised 51 percent or more of the Association's council, and Fletcher Booth soon became its second chairman (the chairman for the first year was Padre Davidson of Toc H). Most of the hearing people on the council had deaf relatives.[33] Rather than having a background executive or finance committee making the decisions, this Association's council had a management committee, composed entirely of Deaf members. Membership was cost-free for all deaf members—the Association's declared policy was that, rather than a fee, "The Council simply look for the good will and support of the Deaf in their efforts on their behalf."[34] The Association published two issues of a magazine called *Onward!* in August 1929 and January 1930, then from December 1930 until 1937, it regularly published a magazine called *The Deaf Advocate*. This magazine, under Deaf editors Fletcher Booth and Ernest Quinnell, soon acquired a national readership. It welcomed letters and articles from those in other states who lacked an outlet for writing about their own grievances, and—for the modern reader—provides a compelling record of the dissident movements in the Australian Deaf community during those years.

The *Advocate* editors made inquiries into other Deaf organizations around the world, to demonstrate that their association was "'in step' with go ahead Deaf organizations" and that the Deaf Society was "out of step."[35] In June 1932, the magazine reported on organizations such as the National Association of the Deaf and the National Fraternal Society of the Deaf (hereafter NSFD), both of which were in the US, and the National Deaf Club in Britain, which they claimed were all "managed by the deaf themselves" or "managed by the deaf exclusively."[36] Organizations, such as the ones they examined, did indeed have similar ideals and used the same rhetoric. The NFSD had asserted as early as 1904 that its work could "give stronger evidence of the ability of the Deaf to manage their own affairs, prove their independence and settle once and for all time the 'object of charity' delusion."[37] The *Advocate* article concluded:

I think I have stated enough for anyone to be convinced of the capabilities of the Adult Deaf in organizing, controlling, or managing their own affairs. IT IS NO LONGER A POSSIBILITY; IT IS AN ACCOMPLISHED FACT.[38]

As the Sydney Deaf community adjusted to their new circumstances, regular club nights and special events tended to be well patronized at both venues. To many Deaf people, that is all the two organizations were—alternate venues. Not all Deaf people understood, or were interested in, the political philosophies behind the two organizations, especially younger Deaf people who had just left school or moved to Sydney from elsewhere. These Deaf people did not have long memories of the Deaf community's efforts to create the Society, and were primarily in search of friendship and entertainment. A series of interviews conducted with older members of the Sydney Deaf community in the 1980s captured some of the memories of people who would have entered the Deaf community in the late 1920s and early 1930s. None of the interviewees volunteered information about the political background of the two organizations, but several remembered the conflicts between them and the disapproval directed at people who attended both. One man remembered:

I went to the Society. There was another place called the Deaf Association. There were two Clubs. I went to one to have a look where my friends went. Then I would go to the other one. People called me "two-faced." They would whisper, "Bob Herman, there's Bob Herman. He goes to the other Club too." I never worried about that. I only wanted to see my friends, my mates so I would go to both of them.[39]

Deaf people probably chose their allegiance for a range of reasons—not only which organization they supported ideologically, but also which one their friends or spouses attended, which had better social functions, which provided the best opportunities for sporting participation (a consideration well exploited by the Society), and—as the Depression took hold—which provided the most practical support.

The breakaway and the establishment of the Association in Sydney had a significant impact on Deaf communities and Societies in other states. Their relationships with the Sydney Deaf community suddenly became more complicated, and a new kind of diplomacy was required when engaging in routine organizational business, such as planning sporting competitions. The seeming success of the Sydney breakaway group provided inspiration or inflammation, depending on one's perspective, to restless and disaffected groups and individuals in other states. A new model for dealing with repression against deaf Australians had suddenly arisen.

Rebellion Spreads

The organizational breakaway in NSW drew attention from Deaf people and organizations around Australia, especially in the adjacent states of Queensland and Victoria. Rumblings of discontent grew louder in many Deaf communities, and found an outlet in *The Deaf Advocate* when it could not be expressed locally. Another breakaway group emerged in Queensland and schisms grew more pronounced in Victoria.

Breakaway Beginnings In Queensland

In Queensland, as in NSW, Deaf community dissatisfaction became more overt after the appointment of a British missioner to the Queensland Adult Deaf and Dumb Mission (the equivalent of the Adult Deaf and

Dumb Society of NSW) in 1927. John M. Paul, the new missioner, was similar to Hersee in many ways—he was also a child of Deaf parents and his father had worked as a missioner and held office in British Deaf organizations. As with Hersee, Paul's progressive views on working with Deaf people were not always compatible with those of the hearing men who dominated the Queensland Mission's board in the 1920s. Paul summarized his views in a succinct comment he made in 1933:

> Every effort which has brought real benefits to the Deaf has been one which enlarged their freedom, increased their opportunities, called for their co-operation and raised their status. The same principles apply to the "hearing" world, so in a sentence it is "To treat the deaf as you treat the hearing."[40]

Paul's experiences in working for the Queensland Mission soon became similar to those of Hersee with the NSW Society. Paul established a firm rapport with the Deaf community, exposed them to ideas about Deaf people's experiences in other states and countries, and was viewed with increasing discomfort by the mission's board. This particular board included a number of teachers of the Deaf, and perhaps because of this, the Mission's rhetoric sometimes echoed that of Australian schools for the Deaf. The Mission's annual reports contain scattered references to Deaf "girls," "boys," and "lads";[41] because the mission seemed to value parental approval, even though its deaf members were adults: "the parents are deeply grateful for all the Mission has done and is still doing for their sons and daughters."[42]

Over the next four years, Paul's relationship with the Mission's board steadily deteriorated. deaf people and their supporters expressed increasing dissatisfaction with the Mission's management methods and treatment of deaf people. In early 1931, a government inquiry was commissioned to review the Mission's management. The commission's report provided revealing insights into competing views of Deaf people. Mr. W. Bradbury, the report's author, after interviews with the Mission board, criticized Paul and his relationship with the Deaf community, cautioning that, "Mr Paul . . . should know that the usually suspicious nature, which is generally apparent in the deaf, should not be inflamed or provoked."[43]

Paul responded to this using angry rhetoric as he pointed out the double standards that were being applied to Deaf people's and their hearing supporters' efforts to seek information and critique the workings of their organizations:

> My deaf friends, it is of no use that you say you have proofs, evidence, first hand information, direct complaints. That according to the moral standards ruling among men of repute you are right. You are only the deaf and dumb, what is praiseworthy among hearing people as a desire for justice, honorable conduct, the upholding of moral standards, the maintenance of common rights IS IN YOU, A SUSPICIOUS NATURE.[44]

The Deaf Advocate in Sydney published this response alongside its detailed coverage of the unrest in Queensland. Deaf leaders in Queensland, such as Alf Eaton, C. C. Garner, and Martha Overend Wilson, as well as John Paul, regularly wrote to *The Deaf Advocate* about their struggles because there were no local Deaf magazines or newspapers in Queensland.

A New Breakaway Association Emerges

The board of the Queensland Mission finally dismissed Paul from his role as superintendent in August, 1931. As in NSW after the dismissal of Hersee, Deaf people and their supporters responded quickly by calling a public meeting to set up an alternative organization. This meeting attracted similar interest from local newspapers, although this time their reporting was thorough and detailed, as Paul interpreted the signing of the Deaf meeting conveners:

> . . . Deaf and Dumb Act . . .
> Members of the Queensland Adult Deaf and Dumb Mission seceded from the organization at a protest meeting held last night . . .
> The meeting . . . was attended by about 100 persons, most of whom were either deaf or dumb, or deaf mutes . . . Convened by Messrs. C. C. Garner and A. Eaton, the meeting was held in the mission rooms, and Mr. G. D. Harrison (a deaf mute) acted as chairman. Consequently, all "speeches" by deaf and dumb members were interpreted by the former superintendent, Mr. Paul. . . .
> The meeting had been convened, stated Mr. C. C. Garner, by the manual language of the deaf and dumb, as a protest against

Martha Overend Wilson. From the collection of Edena Winn.

the dismissal of the superintendent. He had been dismissed and no reason for it given by the committee. They had no faith in the general committee, he said. . . .

The meeting then decided to appoint a provisional committee of four speaking members and four deaf and dumb members, to be augmented later to eight of each. . . .The new name of the society was decided upon as the Queensland Deaf and Dumb Citizens Reformed Association.[45]

The new breakaway association, as in NSW, identified itself as a group of citizens, presenting a clear contrast with the Mission and its paternalistic attitude. Adopting the role of citizens was clearly associated with assuming a greater degree of autonomy and self-management. Garner, a deaf man, later wrote that the actions of the mission committee "inflame[d] the Deaf and provoked them to such extent that they caused us to break away and form a new and free body in which we could have a say in our own affairs."[46]

The breakaway group's management council's records have not survived, but *The Deaf Advocate* reported that it had an equal number of Deaf and hearing councilors.[47] A 1932 newspaper interview with one of the hearing councilors confirmed:

> Our constitution secures to the deaf and dumb representation on the council and the management committee from among their own members. . . . Experience has proved the value of enlisting their sympathy and knowledge of the needs of their fellows in the Land of Silence.[48]

The uneasy coexistence of the new breakaway Association and the initial Queensland Mission led to divisions within some sections of the Deaf community, as had happened in NSW. Young Deaf men were said to taunt those who remained with the original Mission, calling them "scabs."[49] The Mission also allegedly used bribery and intimidation in its efforts to stop their deaf employees from going to the breakaway association, or as a way of enticing them back. M. O. Wilson described "How the Deaf and Dumb stand together in spite of tempting baits held out by the old Society, all the world will be theirs if they will only go back without Mr. Paul . . ."[50] John Paul described the alternatives more starkly: "The Deaf world now knows the fight is on—Fear or Freedom."[51]

Despite the Mission's efforts, it seems that, as in NSW, the majority of Deaf people in Queensland initially supported the new Citizens Reformed Association in its early years. The above-quoted 1932 newspaper article claimed that approximately two-thirds of Deaf people in Queensland had joined the new association.

The upheaval in Queensland drew the attention of other Deaf communities in Australia and overseas. *The Deaf Advocate* in Sydney ran regular reports of the new association and served as a public forum for Paul, Garner and others. The sympathetic editors of the *Advocate* frequently pointed out the similarities between the NSW and Queensland responses to the marginalization of Deaf people, and encouraged Deaf people elsewhere in Australia to take inspiration from them:

> Let us hope that the experiences in New South Wales and in Queensland will be the forerunner of strengthening the Deaf in

other States to safeguard their interests and demand a recognition of their rights, so that they are no longer regarded as incapable of managing their own affairs. These prejudices against the Deaf must be swept away once and for all and co-operation, goodwill, and fellowship must be firmly established.[52]

The *British Deaf Times* also reported on the breakaway in Queensland, concluding one report by saying:

One thing seems paramount from the reports to hand and that is, the status of the deaf needs to be raised in Queensland, and a fuller appreciation of the rights of the deaf to manage their own affairs.[53]

Reports such as this, showing knowledge of events in Australia, indicate that Hersee and Paul were in regular contact with former colleagues in Britain. They also illustrate that the overriding theme of Deaf people "managing their own affairs" was one that resonated broadly during the late 1920s and 1930s, not only within Australia but in other countries' Deaf communities as well.

Progress Slows

The momentum generated by these breakaway organizations had other effects in the Australian Deaf community as well, including the establishment of a new national Deaf organization in 1932—the Australian Association for the Advancement of the Deaf. This organization, and the tactics used by the Deaf societies to isolate and weaken it, are described elsewhere.[54] Its establishment was part of the ferment of activity and new ways of representing themselves that marked the history of Deaf people in Australia at the time. However, this time of political protest and optimism about the possibilities for deaf people's autonomy was short lived.

The general conservative and repressive climate in many western countries during the late 1930s was also reflected in Australian politics and society. For example, during the 1930s, the Australian government cracked down on dissident groups such as communists, by limiting access to public meeting halls, controlling street gatherings and placing restrictions on the kinds of material that could be sent through the mail.[55] Some of the decline in political activism in Australian Deaf communities during the late 1930s and beyond may be attributed to these wider influences, and some situations, such as the dissolution of the NSW Association, were triggered by changes in government legislation that significantly affected Deaf organizations. It was also likely that the small Deaf communities in most states were wearied by the energy required in maintaining opposition to the Deaf Societies, with their connections and resources and control of sites and events culturally important to most Deaf people.

The Demise of the NSW Breakaway Association

The NSW government revised its Charitable Collections Act in 1934. This law set out the conditions under which charitable organizations— such as the Adult Deaf and Dumb Society of NSW and the NSW Association for Deaf and Dumb Citizens—were registered with the state government and authorized to collect subscriptions from the public. The law was revised in an effort to eliminate so-called duplication, and now specified that only one charitable organization for a particular population or cause could be registered. The following year all charitable organizations were informed of the new conditions and invited to apply for registration or exemption under the Act.[56] Both the NSW Association of Deaf and Dumb Citizens and the Adult Deaf and Dumb Society of NSW applied for registration. The Chief Secretary's department replied to both groups, informing them of the other group's application, and of the government's wish to avoid "overlapping and duplication of effort."[57] The two groups were informed that:

> I am desired by the Minister to suggest that the governing bodies of both organizations should make an effort to effect a fusion or amalgamation as this is considered to be the best means of eliminating the possibility of duplication. Furthermore, such a fusion or amalgamation would be in the best interests of the deaf and dumb as well as charitably minded people on whom the institutions are largely dependent.[58]

This set the scene for a long drawn-out and painful amalgamation process between the two organizations, since the new regulations meant that both organizations could not survive financially if they remained separate. Amalgamation negotiations lasted from February 1936 until August 1937. Representatives from each organization met several times in an attempt to come to a resolution that both groups would accept.

Some meetings were chaired by a government representative, since the two organizations could not reach an agreement on their own. All representatives involved with these meetings were hearing men from their respective boards—no Deaf people participated and no records survive of their contributions to the discussions that occurred during the amalgamation process. This absence of their voice starkly contrasts with the richness, variety, and number of records from Deaf peoples' perspective during the early 1930s.

Despite the absence of Deaf people in the negotiations, the issues that the two organizations argued over were essentially about Deaf people's citizenship and ownership of the existing organizations, and how decisions about these matters would be reflected in the new combined organization. The Association representatives initially proposed that both organizations be dissolved, and a new one established, with a provisional committee and an outside chairman. They insisted that Deaf members should have majority representation on this provisional committee and the right to vote.[59] The Society rejected these proposals, assuming that their organization would prevail, with the addition of the Association's members and assets (both of which they obviously saw as theirs by default).

Much of the discussion revolved around each organization's assets and, the associated issues of ownership. The Society detailed their property and other assets, declaring, "It is quite impossible for this Society to give equal representation to an organization with only one-fiftieth part of the Society's Capital." When they reiterated that they brought £38,000 worth of assets to the proposed amalgamation, the Association representatives responded, "That belongs to the deaf."[60] They explained this by saying, "The £38,000 property was raised to a certain extent by our deaf" (i.e., former Deaf members or collectors of the Society who were then Association members). The Association made an intriguing comparison between the situation of Deaf people in NSW and that of the Free Church of Scotland. When this church amalgamated with another to form the United Free Church of Scotland in 1900, a disaffected portion of the original Free Church of Scotland broke away, and were known as the "Wee Frees." This splinter group succeeded in making a valid legal claim for ownership of a proportion of the buildings of the United Free Church of Scotland, since they had constituted part of its original membership.[61] This ingenious comparison was unfortunately dismissed by the government chairperson and thus not pursued, but it was a daring claim. The Society's men considered the assets as theirs; they had been accumulated largely by men of stature like themselves—although their deaf collectors would have done most of the actual fund-raising. The Association's representatives radically proposed that the assets belonged to the workers or those who had toiled to raise the capital for them, and, therefore, the Society could not claim full ownership of the assets. It would be interesting to know if Deaf members of the Association shared their representative's sentiments on this, and to contemplate what might have happened had they decided to pursue such a claim.

Another sticking point in the negotiations was the proportional representation of Deaf people on any new governing body and whether they should have voting rights (since they would always form the majority of the organization's members). The Association's representatives seem to have accepted after a while that their preferred way of forming a new organization would not succeed, and that their task now was arguing for the best deal for their members in the inevitable reabsorption of the Association into the Society. The debate centered on the accommodations the Society should make in the process. One issue was the composition of the Society's board, and the number of Association representatives on it. The Association originally argued that Deaf people should form a board majority, but the Society rejected this out of hand:

> With our knowledge of world wide conditions, we are convinced that this Society must maintain it's [*sic*] present form of administration, and cannot be a party to forming an organization to be controlled by a Council with a balance of power in favor of the Adult Deaf & Dumb.[62]

The two groups eventually negotiated for six Association members out of a total of 16 representatives to serve on the Society's board. Of these six, the representation would consist of three Deaf and three hearing individuals. The Society accepted three hearing people from the Association on its smaller nine-member executive committee, but no Deaf people. Although the Association initially reacted to this offer with indignation, they eventually accepted it.[63] Deaf people's aspirations to manage their own affairs, which had seemed so bright and viable just a few years earlier, slowly became irretrievable.

The Association insisted that Deaf members should have voting privileges, and they argued also that they should pay a lower subscription fee than hearing members. An Association representative maintained that it was reasonable for Deaf people to expect to vote in their organizations, "considering that three-fourths of them are citizens who have a vote in the Government, who have a Municipal vote."[64] However, the Society initially rejected these demands, because Deaf members would always far outnumber hearing members at general organizational meetings. The Society's executive officer reflected their fears of losing control when he expostulated that if they allowed Deaf people to vote, "You would hand the whole thing over to the deaf."[65]

The newly combined Adult Deaf and Dumb Society was granted registration under the Charitable Collections Act in late 1936, but it took several more months of letter writing, meetings, and concessions from the Society before official amalgamation occurred in August 1937.[66] The Society finally agreed to a reduced membership fee for Deaf people and that they would have full voting rights in general meetings; they also promised to employ the Association's staff on a casual basis—with the exception of Hersee. The Association's practice of having Deaf people comprise at least half of the council positions was not adopted, and would not happen again in Australian Deaf societies for more than 50 years.

The NSW Association for Deaf and Dumb Citizens was the first organizational expression of Deaf Australians' desire for autonomy. The debates during its eventual amalgamation with the Society raised unresolved issues of collective Deaf ownership of assets which they had worked to acquire. The Association's articulation of Deaf independence by using the widely accepted "citizen" model influenced Deaf individuals and organizations throughout Australia, and its demise showed the vulnerability of Deaf organizations to the institutions of charity and government.

The Queensland Breakaway Organization's Decline

The Queensland breakaway organization was not affected by similar registration system changes for charitable collections in its state as occurred in NSW. However, the collapse of the NSW breakaway Association and the fledgling national organization contributed to an increasingly negative morale within the Queensland organization. It became more isolated as the state's first Deaf Mission strengthened its ties with other state Deaf Societies and rode out the challenge from its competitor. The Queensland breakaway association survived for twenty-one years, although its membership levels dwindled along with the popularity that it experienced during its early years. When John Paul retired from the association in 1952, the Queensland Deaf and Dumb Citizens Association also closed down.

Conclusion

The Australian Deaf community of the 1920s and 1930s provides a compelling case study of the possibilities and pitfalls in the quest for autonomy. At the time, it was a relatively young Deaf community with some charismatic leaders—and one that embraced the rhetoric of citizenship and autonomy, but encountered opposition from older and more established institutions. These organizations were unwilling to share control or even acknowledge the deaf people's aspirations to collective ownership of these groups. This pattern has played itself out in other minority group struggles, and is always affected by the political and social context at the time.

Australian Deaf communities in two states found that their aspirations for autonomy were incompatible with existing organizations' views of Deaf people , and chose to break away and establish new bodies that explicitly endorsed the identity of Deaf people as citizens. Deaf communities in other Australian states did not follow these two states' lead in establishing breakaway groups, but were influenced by these events and the public debates surrounding them. For a few years, Deaf people's ambitions of organizing themselves as citizens occurred on the national level too, in the establishment of the Australian Association for the Advancement of the Deaf. These efforts proved unsustainable, and the breakaway organizations were reabsorbed into the older Deaf societies with little lasting effect on those institutions' power structures and practices. Indeed, it was not until the 1980s that Australian Deaf communities again established themselves in autonomous organizations and asserted their independence and citizenship in their dealings with others.

The reasons for this brief flowering of deaf autonomy are difficult to isolate. Factors that contributed include the wider context of political unrest in which other marginalized groups also organized and protested as ways of attaining their goals, the arrival of strangers who became catalysts for change, and the emergence of strong deaf leaders who had the resources and skills to channel the Deaf communities' discontent into the momentum needed for the creation and maintenance of the new organizations. Just as equally, the reasons for its collapse are complicated. Perhaps the community was not yet robust enough to sustain such concentrated change, and had not produced enough skilled and energetic leaders to sustain it for future generations. External factors such as rising political conservatism and the random changing of a registration law may have had a disproportionate impact on these small communities. Conflict and dissension are tiring and, over time, can wear down people's resilience, especially when their opponents are well-resourced and powerful. The story of these breakaway groups in Australian Deaf history provides a rich opportunity to study these factors and their interaction with deaf people's assertion of their rights as citizens.

Notes

1. See Lake, *Getting Equal*, 50, 140.
2. Ibid., 139.
3. Davidson, *From Subject to Citizen*.
4. Carty and Thornton, "Deaf People in Colonial Australia," 148–55; See also Branson and Miller, *Story of Betty Steel*.
5. Flynn, "Some Aspects of the Development."
6. Ladd, *Understanding Deaf Culture*.
7. Atherton, "Feeling as Much," 443–54.
8. Carty, "Managing Their Own Affairs."
9. Kennedy, *Australian Welfare*.
10. Conference Notes: Australian (*sic*) Deaf & Dumb Association, October 5, 1922. File No. 253, (John W. Flynn) Collection. (Subsequent references will use JWF Collection.)
11. The name "Toc H" is derived from Talbot House, a "rest and recreation" house for soldiers, which operated in Flanders from 1915. It was usually called T.H., which became Toc H in signalers' code. See Altschwager, *First Sixty Years*, 6.
12. "Our Missioners. 2. Mr. H. V. S. Hersee, Portsmouth," *The British Deaf Times* 19, no. 221–22 (May–June 1922): 39.
13. "Why the Association of Deaf and Dumb Citizens was Formed," *Onward!* (January 1930): 8.
14. Adult Deaf and Dumb Society of New South Wales (ADDSNSW), transcript of Special Meeting of Council held on April 8, 1929, 2–6, JWF Collection File No. 0146.
15. Ibid.
16. See Macintyre, *1901–1942*, 234–54.
17. ADDSNSW, Minutes of Executive Meeting, May 9, 1929.
18. Caption accompanying photo, *Sydney Morning Herald*, May 9, 1929, 12.
19. Fischer and Vollhaber, *Collage*, 9.
20. "Deaf and Dumb. Angry Meeting," *Sydney Morning Herald*, May 9, 1929, 11.

21. Ibid.

22. "Deaf and Dumb. New Society Formed," *Sydney Morning Herald*, May 11, 1929, 21.

23. Minutes of Conference between representatives of the Adult Deaf and Dumb Society and the Association of Deaf and Dumb Citizens [*sic*], May 25, 1936. JWF Collection File No. 0144.

24. "Deaf and Dumb. New Society formed," *Sydney Morning Herald*, May 23, 1929, 12.

25. "Deaf and Dumb Association," *Sydney Morning Herald*, June 19, 1929, 10.

26. See report in *The Deaf Advocate* 2, no. 8 (August 1932).

27. E. J. Davidson, "A Well-Wishing," *Onward!* August 1929: 1.

28. Fletcher S. Booth, "Why the Association of Deaf and Dumb Citizens was Formed," *Onward!* January 1930: 9.

29. "Wild Meeting. Policemen Present," *News*, August 24, 1929. Quoted in *Onward!* January 1930: 13–14.

30. Ibid.

31. "Fooling the Deaf and Dumb! Lively Close to Annual Meeting." *Daily Telegraph Pictorial*, August 24, 1929, 3.

32. Ibid.

33. For example, in February 1933, nine of the fourteen councillors were Deaf, and four of the five hearing councillors had Deaf relatives. Editorial, *The Deaf Advocate* 3, no. 2 (February 1933).

34. Editorial, *The Deaf Advocate* 1, no. 3 (March 1931).

35. "The Deaf A R E Managing their Own Affairs," *The Deaf Advocate* 2, no. 6 (June 1932). (Capitals in original.)

36. Ibid.

37. Francis Gibson, in *The Frat* 1, no. 2 (March 1904). Quoted in Burch, *Signs of Resistance*, 107.

38. "The Deaf A R E Managing their Own Affairs," *The Deaf Advocate* 2, no. 6 (June 1932). (Capitals in original.)

39. Bob Herman, interview in Clancy, *Heritage in our Hands*, 117.

40. John M. Paul, "Birthday Greetings," *The Deaf Advocate* 3, no. 5 (May 1933).

41. For example, Queensland Adult Deaf and Dumb Mission (hereafter QADDM), Report for the Year Ending February 28, 1925; Ibid., Report for the Year Ending February 28, 1933, 17–18.

42. W. R. Kingwell (Committee member of QADDM), letter to A. L. Lonsdale, October 26, 1931. JWF Collection File No. 0255.

43. W. Bradbury, "Inquiry into the Working of the Queensland Adult Deaf and Dumb Mission," (1931). JWF Collection File No. 0255, 11.

44. J. M. Paul, "A letter from Queensland," *The Deaf Advocate* 2, no. 2 (February 1932). (Capitals in original.)

45. "Definite Break. New Body Formed. Deaf and Dumb Act. Protest at Committee Actions," *The Daily Mail*, August 19, 1931, 8.

46. C. C. Garner, "To the Advocate," *The Deaf Advocate* 2, no. 3 (March 1932).

47. Editorial, *The Deaf Advocate* 3, no. 2 (February 1933).

48. "Deaf and Dumb Citizens Reformed Association," *The Cairns Post*, September 1, 1932, 10.

49. QADDM, Minutes of meeting held September 15, 1931.

50. Martha Overend Wilson, "Queensland–A Lady's Point of View," *The Deaf Advocate*, (September–October 1931).

51. J. M. Paul, "Queensland Deaf and Dumb Association News," *The Deaf Advocate* 2, no. 3 (March 1932).

52. Editorial, *The Deaf Advocate*, (September–October 1931).

53. "Overseas Page. Australia," *British Deaf Times* 29, no. 337–38 (January–February 1932): 3.

54. See Carty, 2004.

55. For a description of Australian conformity and repression in the mid- to late 1930s, see Stuart Macintyre, *1901–1942 The Oxford History of Australia*, 307-24.

56. For example, letter from E. B. Harkness, Under Secretary of Chief Secretary's Dept, to ADDSNSW, June 11, 1935. State Records NSW: Colonial Secretary; CGS905, Main series of letters received, 1826–1982; Items [12/7524 No. 1026 and No. 1085]. Copies of items also in JWF Collection File No. 0144.

57. Letter from Harkness to ADDSNSW, December 12, 1935. JWF Collection File No. 0144.

58. Ibid.

59. ADDSNSW, Minutes of Executive Committee, February 19, 1936.

60. Ibid., 9.

61. *General Assembly of the Free Church of Scotland v Overtoun* [1904] AC 515 (HL).

62. Ibid.

63. Ibid., 12.

64. Ibid., 11.

65. Ibid., 8

66. Minutes of General [Deaf] Committee meeting of ADDSNSW, November 4, 1936. JWF Collection File No. 0144.

References

Altschwager, Leila. *The First Sixty Years: A History of Toc H in Australia from 1925 to 1985*. Adelaide: Toc H Australia, 1985.

Atherton, Martin. "A Feeling as Much as a Place: Leisure, Deaf Clubs and the British Deaf Community." *Leisure Studies* 28, no. 4 (2009): 443–54.

Bontempo, Karen, and Josie Hodgetts. *History of the WA Deaf Society 1921–2001*. Leederville, WA: The Western Australian Deaf Society Inc., 2002.

Bourke, John Patrick. *The After-School Problems of the Deaf and Dumb, No. 1: The Problem of a Central Meeting Place for Them*. Melbourne: J. P. Bourke, 1933.

———. *The After-School Problems of the Deaf and Dumb, No. 2: The Problem of Ministering to Their Religious and Spiritual Needs*. Melbourne: J. P. Bourke, 1933.

———. *The After-School Problems of the Deaf and Dumb, No. 3: The Problem of the Impotent Deaf*. Melbourne: J. P. Bourke, 1935.

Branson, Jan, and Don Miller. *The Story of Betty Steel: Deaf Convict and Pioneer*. Petersham, NSW: Deafness Resources Australia Ltd., 1995.

Burch, Susan. *Signs of Resistance: American Deaf Cultural History, 1900 to World War II*. New York: New York University Press, 2002.

Carty, Breda. "Managing Their Own Affairs: The Australian Deaf Community in the 1920s and 1930s." PhD diss., Griffith University, 2004.

Carty, Breda, and Darlene Thornton. "Deaf People in Colonial Australia." In *No History, No Future: Proceedings of the 7th DHI International Conference, Stockholm 2009*, edited by Tomas Hedberg, 148–55. Solna, Sweden: Dixa, 2011.

Clancy, Michael, ed. *Heritage in Our Hands: Stories of the Deaf Community of N.S.W.* Sydney: Adult Education Centre for Deaf and Hearing Impaired Persons Inc., 1988.

Davidson, Alastair. *From Subject to Citizen: Australian Citizenship in the Twentieth Century*. Cambridge: Cambridge University Press, 1997.

Doran, Ella. *Hand in Hand with Time and Change: The Life of Ella Doran and Her Work with the Deaf in Australia*. Woden, ACT: Molonglo Press, 1998.

Fisher, Renate, and Tomas Vollhaber, eds. *Collage: Works on International Deaf History*. Hamburg: Signum Press, 1996

Fitzgerald, Sarah, ed. *Open Minds Open Hearts: Stories of the Australian Catholic Deaf Community*. Lidcombe, NSW: CCOD, 1999.

Flynn, John. *No Longer by Gaslight: The First 100 Years of the Adult Deaf Society of Victoria*. East Melbourne: Adult Deaf Society of Victoria, 1984.

———. "Some Aspects of the Development of Post-School Organizations of and for Deaf People in Australia." MA thesis, La Trobe University, 1999.

Jackson, Peter. *A Pictorial History of Deaf Britain*. Winsford, Cheshire: Deafprint Winsford, 2001.

Kennedy, Richard, ed. *Australian Welfare: Historical Sociology*. Melbourne: MacMillan, 1989.

Koschutzke, Jenny. "The History of the Sydney Deaf Community's Boycott of the Adult Deaf and Dumb Society from 1929 to 1937 and the Establishment of Their Own Rival Association of Deaf and Dumb Citizens." MA thesis, University of Sydney, 1995.

Ladd, Paddy. *Understanding Deaf Culture: In Search of Deafhood*. Clevedon, England: Multilingual Matters Ltd., 2003.

Lake, Marilyn. *Getting Equal: The History of Australian Feminism.* St. Leonards, NSW: Allen & Unwin, 1999.

Loades, Rhonda. "The Establishment and Maintenance of the Deaf Community in South Australia." BA Hons thesis, Flinders University, 1989.

Macintyre, Stuart. *1901–1942 The Oxford History of Australia, Vol. 4: The Succeeding Age.* Melbourne: Oxford University Press, 1986.

Thornton, Darlene, Susannah Macready, and Patricia Levitzke-Gray. "Written into History: The Lives of Australian Deaf Leaders." In *Telling Deaf Lives: Agents of Change,* edited by Kristin Snoddon, 93–101. Washington, DC: Gallaudet University Press, 2014.

Wilson, Sue. *The History of the Queensland Deaf Society: From Mission to Profession 1903–2003.* Brisbane: The Queensland Deaf Society, 2003.

Wrigley, Owen. *The Politics of Deafness.* Washington, DC: Gallaudet University Press, 1996.

Archives

Queensland State Archives

Home Secretary's Office; Correspondence re blind deaf and dumb, general, 1900–1937; Extracts from Minute Book on Training Scheme Verified by & Initialed by Supt. Paul 23-2-31; RSI2383-1-21.

Home Secretary's Office; Statement by President of Q. A. D & D. Mission (Incorp) at the Inquiry held by Mr Bradbury, Home Department 8-5-31; RSI2383-1-21.

State Records New South Wales

Colonial Secretary; CGS905, Main series of letters received, 1826–1982; items [12/7524 No. 1026 and No. 1085].

Legislation

Charitable Collections Act 1934 (No. 59) (NSW).
General Assembly of the Free Church of Scotland v Overtoun [1904] AC 515 (HL).

Other Official Sources

Minutes, Annual Reports, Constitutions, correspondence, and other records of Deaf-related organizations in Australia.

Periodicals

The British Deaf Times, 1920–1932.
The Cairns Post, 1932.
The Daily Guardian (NSW), 1930.
The Daily Mail (Qld), 1930–1931.
The Daily Telegraph (NSW), 1929.
The Deaf Advocate, 1930–1937.
The Deaf Quarterly News (UK), 1925–1928.
Deaf Sports Notes (NSW), 1937.
Onward! (NSW), 1929–1930.
The Silent Messenger (NSW), 1907–1956.
The Sydney Morning Herald, 1929.

12

Divine and Secular:
Reverend Robert Capers Fletcher and the
Southern Deaf Community 1931–1972

Jean Lindquist Bergey

CLERGY THE WORLD OVER are called to assist members of their congregations with issues intimate and infinite. Their doctrinal and personal perspectives on life's transitions are offered as babies are welcomed into a family with holy words and traditional ceremonies, coming-of-age events are marked and rites of passage officiated. For Episcopal priests, baptisms, confirmations, weddings, and funerals, as well as weekly worship, a litany of holidays, and ministering to the sick, frail, and dying, are among the tasks of the position. Deaf clergy have all of these responsibilities, and also take on duties that are specific to deaf congregations. This chapter examines the work of one Episcopal priest, Reverend Robert Capers Fletcher (1900–1988), and his efforts to foster agency within Deaf communities of the South.

Deaf Episcopal priests had served congregations since October 14, 1883, when Reverend Henry Winter Syle (1846–1890) and Reverend Austin Ward Mann (1841–1911) joined the priesthood at the same ceremony.[1] Forty-eight years later, Robert Fletcher became a reverend in 1931 in Birmingham, Alabama, the twenty-seventh deaf person ordained in the church. A description of the ordination by the Rt. Reverend William G. McDowell, Bishop of Alabama, was published in *Silent Missionary*, where he stated it was a "most impressive service" officiated by seven priests and several laypeople. Bishop McDowell wrote: "The Rev. Mr. Fletcher has greatly endeared himself to those whom he serves. There are about 4,000 deaf in the Province of Sewanee."[2]

Named after the School of Theology of the University of the South located in Sewanee, Tennessee, the Province of Sewanee is the largest of the Episcopal Church provinces, and includes dioceses in Alabama, Georgia, Florida, Kentucky, North Carolina, Mississippi, South Carolina, Tennessee, and part of Louisiana.[3] Deaf Episcopalians from this wide swath of the United States were served by one priest from 1931 to 1951. Traveling by train on a minister's free Louisville & Nashville Railroad pass along the network of rails that crisscrossed the farms and towns of the American South, Fletcher maintained deaf congregations. For deaf people residing in areas far from Birmingham, church services, baptisms, weddings, and sometimes even funerals, meant waiting until Fletcher could arrive.

Background

Born June 11, 1900, Robert Fletcher grew up in the farming community of Arab, located in the northeast part of Alabama. According to family lore, he had become deaf at the age of four from a lightning strike. One of Fletcher's daughters, Roberta, explained that her father may have been closer to five or six years old when he became deaf and, although the lore included deafness due to a lightning strike. He had fallen while on the porch during a storm and lay unconscious for several days, which suggests that he probably had meningitis.

Fletcher's mother did not want to send her son away to a residential school and worked closely with him at home on his school work. Fletcher recounted stories of his mother's tapping out rhythms on the table to teach him patterns of speech. He stayed in Arab with his family and attended the local one-room schoolhouse. Fletcher described his studies there as "staying in the 4th grade for 4 years."[4]

As a boy, an accident with scissors left Fletcher blind in one eye. At the age of twelve, his mother died of tuberculosis, as did the youngest of his three sisters. It was then, that his father chose to enroll him at the residential state school for deaf students in Talladega, nearly ninety miles from home. In a 1986 family film, Fletcher described this experience and his introduction to deaf people: "I went to a public school until age 12. When my mother died, my father took me to the deaf school. I had never seen deaf people before. There was fluttering of hands and tapping me on the shoulder and clasping my hands."[5] This new school was the Alabama Institute for the Deaf and Blind. He stayed there for nine years, graduating in 1921 at the age of twenty-one.

Fletcher went on to Gallaudet College in Washington, DC, graduating with his bachelor's degree in 1926. During his undergraduate years

Estelle Caldwell and Robert Fletcher
during their Gallaudet College years.
Courtesy of Gallaudet University
Archives, Collection of Rev. Robert
and Mrs. Estelle (Caldwell) Fletcher.

he assisted Reverend Henry J. Pulver of the St. Barnabas Mission to the
Deaf as a lay reader. Fletcher's readings were described in the *Silent
Missionary* as instructive and interesting. "Though a very young student,
he was a very forceful speaker."[6] It was at Gallaudet that Fletcher met
Estelle Caldwell, who had come to the college from the Texas School for
the Deaf. The two became sweethearts and remained together for the
rest of their lives.

Church Work and Family Life

Following graduation from Gallaudet College, Fletcher went on
to attend the Philadelphia Episcopal Seminary, studying theology, the
scriptures, social issues, and church management. Upon completion

of his graduate studies, dimensions of his personal life would quickly change with marriage and children and his work with congregations on the horizon.

Description of the large Bryan, Texas wedding of Estelle Caldwell and Robert Fletcher in August of 1930 filled almost one column in the *Deaf-Mutes' Journal*. The story noted that "the bride, Miss Caldwell, had been a popular young belle at Gallaudet College, where she first met Mr. Fletcher, and the bridegroom was gaining attention among the deaf in the South for his missionary zeal and good sermons."[7] It was not long before the family grew and their children John (1931), Louise (1934), Roberta "Bobby" (1937), and Georgianna (1939), were born. John was born in Texas, where Estelle (Caldwell) Fletcher had gone to be with her mother for the birth, a necessary separation given her husband's extended travel. The rest of their children, Louise, Bobby, and Georgianna, were all born in Birmingham.

Estelle cared for her active family and kept a busy household, which included "roomers," unmarried women who paid to board in the family's spare bedrooms. "Mother managed this household on very little money, no car, Daddy often gone, and a little grocery store four blocks away," explained daughter Bobby.[8] Part of managing the house also included budgeting during difficult economic times. "My parents were always strapped," added Bobby. When first married, the Fletchers lived in St. Mary's on the Highlands Church. During the Depression, the couple and their children lived in a rented apartment until they could finally afford to move into a house of their own.

Supporting church work, Estelle taught Sunday school, performed in or directed the choir, participated in the women's auxiliary functions, and hosted events. Cooking was also a significant task for Estelle and the other women of the congregation, and in one archival film Reverend Fletcher is shown thanking Estelle and other women for a fine meal.[9]

A detailed organizer, Estelle assisted her husband by keeping directories of members as he served multiple congregations. For deaf people who communicated via letters, keeping directories was essential for a functional church. In the Fletcher household keeping church directories was a formidable task as it was not one or two congregations but addresses for deaf people from Louisiana to Kentucky and up the eastern seaboard. Outside of Alabama, she organized membership directories by state. Her daughter Bobby wrote that "at Christmas or Easter, or when it was time to notify the congregations of Rev. Fletcher's schedule, she addressed each card, and every Christmas or Easter letter—

hundreds of them. We all stuffed the envelopes at the dining room table, which was cleared annually—in time for Christmas dinner."[10]

In church, Robert and Estelle Fletcher often signed in unison during services. For the hearing, singing together is one way that congregations connect as individuals listen to their voice blended with others, affirming faith. For Deaf congregations, spiritually moving expressions of faith are sometimes seen by signing in unison. This was the case at St. John's Church in Birmingham, where those who had practiced hymns signed together. The congregation also would sign the Lord's Prayer in unison.

In 1933, Episcopal Bishop William McDowell presented "Old St. John's Church" in Birmingham to Reverend Fletcher and a small congregation of three deaf parishioners.[11] By 1940, Fletcher reported that in just seven years the membership had grown to fifty-eight. "The church has a vestry, woman's auxiliary, Bible class, and five lay readers who take turns in conducting services" stated Fletcher.[12] Lay leaders were critical given the number of Sundays Fletcher traveled to other congregations and schools for deaf students in nine states. Within the congregation, members had to assume roles of lay ministry.

Preaching for multiple congregations required documentation of particular stories or statements. The Episcopal Church sets lessons and Gospel readings by the church calendar and these are often accompanied by the minister's message. To keep track of use of the passages, Fletcher often jotted down a sentence combined with the beginning and end of a scripture line, such as "Thou _____ with me," which would then continue: ". . . because God is Love. Which explains it, if you think it out." These reminders to himself were often followed by a list of places the lesson was given. For example, "St. John's, Birmingham, Talladega, Nashville, Memphis, Mobile, Chattanooga, Charlotte, Hickory, Morganton, and Asheville."

Even during the weeks Reverend Fletcher preached only in Alabama, his schedule was grueling. For the earlier years of his services, he rode the railroad, and later buses. However, in his summary report to the diocese in 1947, he requested the purchase of a car, explaining that bus schedules between Birmingham and Talladega did not allow sufficient time for services. His proposed Sunday schedule, with a car, was listed as:

11:00 A.M. Holy Communion, Birmingham, St. John's Church for the Deaf

2:00 P.M. Service for Deaf Negroes—Adults—about 20

3:15 P.M. Holy Communion, St. Peter's Church, Talladega
6:00 P.M. Talk in School Chapel to deaf Negro children
7:00 P.M. Talk in School Chapel to White deaf children

Segregated services both in the city of Birmingham and at the school
chapel at the Alabama Institute for Deaf and Blind in Talladega increased the number of sermons given. Court-ordered desegregation
in 1967 required closing the segregated school in 1968, thus allowing
Reverend Fletcher to finally offer a single, combined worship service.[13]

Communicating

Contact with parishioners, church officials, and the public was maintained in several ways. Besides the US postal service, long-distance communication in the 1930s required that telegrams be sent to the Fletcher
home. A light attached to the doorbell alerted the family to postal workers or visitors at the door. In 1941, the Fletchers had a telephone installed
and their hearing children would take and occasionally make calls for
their parents.[14]

Reverend Fletcher often handwrote notes of correspondence to congregants. He also used a printed postcard that said "We missed you!" in
text with drawn illustrations of signs. The card showed a priest signing
"We," "missed" was illustrated with a hand fingerspelling, and "you"
was expressed with a drawing of a hand pointing to an empty pew.

To reach out to hearing individuals whose names appeared in the
Birmingham newspaper, Fletcher would mail a functional, envelope
sized, absorbent ink blotter that read, on the cardboard side, "Good
Morning! I am glad to read about you" next to a drawing of three small
bibles. It included Fletcher's name and title "Missionary to the Deaf of
Alabama" and his address next to a space for handwritten notes. These
remarks were intended to introduce notable residents of Birmingham
to the existence of a deaf ministry.

To connect with hearing people he saw in town and while traveling,
Fletcher distributed fingerspelling cards printed by either the Alabama
Association of the Deaf or the Episcopal organization: Conference of
Church Workers Among the Deaf.

Fletcher's daughter Bobby recalls her father as a skilled lipreader
who often conversed with hearing people using his voice. Within the
family he would sign and speak, except when in private conversation

with his wife, in which case the couple would sign faster than the children were able to follow. During his sermons, Fletcher would use only sign if the entire attendance that day was deaf, adding voice when needed to accommodate hearing visitors.[15]

A Dixie Home

A critical 1930s social need for all people, but with specific requirements for the deaf population, was care for elders. In 1930, an estimated 5.4 percent of the United States population was over sixty-five years, and that percentage was rising.[16] Care for aging Americans often came from younger family members, but not all elders had families who were able to provide care, and deaf people frequently experienced limited communication with hearing family members.

President Franklin Delano Roosevelt addressed Congress in January 1935, outlining legislation protecting the economic security of US citizens "against certain hazards and vicissitudes of life."[17] The Social Security Act of 1935 became law, although it would take years for regulations to be approved and a system created to educate the public and distribute funds. In 1938 Roosevelt reported via national radio on the program's progress, explaining that forty million applications had already been received.[18] Describing what the situation meant for older citizens, Roosevelt stated, "Long before the economic blight of the depression descended on the Nation, millions of our people were living in wastelands of want and fear. Men and women too old and infirm to work either depended on those who had but little to share, or spent their remaining years within the walls of a poorhouse."[19] Social Security applications were starting to be processed and the administration had begun distributing cards with Social Security numbers, however checks would not be issued until 1940.[20] In lieu of government and family aid, the challenge of caring for older deaf citizens was taken up by other community members, including Reverend Fletcher.

Depending only on family or charity in the post-depression years was not feasible for many older Americans. Deaf people who often had limited incomes had the added challenge of communicating with non-signing family or caregivers. A solution proposed was the creation of a care home designed specifically to serve older deaf individuals, enabling them to live together in a beautiful setting where communication was clear. The Dixie Home for the Aged Deaf was established in

Moultrie, Florida, near St. Augustine, with funding from private donations, which included support from architect and 1889 graduate of
Gallaudet College, Thomas Marr. Several Deaf men and women had
moved in to the large Dixie Home, but additional finances were needed
to maintain the property.

Reverend Fletcher served as chairman of a funding campaign. He
called on the southern Deaf community to support the recently purchased home in Florida through associations and the networks of school
alumni. In a two-minute fund-raising film titled, *Dixie Home for the Aged
Deaf*, made by Fletcher in the early 1930s, he explains the need for the
home:

> Long ago, Jesus made a deaf man hear. We have seen deaf people
> moving up in character, heart and mind—going to school and col-
> lege, and we have our churches. Now we want to change Jesus'
> parable into action. We've seen many deaf elderly people who
> can't find a home where they can get care. They want to move to
> one place where they will be supported and happy and content.[21]

In this film, Fletcher goes on to make the case for donating financial
support to the Dixie Home:

> Why should you support this home? First, [you should support
> it] because you want to have a place where you can go when you
> grow older. Maybe something will happen to you. Maybe you will
> become ill. Maybe your children will be far away and leave you
> alone. Now you will have a place you can go. And, you can work
> hard now to make a nice name for yourself. As an older person you
> may need to move there and will be able to look back on yourself
> as someone who did good things. Furthermore, we can show the
> hearing world that deaf people can succeed on an equal level. For
> all those reasons— with this noble action we can be proud of our
> deaf [community] and proud of something we accomplished in
> our lives.

In addition to reaching out to the southern Deaf community, Fletcher
used the alumni networks of schools and parents of deaf children to
advance the cause of the Dixie Home. As the funding campaign chairman, he distributed a letter to parents that called for their donations on
behalf of their child and older deaf citizens. Conjuring images of life in

an almshouse, Fletcher implores families to contribute coupons that can be turned in for funds.

Dear Parent:

Your child wishes to do a good deed. We wish to teach your child to be charitable and are asking that you help us.

We have a Home for our Aged and Infirm Blind and Deaf people in the South. It is located at Moultrie, Fla. The Alumni of this School are trying to support the Home the best they can. The Octagon Company has promised to help them financially if they will collect the coupons from the products listed on the reverse side of this circular. The Company gives the Home $4.00 for every 1,000 coupons sent in. The Alumni are seeking your aid through your deaf child. The child is happy to help but he has no coupons. You can supply him with coupons and the child can give them to the Principal of this School for the Deaf.

We wish to build the Home and make it larger for the increasing number of Aged and Infirm Deaf who are now without Homes and are lonesome in almshouses. Your child may become sick and helpless when you are gone from this earth. If so, your child will have this home to go to.

Send your coupons to the School for the Deaf or to your Child. Let your child be made happy by having the privilege of giving.

Rev. Robert C. Fletcher, Campaign Chm.
Missionary to the Deaf in the South

The Dixie Association of the Deaf had several chapters throughout the South and each was charged with collecting coupons from products including Luzianne tea and coffee, Octagon soap, Rumford baking powder, Knox gelatin and Borden's condensed milk. By tearing off and sending in 1,000 coupons the Dixie Home for the Aged Deaf could collect $4.00.

Every possible means of garnering support for the Dixie Home was employed. During very lean times, Fletcher used fear, guilt, compassion, and the pleasure that comes from giving to financially bolster a home for deaf elders who could not support themselves. He also used pride in showing that deaf people could create a care home that serves their community. Fostering self-determination he asked deaf people to assume responsibility for supporting the Dixie Home. His film attempted

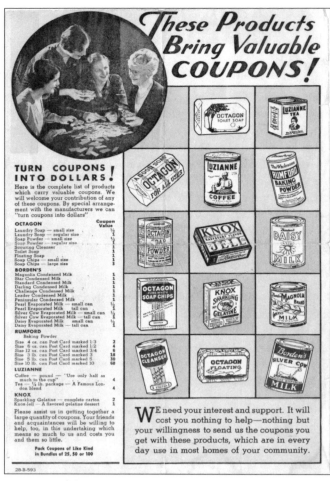

Coupon campaign flier. Courtesy of Gallaudet University Archives, Collection of Rev. Robert and Mrs. Estelle (Caldwell) Fletcher.

to raise money and also touched the very heart of what deaf people at the time strived to demonstrate—parity with hearing people. Eighteen deaf elders had lived at the Dixie Home. In a 1977 report Fletcher wrote: "When the United States Government began paying Social Security these aged people were called home by their children who would not support them before. The Home was moved to Atlanta and later was closed."[22]

Proof of Ability

To many outside the Deaf community, the Fletchers demonstrated that deaf people could be good parents. A compilation film of their growing family shows son John, at approximately 7 years of age, wearing a white shirt and suspenders riding a scooter; daughter Louise is wearing a cotton dress and a bow in her hair as she rides a tricycle. A baby at this time, Bobby plays with a rattle, and is seen smiling in a rattan carriage and taking a bath in a basin. In one scene she is placed on a blanket on the ground by an African American woman, who was likely hired by Estelle's mother.[23] Also in the film, Fletcher remarks on the couple's wedding anniversary; his wife corrects him on the date.

The children appear in several such films made just for family. Georgianna, the fourth child was born. Footage shows John as a handsome teenager in a tuxedo, playing the piano. Louise stands in a stunning, massive pale lavender prom dress. Bobby has a purple ballet recital dress and Georgianna sports a red tap dancer outfit. In the films, the daughters speak to each other and their grandmother, and sign when conversing to their parents.[24]

In *Out of Silence and Darkness*, a written history of the Alabama Institute for the Deaf and Blind, the authors note that Fletcher was referred to as a parenting role model. They commented that "he also showed that the deaf could raise successful children." Dr. Fletcher's daughter, Louise, became an actress and won an Academy Award for her role in the noted movie *One Flew Over the Cuckoo's Nest*.[25] Receiving the award, Louise signed to her parents, thanking them for teaching her "to have a dream."[26] At a time when the public questioned deaf people's ability to parent, the Fletchers were held up as evidence to the contrary.

Sacred and Secular Work

In 1947, Fletcher reported to the bishops in the Province of Sewanee on services from the previous three years, stating, "As your missionary, I beg to submit the following statistical report for my work throughout the province in the three-year period: Pastoral calls, ca. 2,033; sick calls, 143; baptisms, 52; candidates presented for confirmation, 82; Holy Communion services, 242; other services, 291; attendance at all services, ca. 24,106; offerings $2,232.62; miles traveled, 88,805."[27] His travel schedule was exhausting and it taxed the family. However, it also brought Fletcher into contact with much of the Southern Deaf community, making him aware of their needs and resources. He was instrumental in spreading information, carrying news from congregations and word of opportunities, helping deaf people find jobs, homes, and spouses.

Doing work that met the physical needs of congregants, Fletcher helped connect business owners with deaf people seeking jobs. Wearing his priest's collar while out paying social calls to local businesses, he connected deaf typesetters, mechanics, carpenters, and bakers with potential employers. He also helped families find much needed homes and participated in meetings between congregants and their lawyers or doctors.

Through church camps Fletcher brought together wider circles of deaf people. In the film *Bishop Murray and Bishop Carpenter Church Camp*, Bishop Murray can be seen leading the Lord's Prayer in strained signing, this is in contrast to Fletcher's fluent signing of prayers. At the camp parishioners parade past the camera, on occasion thanking the Reverend and proclaiming to return in subsequent years. Matchmaking was a role the Fletchers adopted and one young couple smile at each other while the man signs "thanks to Fletcher for bringing me to see her today."

Missionary work included advocacy for deaf education. Fletcher wrote to state legislators and encouraged others to do likewise. *A History of the Alabama Institute for the Deaf and Blind* reported, "The Alabama Association of the Deaf also supported increased state appropriations. Robert C. Fletcher, president AAD, encouraged each deaf alumnus of the Alabama School for the Deaf to contact his legislator and ask him to increase per capita appropriations."[28] Visits to schools brought Fletcher into contact with hundreds of deaf children and youth. State residential schools offered students an education that would most often lead to a job in a skilled trade for boys and domestic work for girls. A select few would go on to Gallaudet College.

In each of the nine states within the Province of Sewanee the education system was racially segregated until the mid-1960s. For instance, in Louisiana there was no school for Black deaf students until 1938 and it remained segregated until 1978.[29] Black students in segregated schools often received less support and services than white students. The principal of the Alabama School for the Negro Deaf and Blind filed a formal complaint in 1945 that his student's education was suffering because they were called upon to do chores previously done by hired hands.[30] During the 1950s, Black deaf girls in the segregated Alabama Institute were taught laundering, cooking, and sewing, while boys were taught mechanical arts, "dairy arts," and barbering.[31] For Fletcher, visits to these schools generally meant segregated services for students.

Black or white, education beyond the primary and secondary residential school programs was needed for most deaf adults to secure gainful employment. In a report by Fletcher titled "Rehabilitation Needs As Seen By The Deaf" he stresses the need to establish continuing education programs for deaf adults. This undated document begins with: "Who can speak with greater insight about the problems of the Deaf than the Deaf themselves?" Speaking for the Deaf community on the subject of vocational rehabilitation, he points out the barriers to job training, or retraining when jobs become obsolete, explaining that deaf workers do not have the same opportunities as hearing people to grow educationally. Fletcher explains that "automation and technology are eliminating many long standing jobs and creating new ones at an amazing rate. This means that the workers will have to be flexible and learn entirely new trades. The first step in the levels of achievement is a test in English and Mathematics. This is where many will stumble."[32] A solution, Fletcher proposed, is creating a junior college explicitly for Southern deaf people. However, such a college was never founded.

In the same report, Fletcher clarifies the inextricable link between education, employment, and family communication. "We should have School Rooms for Adults. There is so much the Deaf need to learn. Today they realize what they missed in school. To give the deaf children a fair vocabulary while young I think all hearing parents should learn to spell with their fingers. This system will help their deaf child grow intellectually and its little mind will be able to understand what is going on in the home." Fletcher closes the report declaring his authenticity and authority on the subject, "as a deaf man I have spoken for the Deaf and the Counselors."[33]

Fletcher outlined changes in social service roles of the church and state and federal government in a summary report on St. John's Episcopal Church of Birmingham. Written approximately 1977, following retirement, Fletcher looks back on earlier times, writing that "St. Johns recalls the days when we had to search around to find jobs for our deaf fellowmen. Today the Vocational Rehabilitation Service provides training for the deaf so they can make their living. At times food was needed and we asked our members and friends to donate food and money with which we kept many alive. Food disposition is now the task of the Welfare Departments. We sent small donations to our college

Rev. Robert Fletcher in "new" St. John's Church, 1950s.
Courtesy of Gallaudet University Archives, Collection of
Rev. Robert and Mrs. Estelle (Caldwell) Fletcher.

students at Gallaudet College, the only college for the Deaf in the World, Washington, DC. Today the U.S. Government through its Vocational Rehabilitation Service offers education to our deserving deaf students."[34]

Outside of the Province of Sewanee Fletcher remained connected to the wider church network by traveling to attend ordinations of new missionaries, church anniversary celebrations, and meetings of the Conference of Church Workers Among the Deaf (CCWAD) organization. In 1949, Fletcher was elected second vice president of the CCWAD and remained involved for decades.[35] He also maintained connections with colleagues in Washington, DC, and fellow Gallaudet College alumni. In 1945, was elected to the Executive Board of the National Association of the Deaf.[36]

A persuasive presenter, Fletcher used his skills to gather financial support and services. The year 1951 was momentous when "Old St. John's" Church was replaced by a new St. John's. The old church was too small for the growing congregation and when construction began termites were discovered. They had eaten through the walls and the building was condemned.[37] New church construction would cost $35,000, a tremendous sum to raise. Fletcher knew that it was badly needed, but beyond the financial scope his congregants could supply. At the 1949 meeting of the Jefferson County Episcopal Churchmen's Association, Fletcher used his speech to request funds. His plea was successful, and thanks to the Association members, he acquired enough backing to build a new structure designed for the church's deaf parishioners.[38]

Shortly after "new St. John's" opened, Fletcher's work obligations changed. He was no longer required to serve nine states. Declining health and the strain of unrelenting travel compelled a diminishment of his region of service to the state of Alabama. For 21 years, from 1951–1972, a period of great social change and civil rights struggle, Reverend Fletcher served only two Deaf churches in Birmingham, Alabama, one was African American (St. Mark's) and the other was white (St. John's); he also served a third church in Mobile, over 250 miles away. A car made Fletcher's new routine of local and intercity travel possible.

Life on Film

The *Dixie Home for the Deaf* film documented one topic, time, and location. It was one of seven films donated to the Gallaudet University Archives by members of the Fletcher family. Three of the film reels are compilations of spliced footage spanning many years. Two films that were not restored included one post-1956 reel showing family footage of a Jamestown trip and a wedding, and another reel of Reverend Fletcher performing a funeral for a baby, approximately 1956. One film shows Fletcher at 86 years sending greetings.

While film from the 1940s and 1950s is rare for all communities, it is especially rare within the African American Deaf community. Particularly noteworthy in the collection is footage of Deaf workers in front of "Perfection Laundry," circa 1956, where Fletcher had worked to get jobs for African American Deaf people in the Birmingham area. Brief footage of the outside of St. Mark's Church, an African American Deaf congregation, is also included.

In one film, shot in 1946 or shortly after, Estelle, who loved to perform, signed the song "Dixie" while shuffling through a dance in blackface and dressed in tails and comically long pointy shoes. Fletcher's
daughter Bobby described the outfit,

> Mother borrowed the entire costume, shoes and all, from Uncle
> George Long, her sister Louise's husband, who lived in Bryan,
> Texas—where Mother was born and where her family always
> lived. . . . It was made of stiff striped fabric like mattress ticking
> and was very hot and uncomfortable to wear. I don't know why
> he had it made, but I know that my parents thought it was a great
> costume.[39]

The visible portion of the white audience seated behind the performer
strains to see and chuckles at her knee-slapping antics while she signs
"Look away, look away, look away, Dixieland." This "Saturday Night
Review" show, and Estelle's choice of costume, is representative of the
times. Considering the use of blackface and the song "Dixie," Bobby
explained that was probably because she, [her mother] had that costume
available, Al Jolson was hugely popular, and she and others of her generation had grown up with a continuation of a popular nineteenth- and
early twentieth-century type of entertainment—performing in blackface. "I don't think she thought it was particularly funny, I just think
it was a still a fairly conventional type of entertainment at the time. . .
. Mother had the attitudes about race and class typical of the time and
place of her upbringing, I think. She had grown up with having black
servants in her parents' home. . . . She was always kind to everyone and
deplored the later horrors that were carried out in Birmingham in the
civil rights struggle in the 1960's. But I do not believe it would have occurred to her to think her performance would be seen as offensive by
anyone—white or black—or she would never have done it."[40]

The signed "Dixie" performance illustrates how the Fletchers' lives
and actions were influenced by twentieth century narratives on race.
"Blacking up" for performance in the mid-twentieth century was not
uncommon. Gallaudet alumni tell of a performance by a white, male
classmate in blackface on the college campus in 1955.[41] What makes this
rendition of "Dixie" rare is that a white woman dressed as a Black man
performed. While the gender difference was unique, the cultural phenomenon of white performers in blackface, and the example of Mrs.

Fletcher's approving audience, demonstrates racial demarcation typical of the times.

National Spotlight

Congressional recognition of the Deaf community and public prayer in sign language occurred when Reverend Fletcher became the first deaf minister to open the US Senate on March 26, 1952. A signed invocation was novel for the Senate, and it was a symbol of Deaf community validation. Fletcher prayed, "Bless our land with honorable industry, sound learning, and pure manners. Defend our liberties, preserve our unity." He asked God to bless each member of the Senate and "replenish them with grace." He also asked the Heavenly Father to "Endue them plenteously with heavenly gifts and make them ever mindful of their calling to serve our people" as a reminder of the work to be done.[42]

Stepping back from service, Reverend Fletcher retired in 1972. He was bestowed the title "Canon Ordinary," the first to receive this life honor in the Diocese of Alabama.[43] In the last film he made, at age eighty-six, Fletcher sent signed greetings back to his alma mater the Alabama Institute for the Deaf and Blind, with apologies for being unable to attend his induction into their Hall of Fame; two of his daughters attended in his stead. Remarking on his "Alabama start in life," he said: "God has been good to deaf people of Alabama." As he grew older, Fletcher decried the rise of new evangelical churches that fragmented the small Deaf church-going community. Reverend Robert Capers Fletcher died in 1988, at the age of eighty-eight.

Studying the life and work of this one missionary reveals issues of religion, race, the role of women, and social support within the Deaf community. Fletcher supported southern notions of hierarchy and privilege while also disrupting circumscribed ideas of Deaf participation in society. He advocated and pushed others to advocate for greater access. His life's work argued that everyone needs a family with whom they can communicate, an education, a job, a place to live, and, if they choose, a spiritual home. Fletcher's missionary work addressed Deaf-specific access to universally human issues of body and soul.

Notes

1. Otto B. Berg. *A Missionary Chronicle: Being a History of the Ministry to the Deaf in the Episcopal Church (1850–1980)*. Hollywood, MD: St. Mary's Press, 1984, xxvii. Reverend Otto Berg presents the history of the early years of the Episcopal

Conference of the Deaf, relying heavily on the *Deaf-Mutes' Journal* and *Silent Missionary* for primary source documentation.

2. Berg, *A Missionary Chronicle,* 119–20.

3. Province IV of the Episcopal Church Province of Sewanee. Last modified 2014. Accessed August 15, 2014. http://www.provinceiv.org/.

4. Roberta "Bobby" Fletcher. Interview by the author. Gloucester, VA. September 18, 2014. Review of primary source material held by the Fletcher/ Ray family.

5. Robert Capers Fletcher, signed performance of "Reverend Fletcher at 86 Years." Performed by Robert Capers Fletcher. 1986. Washington, DC: Gallaudet University Archives, 1986. Videocassette.

6. Berg, *A Missionary Chronicle,* 102.

7. Ibid., 117.

8. Fletcher, Interview, September 18, 2014.

9. Robert Capers Fletcher, prod. "Reverend Fletcher's Movie Archive Bishop Murray and Bishop Carpenter Church Camp, Reel 11," produced by Robert Capers Fletcher. Gallaudet University Archives. Composite DVD of multiple scenes, 1955–1958.

10. Roberta Ray, Memorandum, March 7, 1988. Collection of Reverend Robert and Mrs. Estelle (Caldwell) Fletcher, Box 2. Gallaudet University Archives. Washington, DC. Unpublished speech given on the occasion of a major gift to St. Johns and St. Mark's Churches in honor of Reverend Fletcher.

11. Berg, *A Missionary Chronicle,* 125.

12. Ibid., 140.

13. Robert Hill Couch and, Jack Hawkins, Jr., *Out of Silence and Darkness: The History of the Alabama Institute for Deaf and Blind 1858–1983* (Troy, AL: Troy State University Press, 1983), 216–17.

14. Roberta Ray, interview by the author.

15. Ibid.

16. Larry W. DeWitt, Daniel Beland, and Edward D. Berkowitz, *Social Security: A Documentary History* (Washington, DC: CQ Press, 2008), 52.

17. Ibid., 56.

18. Ibid., 124.

19. Ibid., 125.

20. Social Security Administration, "First Social Security Beneficiary" *Social Security History*. Accessed January 24, 2015, from http://www.ssa.gov/history/imf.html.

21. Robert Capers Fletcher, prod., "Dixie Home for the Aged Deaf," Gallaudet University Archives.

22. Robert Capers Fletcher. Memorandum, "St. John's Episcopal Church for the Deaf," 1977, 5. Collection of Reverend Robert and Mrs. Estelle (Caldwell) Fletcher, box 2. Gallaudet University Archives, Washington, DC.

23. Roberta Ray. Interview by the author. Gloucester, VA. September 18, 2014.

24. "Fletcher, Robert Capers, prod. Uuntitled, Reel 3," produced by Robert Capers Fletcher. Gallaudet University Archives. Composite DVD of multiple scenes, 1938–1958.

25. Robert Hill Couch, Jack and Hawkins, Jr. *Out of Silence and Darkness: The History of the Alabama Institute for Deaf and Blind 1858–1983*. Troy, AL: Troy State University Press, 1983, 313.

26. Berg, *A Missionary Chronicle*, 222.

27. Ibid., Berg, *A Missionary Chronicle*, 155.

28. Couch and Hawkins, *Out of Silence and Darkness: The History of the Alabama Institute for Deaf and Blind 1858–1983*. Troy, AL: Troy State University Press, 1983, 152.

29. Carolyn McCaskill, Ceil Lucas, Robert Bayley, and Joseph Hill, *The Hidden Treasure of Black ASL: Its History and Structure*, Washington, DC: Gallaudet University Press, 2011, 20.

30. Couch and Hawkins, *Out of Silence and Darkness: The History of the Alabama Institute for Deaf and Blind 1858–1983*. Troy, AL: Troy State University Press, 1983, 138.

31. McCaskill, Lucas, Bayley, and Hill, *The Hidden Treasure of Black ASL: Its History and Structure*. Washington, DC: Gallaudet University Press, 2011, 39.

32. Robert Capers Fletcher, Memorandum, "Rehabilitation Needs As Seen By the Deaf," n.d. Collection of Reverend Robert and Mrs. Estelle (Caldwell) Fletcher, box 2. Gallaudet University Archives, Washington, DC.

33. Ibid.

34. Ibid.

35. Berg, *A Missionary Chronicle*, 157.

36. Ibid.

37. Robert Capers Fletcher, Memorandum, "St. John's Episcopal Church for the Deaf," 1977, page 2. Collection of Reverend Robert and Mrs. Estelle (Caldwell) Fletcher, box 2. Gallaudet University Archives, Washington, DC.

38. Berg, *A Missionary Chronicle*, 162.

39. Roberta Ray. "Fletcher Family Story." E-mail message. October 4, 2014.

40. Ibid.

41. Gannon, Jack R. "Question for a Chapter." E-mail message. November 17, 2014

42. Robert Capers Fletcher, "Invocation." Unpublished typescript, March 26, 1952, Gallaudet University Archives, Washington, DC.

43. Robert Capers Fletcher, "Reverend Robert Capers Fletcher." Unpublished typescript, August 1982. One page personal statement, Fletcher collection, Gallaudet University Archives, box 2.

CONTRIBUTORS

Robert Bayley is professor of linguistics at the University of California, Davis. He has conducted research on variation in English, Spanish, Chinese, ASL, and Italian Sign Language as well as ethnographic studies of language maintenance and shift in US Latino communities. His recent publications include the *Oxford Handbook of Sociolinguistics* (ed. with R. Cameron and C. Lucas, 2013) and "Variation in Italian Sign Language: The Case of wh-Signs" (with C. Geraci et al.), *Linguistics* 53(1), 2015.

Jean Lindquist Bergey, associate director of the Center for Deaf Documentary Studies at Gallaudet University, has directed the *History Through Deaf Eyes* project, curated the Gallaudet University Museum exhibition *Making a Difference: Deaf Peace Corps Volunteers*, and served on the exhibit curatorial team for *Deaf President Now: A Pivotal Moment*. Publications include (with Douglas C. Baynton and Jack R. Gannon) *Through Deaf Eyes: A Photographic History of an American Community*.

Breda Carty is a lecturer in special education at the RIDBC Renwick Centre (affiliated with the University of Newcastle) in Australia. Her doctoral dissertation explored the development of the Australian Deaf community and its organizations in the early twentieth century. She has also co-authored articles on deaf people in early colonial America and Australia.

Brian H. Greenwald is professor of history and director of the Center for Deaf Documentary Studies. He is co-editor of *A Fair Chance in the Race of Life: The Role of Gallaudet University in Deaf History* and has published articles and chapters on topics in Deaf history.

Joseph Hill is assistant professor in the Department of ASL and Interpreting Education of the National Technical Institute for the Deaf (NTID) in Rochester, New York. His research interests are sociohistorical and sociolinguistic aspects of the Deaf African American community and Deaf individuals' language attitudes and ideologies about signing varieties in the American Deaf community. His contributions include *The Hidden Treasure of Black ASL: Its History and Structure* (2011), which he co-authored with Drs. Carolyn McCaskill, Ceil Lucas, and Robert Bayley, and *Language Attitudes in the American Deaf Community* (2012).

Motoko Kimura is associate professor of special education at Gunma University, Japan. She was associate professor at the University of Miyazaki until March 2016. She received a PhD in disability science from University of Tsukuba, Japan in 2011. Her dissertation examined the history of the Chicago day schools for deaf students that developed under the influences of the urban public school system.

Jannelle Legg is a PhD student and digital history fellow at George Mason University. In 2011 she received dual MA degrees from Gallaudet University in Deaf cultural studies and Deaf history. Her research interests include digital history and Deaf religious history in the late nineteenth and early twentieth centuries.

Ceil Lucas was raised in Guatemala City and Rome, Italy. She is professor of linguistics, emerita at Gallaudet University, where she taught from 1982 to 2013. She is a sociolinguist with broad interests in the structure and use of sign languages. She has co-authored and edited many articles and books, including the *Linguistics of American Sign Language,* fifth ed. (with Clayton Valli, Kristin Mulrooney, and Miako Rankin, 2011).

Melissa Malzkuhn is a storyteller, digital strategist, and creative director interested in languages, cultures, history, and immersive storytelling. She holds an MA in Deaf studies, with an emphasis on history/culture from Gallaudet University; and an MFA in visual narrative from the School of Visual Arts in New York. Melissa leads development of research-based bilingual products for Deaf children at the Science of Learning Center on Visual Language and Visual Learning at Gallaudet University.

Carolyn McCaskill is professor in the ASL and Deaf Studies Department at Gallaudet University. She has conducted numerous seminars and workshops related to multicultural issues in the Deaf community and on Black Deaf history, community, and culture. She is co-author of *The Hidden Treasure of Black ASL: Its History and Structure,* published in May 2011. Dr. McCaskill and the co-authors have given over twenty-two presentations related to various aspects of Black ASL on a local, national, and global level.

Kati Morton Mitchell earned a bachelor's degree in Deaf studies from Utah Valley University and a master's degree in Deaf studies with an emphasis in Deaf history from Gallaudet University. Her master's thesis focused on the life and advocacy of Alice Taylor Terry. She currently works at Gallaudet University doing government and community relations.

Joseph J. Murray is associate professor in the ASL and Deaf Studies Department at Gallaudet University. He is the co-editor of *Deaf Gain: Raising the Stakes for Human Diversity* (University of Minnesota Press, 2014) and has published in the fields of Deaf history, Deaf studies, and human rights.

Octavian Robinson is assistant professor of American Sign Language and Deaf studies at the College of the Holy Cross. He holds the college's first tenure-track position in Deaf studies. He has chapters in three collections from Gallaudet University Press in addition to published work with Sage Publications and Facts on File Press. He holds a PhD in history from The Ohio State University.

Marion Schmidt is a PhD candidate at the Institute for the History of Medicine at Johns Hopkins University, working at the intersection of medical, Deaf, and disability history. Her dissertation, a history of genetic deafness, follows how different professional groups and deaf people negotiated the meaning of deafness in the twentieth century and traces the implications of different professional paradigms on deaf people's (reproductive) agency. She teaches classes on disability, gender, and reproduction and is on the editorial board of *Considering Disability*.

Anja Werner (née Becker) is a research associate in the history of medicine at Martin Luther University Halle-Wittenberg (Germany). Her research interests revolve around transatlantic transfers of knowledge in the eighteenth to twentieth centuries with a special emphasis on deaf and black perspectives. Among her major publications are *The Transatlantic World of Higher Education: Americans at German Universities, 1776–1914* (2013), which includes a chapter on deaf Americans, and, together with Kendahl Radcliffe and Jennifer Scott, *Anywhere But Here: Black Intellectuals in the Atlantic World and Beyond* (2015).

INDEX

Note: Page numbers in *italics* indicate illustrations and tables.